Bobby Groves is the head of oysters at London restaurant Chiltern Firehouse. Born in Maldon, Essex, Bobby began working at his local oyster farm, Maldon Oysters, in 2006, cultivating, delivering and exporting shellfish. He has also worked as an oyster shucker for various London food markets, shucking thousands of oysters per day.

As part of his research for *Oyster Isles*, Bobby undertook a 5,000-mile journey around the coastlines of the British Isles and Ireland on a Triumph motorcycle. Bobby lives in London, supports Newcastle United and also plays the banjo in folk band Beans on Toast.

Instagram: @bobby__banjo / @bobbysoysters
Website: www.bobbysoysters.com

As a country boy
in rural England, I was lucky enough to
watch you skate vert demos in London in
the 2000s!

"Stay Rad!!!"

: And thanks
for helping to
save Southbank,
in London.

Los Angeles
March
2022
Bobby

Oyster Isles

A Journey Through Britain and Ireland's Oysters

BOBBY GROVES

Dear Tony

Please accept this oyster book I wrote as a gift from me to you. The last sentence of the 80,000 words I wrote is a thank you in the acknowledgements to Bad Religion for decades of punk music (that has nothing to do with oysters, it was just an opportunity to express thanks). Anyway, if it wasn't for your THPS games, I would have never found the song "You" or the band who changed my life. Thank you !!!!

Cheers   BOBBY x

CONSTABLE

CONSTABLE

First published in Great Britain in 2019 by Constable
This paperback edition published in Great Britain in 2020

3 5 7 9 10 8 6 4 2

A CIP catalogue record for this book
is available from the British Library.

ISBN: 978-1-47212-907-9

Typeset in Sabon by Hewer Text UK Ltd. Edinburgh
Printed and bound in Great Britain by Clays Ltd, Elcograf S.p.A.

Papers used by Constable are from well-managed forests and other responsible sources.

Constable
An imprint of
Little, Brown Book Group
Carmelite House
50 Victoria Embankment
London EC4Y 0DZ

An Hachette UK Company
www.hachette.co.uk

www.littlebrown.co.uk

To Nichola, for your endless love, care and support.
Thank you believing in me and indulging me in my capers.

To the resilient, wonderful Groves family
and our very own Portland Pearl, Joan Barons.

For oyster folk everywhere.

BOBBY'S JOURNEY

Shetland Islands

Skara Brae

Orkney Islands

Outer Hebrides

Ockran

ATLANTIC OCEAN

THE MINCH

NORTH SEA

Mull (Muile)

Loch Creran (Loch Criathrain)

Colonsay (Colbhasa)

Loch Fyne (Loch Fine)

Islay (Ìle)

Lindisfarne

Lough Foyle

Loch Ryan (Loch Rìoghaine)

Donegal (Dún na nGall)

Strangford Lough

Morecambe Bay

Sligo (Sligeach)

Carlingford (Cairlinn)

Achill Island (Acaill)

IRISH SEA

Galway (Gaillimh)

Menai Strait (Afon Menai)

Brancaster

Flaggy Shore (Na Leacacha)

Butley Creek

Moyasta (Maigh Sheasta)

ST GEORGE'S CHANNEL

Deben

Colchester

Tralee (Trá Lí)

Dungarvan (Dún Garbhán)

Maldon

West Mersea

Rossmore (An Ros Mór)

Hook Head (Rinn Dúáin)

Mumbles

Faversham

Whitstable

Sherkin Island (Inis Arcáin)

BRISTOL CHANNEL

Porlock Bay

Poole

Torridge

Porthilly (Porthhyli)

Yealm Estuary

River Teign

Portland

River Fal (Dowr Fala)

ENGLISH CHANNEL

CELTIC SEA

Herm

Guernsey

Jersey

St Malo Bay

Contents

Introduction

It is the mid-nineteenth century and you find yourself standing on a misty river bank of a cobbled industrialised city. Squealing, scampering children – some in rags and others in smarter clothes – are chasing each other through hordes of merchants in the bustling market as folk scramble for a deal at wooden barrows lining the water's edge. The sound of salt-spattered masts and sails clinking and slapping in the breeze carries through the air as men, women and children heave wicker baskets loaded brimful with oysters from boat to harbour. The repeated thud of timber knocking the jetty is added to the clamour as thick serpentine ropes wrestle boats still. Not far away, plumes of soot bellow from the raven-black chimney of a giant steam train as it grinds to a halt in the central station where, too, even more oyster bushels are being unloaded and ferried down to market. The townsfolk are thankful that fresh oysters from the coast are now arriving from beach to barrow in record time thanks to the railway. Looking down at your shoes, the cobbled market place is awash with saline oyster liquor and piles of discarded shells are strewn everywhere at the feet of both gentry and beggars – oysters, unlike many aspects of society, are attainable and devoured by all classes. Welcome to the boomtowns at the height of oyster production of the British Isles and Ireland 150 years ago where the oyster is ready to feed the ever-growing population.

Our very language provides evidence of the oyster's presence in our lives beyond the gastronomic institutions. The word oyster comes from the word '*ostrea*', which is a Latinisation of the Greek '*osteon*' meaning 'bone'; this derives from the beautiful bone-like colour of the mother-of-pearl interior of the oyster shell. The term 'ostracised' was first coined in Ancient Greece; voters would elect to banish another citizen by writing that person's name down on an old oyster shell. Those receiving enough votes would then be exiled from the state, usually for ten years. As over half of the English language is derived from a melting pot of Greek and Latin roots (and a significant number of Germanic, too), these oyster-embedded words from classical civilisations have stayed with us. And as the centuries rolled on, the oyster continued to capture the imagination, including William Shakespeare. In 1602, he coined the phrase 'the world is my oyster' in his play *The Merry Wives of Windsor*, which is still used today. Now, in twenty-first-century London, millions of journeys on the city's buses, Tube and trains are made using the contactless Oyster card. The influence of the mollusc is everywhere.

But what is an oyster? In short, the shellfish creature is a sessile, filter-feeding, saltwater bivalve mollusc with a rough shell. It filters large amounts of water to feed on the phytoplankton suspended in the water. It loves brackish water (water that has more salinity than freshwater, but not as much as seawater) and marine environments and can produce a pearl, and they have been highly prized for both the pearl and their nutritious qualities throughout the ages. It might not be so obvious, but oysters are interwoven into the fabric of our past, sometimes quite literally. The same way builders today use hardcore and aggregate for foundations, the floor surfaces and pathways of the past would also have been constructed mainly from shell. Not only has the creature survived on this planet for around 500 million years but, long before the onset of agriculture, our ancestors would have feasted on the energy-packed meat between an oyster's shells before venturing away from the safety of the coast and making their way inland through the dangerous forests.

In the far northern reaches of Scotland at the coastal settlement of Skara Brae, oyster shell remains have been discovered cast aside in a Neolithic village from 5,000 years ago. In extinct subterranean rivers beneath London today, there have been discoveries of oyster shells from the Roman Londinium in layers of earth 40ft below present-day street level. In Ireland, the origin of the name Sligo (the county, castle and town) is derived from earlier versions of the Gaelic 'sligeach', meaning the 'place abundant with shells'; in Wales, there is a town simply called Oystermouth on the southern coast. In the British Isles and Ireland, there is a profound cultural dependence on the oyster.

If we look very briefly further back into the history of our island nations, it is a simple truth that because north-west Europe is surrounded by water, the first inhabitants of the British Isles and Ireland would have exploited the coastal areas for sustenance, with nourishing oysters being plentiful in the temperate waters. As we move closer to the present day from about 10,000 years ago, the link between local inhabitants and the oyster becomes much more obvious in the form of shell remains in middens (or 'kitchen midden', a literal translation from the Danish 'kjökkenmödding' which refers to prehistoric refuse heaps which often contain animal bone and shells). These comprised the discarded detritus of hunter-gatherers who would have used the presence of oysters as clean-water indicators to sustain and nourish them, particularly on the west coast of Scotland and Ireland.

In more recent history, oysters from Essex, Kent and Hampshire were important enough to be mentioned in the Domesday Book of 1086 and, in the seventeenth century, they crept into the first printed texts as oyster recipes right the way through to the Victorian era. They have been both an 'everyman' food when in abundance before industrialisation, and then a food of decadence once they became scarce at the turn of the twentieth century. Once an affordable food for the poor, the bountiful availability of oysters transcended into culture, as documented by authors such as Samuel Pepys in his diary entries of the 1600s and Charles Dickens' descriptions of working-class life 'that poverty and oysters always seem to go together' in *The Pickwick Papers* (1837). Even pecks of oysters are mentioned among the costermongers and chimney sweeps in Henry Mayhew's *London Labour and the London Poor* (1851).

If you walk along the River Thames foreshore today, you can see thousands of oyster shells amongst the brick, bones and fragments of pottery from when the Thames was used as a rubbish dump. Even Charles Darwin used oysters from Newhaven in his experiments at the University of Edinburgh, which would eventually lead him to develop his evolution theory. Since the 1960s, the oyster has become accessible once again to all strata of society after hatcheries were established and farming oysters became more commercially viable. In the last ten years, oyster culture has experienced a renaissance with oyster bars popping up once again in all of our towns and cities.

But what is behind us rediscovering a native food which was once so much more commonplace and available to everyone? If oysters have been so bountiful in times gone by, what made us lose that desire or ability to harvest them in such abundance? The jagged shell and smooth flesh of the animal is a world away from the processed plastic food so prevalent in our high streets and fast-food outlets. The salty sea notes of a fresh oyster can take us straight from the oyster bar to the water's edge, harking back to our ancestral roots on the edge of the sea, foraging between the tides before great forests were felled and towns were built.

Despite the mainland British Isles having over 11,000 miles of coastline and Ireland's being around 4,500 miles in total (according to the best current estimates), it has become apparent that we are not widely renowned for the oysters we produce on a world stage dominated by France, Asia Pacific and North America. China is by far the biggest producer of oysters worldwide, harvesting over 58 million tonnes of molluscs a year. Apart from a select few fisheries and farms in the British Isles and Ireland, it really is the case that most people are simply unaware of our wonderful indigenous oysters, both domestically and internationally.

Having grown up in Essex working on my local oyster farm, buying and selling local produce was just a way of life. Once I started to deal with a broader spectrum of clientele, such as restaurateurs, I was astounded at how little was known about the salty treasures from our lochs, bays and creeks.

If I had a pound for every time I am asked if I'm serving Fine de Claire oysters in London, I could probably buy enough oysters to give one each to the capital's nine million inhabitants. But let's be fair – the Fine de Claire (translated literally as 'delicacies of the pond') from the west coast of France is the most famous of the French oysters along with its more elusive and seasonal neighbour, the Belon from Brittany. They would both easily make the list of the top ten most famous oysters in the world. However, it has been astonishing to me how many people of different nationalities would often fail to ask for oysters from British and Irish shores. Somebody coming to a UK or Irish oyster bar with a fully stocked menu of incredible local produce and asking for Fine de Claire is like going into a Belgian chocolate shop in Brussels and asking for a bar of Cadbury's Dairy Milk!

Customers can be forgiven for asking for French oysters on my watch, though, because at least they have heard of them before. The French are romantic about their food and, in particular, their oysters. They also enjoy warmer temperatures, more suitable for growing oysters in the wild using tried-and-tested Roman techniques. Historically, by focusing on aquaculture during shortages, not only did the French government respond to historical overfishing scares much more successfully than

Britain (who, at the time, governed Ireland), but the French do a fantastic job at celebrating France and exporting their products and culture to the rest of the world – such examples include champagne, foie gras and Camembert. France is one of the leading oyster-producing nations that together cultivate over 90 per cent of the global supply – the others are China, Japan, Republic of Korea and the USA. Ireland comes in around twelfth, the UK seventeenth and the Channel Islands are twenty-second on the same list published in 1999.

Today, all around the coasts of England, Ireland, Scotland, Wales and the Channel Islands we have working oyster beds and farms. Oysters also occur naturally in our waters with the indigenous species being the native, also known as flat oyster or *ostrea edulis*. There are also extinct oyster species in Dorset's Jurassic stone and others scattered across the country as relics called *gryphaea* (commonly known as 'devil's toenails').

When the Romans came to Britain in AD 43, they famously introduced many new things, including straight roads, broccoli, rabbits and, of course, Latin. Another key introduction to our way of life was a knowledge of aquaculture, which helped to develop efficient oyster cultivation; while the Chinese are believed to be the inventors of aquaculture, it is a Roman Praetor called Orata in 97 BC who is credited with being the first to lay out artificial oyster beds in Europe. And while struggling to come up with anything positive to say about life in Britannia, the Roman politician and historian Sallust did at least manage to note in AD 50: 'Poor Britons . . . there is some good in them after all . . . they produce an oyster.' And from archaeological records in Rome, it is widely recognised that Colchester native oysters were a highly prized delicacy and so desired that they were exported back to Rome for lavish consumption by the ruling élite. The Essex town of Colchester was established as the first capital city of Roman Britain (known then as Camulodunum) and lies at a meeting of three rivers – the Pyfleet, Blackwater and Colne. A couple of thousand years later, it still has a thriving oyster industry and this is the part of the world I call home.

I was born on the Blackwater in the town of Maldon, Essex, just nineteen miles from Colchester by road and about half that by boat. Maldon is an old Saxon town on a hill flanked by the gentle rivers Chelmer and Blackwater. Both rivers flow into the Blackwater Estuary that, in turn, drains into the North Sea amongst the sprawling mudflats, windswept halophytic plants and silent creeks. I grew up just out of town in the village of North Fambridge on the River Crouch. Between the Thames and the Blackwater, the rivers Crouch, Roach and all the creeks in between – where the famous medieval Walflete Oysters were harvested – are rich in oyster heritage and smuggling. Just along from Fambridge is the oyster spot Brandy Hole, a place that gets its name from smugglers stashing their contraband brandy in a secluded area of marsh safe from Customs boats on the waters. Smugglers would leave the brandy there until the coast was clear and then move on.

What was good for brandy was good for the oyster, which flourished in the sequestered bays of the salt marsh and mudflats away from the hustle and bustle of open water. After the last Ice Age, it was the forming of the salt marsh-lined estuaries of East Anglia, Essex and Kent which created an ideal sheltered environment for the native oyster to thrive. An aerial photograph of these areas at high tide looks a bit like a barcode or arteries of water and mud snaking through the grass.

As a family, I remember walking the sea walls along the river with our dog Ben the Border Collie after we had seen off a pub lunch at the Ferry Boat Inn (cheese and pickle on granary for me, every time). At the end of our walk, my siblings and I would scramble through the boat yard to the end of the boardwalk until we could go no further. There we would sit with our legs dangling over the edge inches from the murky water of the Crouch. Watching the terns, gulls and the many wading birds going about their business, we'd scour the mudflats in among the samphire and the weather-boarded boathouses with our buckets and crabbing lines (and some scraps from the Ferry Boat lunch) to catch some last-minute Essex crustaceans before the tide came in and swallowed up the road back to the pub.

Our family then moved to an old disused cattle farm called Great Canney on Hackmans Lane between the mid-Essex villages of Purleigh, Cock Clarks and Cold Norton. It was next to a big white water tower that you could see for miles around. I used to do agricultural work on the neighbouring farms – grain carting, rolling fields, mulching hedgerows, bud rubbing in the vineyards, that sort of thing – as well as labouring for my dad's building firm. Then one day in 2006, I received a call from my sister's friend's father, Richard Emans, who owned the local oyster farm, Maldon Oysters. Their plant was at the other end of Hackmans Lane just over a couple of miles away. They needed someone to run their oyster shack in Maldon's Promenade Park along from Hythe Quay, which took its name from the Saxon 'hythe' meaning landing place and, today, a multitude of sailing barges are seen moored there with their masts clinking in the breeze. Right up until the mid-twentieth century, oyster smacks (boats) would be moored up along the Hythe Quay, a cockle's throw from the shack.

I took the job and was thrown into a world of bivalves, dressed crabs and potted shrimp. I had always known of the oyster fisheries in Essex, but now being involved with one was incredible – a little bit like living in the Champagne region all your life and then starting to work one day for Dom Perignon.

While working there, I was fascinated by the combination of science and nutrition involved in oysters and the act of celebration that came with eating such an amazing food source produced in the very creeks where I grew up. Over the years, I would shuck hundreds of thousands of oysters at London markets, and drive many miles nationwide to deliver the little critters to locations between the banks of the Blackwater and the restaurants of the capital, and much further afield.

Almost fifteen years have passed since I started out in the oyster industry. Up until 2014, I was working the London food markets popping open thousands of bivalves a day for Maldon Oysters in Chelsea and in Borough Market for Richard Haward's of West Mersea, while also doing my own Bobby's Oysters events in the City. In 2015, I launched the oyster programme at the Marylebone restaurant Chiltern Firehouse for American hotelier André Balazs and Michelin-starred chef Nuno Mendes. It is at Chiltern Firehouse that I now get to showcase incredible oysters every day on the oyster cart. I plate them up in sixes, twelves or more perched on a bed of crushed ice on silver platters. I whisk them into the heaving restaurant and courtyard and position the plates on the marble tables as the centrepiece of the feast. While standing beside the guests, it's a pleasure to share one or two of the wonderful stories that have accompanied the precious bivalves on their journey from tide to table. By spending time with our diners, I can also help to instil more of an understanding of how the unique flavour profiles of the different oysters are intrinsically linked to each oyster's provenance. For example, how an estuary oyster's brackish notes can be indicative of a marshy lowland; or how an opaque, creamy-coloured flesh means the oyster has been fattening up in spring and will give a sweeter taste than that of a translucent oyster at the end of summer after spawning. Between shucking, enjoying the privilege of being a storyteller is a gift. Being able to conjure up images of the oyster farmers and the natural beauty surrounding the oyster beds and rivers is an absolute delight, and people always want to know more, often asking for directions to these wild and largely unknown pockets of the world.

One of the most celebrated chefs in the world today, René Redzepi, the owner of the two-Michelin-starred Danish restaurant Noma, wrote in his cookbook, 'When you can no longer afford to import raw materials, you automatically look to see what you have yourself that you can do something with and how you can be self-sufficient.' René Redzepi was referring specifically to Icelandic produce and cuisine while on a research trip for his Copenhagen-based restaurant. In today's economic climate, though, and with an exponentially growing population, this philosophy can definitely be applied to British and Irish food trends with the resurgence in interest of localism, foraging and home-grown produce – and the oyster perfectly fits this idea of sustainably harvesting quality ingredients.

Throughout my time in the oyster industry, I have consistently felt a groundswell of interest in shellfish, but this hasn't always been the case; the oyster in the British Isles and Ireland has been both popular and unpopular at various points in our history. So I invite you to come on a journey with me, deep into the oyster regions of the British Isles and Ireland, where we will uncover the history of the oyster, the role it plays in the environment and our interaction with this unique superfood. As well as delving into the distant past, we will uncover the significance of the oyster today, and we can sample the delights of the specialist establishments that prepare and serve this most nutritious shellfish to their customers. Then, having cast our net as wide as we can, we'll look at what the future has in store for the British and Irish oyster.

1

Maldon

Location: *Goldhanger, Blackwater Estuary, Essex, England*
Natural habitat: *Brackish and marshy estuary*

The trip from central London to Essex is a great motorcycle ride and one I have made many times throughout my life. Cutting through Mayfair to Hyde Park Corner, I head down to The Mall, passing some of the capital's legendary oyster restaurants: Wiltons (1742); Rules (1798); Sweetings (1830); Scott's (1851); and J. Sheekey (1890s). All hark back to a time when oyster houses began to spring up in the city during the boom years of oyster production. And in the nineteenth century, London was one of three oyster capitals of the Western world – the others being New York and Paris.

Beneath me, the Triumph Bonneville's 1200cc engine gently throbs as I glide through the oldest part of the city along the river, my leather panniers sufficiently stocked to carry me eastwards to Maldon. I can't think of a better way of uncovering the treasure trove of oysters that our coastal territories have to offer than astride this sleek example of British engineering.

I can almost taste the beef and oyster pie being served up to Victorian Londoners as I snake along the Thames on the north side towards the old Roman city, better known as the Square Mile today. At Cannon Street Station, there is a small street running north–south called Walbrook. Directly below here is one of the city's many extinct rivers, the River Walbrook (now part of the London sewer system) which used to drain into the Thames. It was on the banks of the Walbrook (40ft below modern street level) that Roman oyster shells were found dating back to 2,000 years ago. Passing London Bridge there is the beautiful Fishmongers' Hall and then just beyond Bank Station on Lower Thames Street is Old Billingsgate Market where the Greek God of the Sea, Poseidon, sits presiding over the huge building.

I pull over to Billingsgate Walk just off the main road and ride up to the Thames to take a moment to imagine the bustling port here in the mid-nineteenth century. Exactly where I am standing is where fishermen would have hauled their catch from the day boats bobbing up and down on the murky river and then sold their haul to the people of London. Costermongers and oyster ladies would have lined the streets shucking to order to feed hungry Londoners. A stone's throw away is Fish Street where fishmongers were situated and over there is Pudding Lane, the site of something similar to today's Borough Market. Waterfront trading of oysters is thought to have been responsible for the substantial discovery of oyster shells around the Roman Thames-side piers beneath Pudding Lane.

The row of oyster boats moored at Old Billingsgate were nick-named 'Oyster Street' and, just north of here near Liverpool Street Station, is the Dirty Dicks pub, which dates to 1648 as an oyster house. It is now more a city boozer, but it has a long history with oysters. My mum has an annual tradition with my brother on his birthday to take him there for a pie and a pint where they sit gossiping below the wooden rafters.

A more famous London tradition is the city's iconic Pearly Kings and Queens who sew mother-of-pearl buttons on to their clothes and accessories in the most wonderfully intricate patterns. Originally associated with the Victorian costermonger community, the original Pearlies used this innovative method of decoration to draw attention to themselves when collecting money for orphanages and hospitals while imitating wealthy West End society, who, by the early nineteenth century, had developed a fashion for wearing pearls.

Now firmly in the East End, just a few blocks away from the river, today you can find the Oyster Boy shucking on the cobbles between the historic brick houses of Colombia Road Market on a Sunday. Riding past the Tower of London, through Wapping, I emerge from the Limehouse Link Tunnel to Canary Wharf which is now the site of the modern Billingsgate Market, a place I know well. Gliding past Barking and Dagenham, I beep two blasts of my horn and I'm into the county of Essex. It is customary in my family to sound the horn twice as we go past the county sign in the tradition of my late grandfather Billy Barons.

The Thames Estuary is teeming with history and stories, and we can be sure that the native oyster indigenous to the river would have filled many stomachs over the millennia. Imagine Essex as a pie cut into thirds: the Thames corridor at the bottom is predominantly made up of London's East Enders, new towns, commuters and industry; in the east, you have the ever-expanding Greater London claiming more of the county each couple of decades; and in mid/north Essex you will find swathes of arable land peppered with rookeries, pubs and salt marsh carving into the North Sea just 130 miles from the Netherlands.

Maldon is a town just fifty miles east of London, but it is a world away. Riding into the town one can't help but notice its presence within the surrounding area as the incline of the road increases. It sits on top of a hill above the green lowlands that flank the rivers Chelmer and Blackwater. The town gets its name from the Anglo-Saxon word 'Maeldune' translating literally to 'monument on the hill', but the first people here were from the

13

Bronze Age and then the Romans. There is still the Moot Hall in the high street that is in use as a meeting place on the hill.

Hundreds of sheltered creeks wind in among the boggy mudflats topped with sea herbs, stretching from Maldon all the way along the Blackwater to the North Sea. There is no doubt the intertidal bivalve from these precious habitats would have sustained people from the Bronze Age right up to the present day.

Despite its train lines having been disrupted twice, cutting Maldon's connection to the outside world (the South Woodham Ferrers line in 1939 because of wartime money-saving measures, and the Witham line in the 1960s because of the Beeching Cuts), this small Essex town comprises a heartland of food producers that could give Essex a status of 'The Larder of England' to rival Kent's 'Garden of England'. Ironically, a couple of centuries before, the onset of train travel accelerated oyster production in the Blackwater. Luckily, the waterways and the proximity to London were a lifeline for trade and kept the town connected to the wider world.

Today, some of our nation's most celebrated food producers have made their home here: Maldon salt; Wilkin and Sons jam in Tiptree; Kelly Turkeys in Bicknacre; Osborne Bros cockles in Leigh-on-Sea; New Hall Vineyards in Purleigh; Wicks Manor sausages in Tolleshunt Major; and the many breweries around Maldon (Farmer's Ales being my favourite). This area has always been rich in food production and one of the biggest players is Maldon Oysters.

In 2006, I ran the seafood shack for Maldon Oysters during the summer months before university in London where I then spent time at the food markets in the city. The old oyster boys were very colourful characters indeed. Ian, who was from Brightlingsea, was in his sixties when I met him; he had a rural Essex accent that could be mistaken for a West Country twang and had worked with oysters all his life. He showed me the 'hinging' technique of shucking and recommended I flip the oyster to show the customer that the adductor muscle had been cut and the oyster was ready to slip out of the shell. My other mentor was Maurice, who would drive up to Duke of York Square Market on King's Road every Saturday, and then provide one of the more authentic ways to eat oysters in London. It was reminiscent of a Hogarth painting when oyster sellers lined the wonky, gin-soaked streets of London shouting, 'Alive . . . alive O!'

Maurice was a stooped, small-framed man with thick grey hair, smoked for England, lived in a caravan at the oyster plant and enjoyed a glass of red wine of an evening. It was Maurice who taught me the art of simultaneously serving, shucking and chatting while opening 2,000 oysters a day. He was a good salesman, and I was his wing man.

After my studies, I went back to the oyster fishery full time. I packed and purified in the processing plant, handled deliveries, made some sales and represented the company at many events, industry tastings and oyster festivals. I was a fully fledged oyster boy. On a usual day in Essex, we would start at 8.00 a.m., open the oyster plant and heave the boxes of roughly 150–200 oysters out of the purification tanks and on to the trolley for packing. The lads and I would switch on Essex FM radio and, for the next couple of hours, furiously pack boxes of 25, 50 and 200 oysters. We'd bag up Palourdes, Cherry Stone clams and, when in season, mussels as well (from September to March). At 10.00 a.m., we'd stop for tea and cigarettes and squeeze into the mess room to put the toast on. Eddie, the fifty-year-old Glaswegian blockman (fish filleter), would always brew the tea and, despite me only ever wanting one sugar, he'd put at least seven in my cup. He was good with fish though, and worked hard. I will always remember him fondly for having consumed an entire sausage roll sandwiched between slices of thickly buttered white bread, and managing to smoke two cigarettes before the tea break was over. Impressive!

After the break, I'd step out of the production line and load up the Sprinter with shellfish, get all my consignments in geographical order and start my deliveries. I'd leave the oyster plant as soon as possible and set off for Southend/Leigh-on-Sea then Ongar, head into London and make about twenty drops city-wide before popping out at Billingsgate to unload the wholesale pallets and then crawl home down the A13 and finish around 7.00 p.m. On busy days, I'd have to add Heathrow and Gatwick to the run as well. Apart from huge deliveries to Billingsgate Fish Market and restaurants in London, Maldon oysters are in demand in Hong Kong and European wholesale markets.

I enjoyed the graft and the physical side of working with oysters, but one of my favourite aspects of the job was walking in and out of the kitchens of London's best restaurants and having fleeting chats with the chefs who were working with the product I knew so well. I would usually deliver to the rear of the restaurants or hotels, but sometimes I'd peer into the low-lit dining rooms with their vibrant, bustling atmosphere. The oyster showed me that it is the perfect marriage between the wild coasts and the busy, cutting-edge centres of commerce.

Today, as I arrive at the state-of-the-art oyster plant, I ride through the farmyard gate into the yard and I am flooded with memories of my time here as a young lad. I remember when the whole yard was iced over one December; working with oysters at that time of year is a tough job and there was nothing better for bringing the blood back to your fingers after constantly dipping them in icy water than a warm pub and a pint of east coast Golden Ale.

The oyster plant is one enormous, hangar-like green building containing various fridges and purification tanks. It has a slight smell of ozone (almost like faint chlorine at the swimming pool) and there is a variety of scientific-looking equipment attached to the metal tanks to control the ozone and UV light used in the purification of the oysters. Each tank is the size of a small van and can accommodate thousands of oysters at a time. It is in this building that the shellfish are processed and packed before being sent out. I have spent many an hour in here methodically packing exactly 25, 50, 100 or 2,000 oysters in boxes or scraping barnacles from mussel shells. Then there's the production line, which enables the grading of oysters by weight and then the rolling of boxes for strapping.

Other oyster farmers also use the plant to purify their oysters for market, and Maldon also runs a smokehouse on the site. The sliding door to the smokehouse scrapes open to reveal a walk-in area the size of an average bedroom. The room is dark and has an overwhelming smell of charred oak chips – one of the woods used to cure the fish. In the smoker currently there are kippers and mackerel hanging on metal racks, with Maldon Oysters smoking a whole range of seafood. One of the best products from here is the smoked eel. The flesh of the eel is white and grey in the centre and purple towards the outside, and the natural oiliness of the fish is exquisite. Just as in Billingsgate a hundred years ago, the preserved, smoked fish would have offered sustenance to many during the colder months.

Leaving the plant, it is a short journey through the fields of rural Essex to the estuary where the oysters are grown. The journey takes us through the town of Maldon and its neighbour Heybridge and on to the northern side of the Blackwater Estuary (previously called the Pont). A quick right turn off the B1026 towards Tolleshunt D'Arcy takes us down a shingle road and past a farm towards the sea wall, where there is a little white weather-boarded outhouse that looks over Goldhanger Creek. These weather-boarded buildings are typical of this part of England and have a charming, simplistic feel about them. They will always have a special place in my heart.

Parking the bike next to the mud-splattered Maldon Oyster flatbed, I walk through the long grass up to the top of the sea wall and, there before me, are rows upon rows of oysters in mesh bags on metal racks half submerged by the brackish water. The tractor is busy chugging up and down the racks (as fast as giant tyres in mud will let it) attending to the different bags.

There is something really special about being beside the Blackwater. It is an unassuming, almost forgotten land that goes about its business flowing gently to the North Sea while hosting an impressive range of wetland birds and other wildlife. In summer, it is a beautiful place of waving long grass, babbling water and trilling birdsong, while in winter it is desolate and deathly quiet.

The Maldon Oyster Company manages its beds in the Goldhanger Creek, which is a large part of the Blackwater Estuary surrounding both sides of Osea Island. The rights to gathering oysters at Maldon go back to the twelfth century when King Henry II gave Maldon the rights to Blackwater and nearby Southend, Leigh and Hadleigh. Historically, the native oyster was originally the only species in the river, as was the case with all European oyster fisheries. But, today, the company is one of the largest producers of the Pacific oyster in the UK, having been founded as a co-operative between local fishermen in the 1960s, and then introducing millions of Pacific oysters to the Blackwater in the 1980s under the management of David Coward-Talbott. In 2002, David joined forces with current owner Richard Emans, who now runs the business alone.

Richard has successfully re-established the native oyster stocks on the beds. He also harvests other shellfish, such as clams and wild oysters, while maintaining large numbers of the rock oysters in stock. By far my favourite oyster from this farm is the Maldon or Blackwater Wild. The thick, irregular-shaped shell with a deep cup allows the growth of a truly plump and meaty oyster. This rugged bivalve really stands out as unique to this part of the world. The wild varieties are generally available all year round and are dredged by boat and then re-laid in special beds to fatten for market, then gathered from the beach at Goldhanger and graded into size. To me, this oyster embodies the elements of the salt marsh and the winding, brackish mudflats of the Blackwater. The flesh has a distinct mineral taste with subtle notes of driftwood, a firm texture and a slight gamey finish. If you can get your hands on a Blackwater Wild, take the time to indulge yourself in some pure Essex gold.

The Maldon native oyster, when in season, is a highly prized product. I also have a very soft spot for this oyster as I myself am a Maldon native. I love serving these when Maldon salt is on the table as well, as it completes a triumvirate of items from Maldon: the oyster, the salt and the shucker.

The Maldon rock (Pacific) is the most popular product the fishery produces, growing to market size in two seasons. They can be found far and wide and are a very palatable 'first oyster' for anyone to try. Their flavour profile is distinct enough to give them a slight brackish aroma (leaning more towards the salty side) while being not too overbearing. They are the foundation of the business and are worked very hard from their intertidal rack-and-bag aquaculture to the tables around the world. The rock is an oyster for everyone – its flavour is easy, fresh and sprightly, evoking bracing maritime breezes and seawater. Although less intensely flavoured than the native, the rock is equally seductive.

After a busy day traversing the mudflats and oyster plants, I ride back to Maldon to take refuge in the Blue Boar Hotel at the top of the antiquated high street. Juddering along the cobbles, the Bonneville glides through the graceful stone archway to rest. This beautiful old building dates back to the fourteenth century and has been a coaching inn for weary travellers since the 1500s, with Henry VIII being rumoured to have stayed here a few times. Today, the pub serves the local Farmer's Ales, supplied by the Maldon Brewing Company, a microbrewery just a couple of yards away. It supplies the pub with freshly brewed barrels of beer that are literally rolled across the cobbles to be housed in the bar.

As I order my pint of Puck's Folly and settle into the corner by the fireplace, I raise my glass, and allow myself a little glow of pride and gratitude for the rich cultural and gastronomic heritage of this corner of Essex.

2

West Mersea

Location: *West Mersea, Mersea Island, Essex, England*
Natural habitat: *Brackish creeks and estuary*

The village of Tollesbury between Maldon and Mersea was mentioned in the Domesday Book for having a notable oyster industry. This means that in 1086, a group of Norman soldiers under William the Conqueror's command were travelling the same route as mine today to take stock of Essex's oysters. I ride north on the Maldon Road round the Blackwater Estuary Nature Reserve, and even now this area of deep-green-brown, littoral vegetation has a charmingly eerie feeling of outlaws, smugglers and an overwhelming sense of mother nature being in command. Salt marshes and mudflats are two of Britain's last natural wildernesses; they form as rivers deposit their load of fine silts and sands in the estuaries and, where the silts become exposed due to the ever-moving tidal currents, large areas of mudflats are created, providing the most productive and protein-rich habitat in the UK. No wonder the oyster loves this kind of environment – the perfect marriage of food and shelter.

This is the large chunk of rural Essex that makes up the central, north and eastern part of the county. This is my Essex, the ages-old blankets of flat land with salty air and big skies on the fringes of East Anglia. Steering south-east before Peldon on to the Mersea road, the black tarmac becomes a little more pastel grey and brown from being just inches from sea.

In front of me lies the Strood, a short stretch of causeway which cuts through the marshland. About a mile in length, it becomes submerged at high tide, cutting Mersea Island off from the main-land twice a day. At low tide, the Strood is an eerie place, with the faint sound of trickling murky water seeping through the muddy creeks and marshes. People travelling over the road have reported hearing sounds of swords clashing in the night and legend has it that the ghost of a Roman centurion haunts the Strood at midnight, particularly in autumn and spring. It is thought that he is guarding a Roman burial barrow on the island that dates back to AD 100–120 known as the Mersea Mound.

Eventually, the ribbon of road winds through the island community of Mersea, leading me to my destination, The Company Shed. This black weather-boarded shack sits on the western side of Mersea Island and is run by seventh-generation oysterman Richard Haward, his wife Heather and their family. The wooden-clad restaurant is a cult favourite among foodies both locally and nationwide and has received rave reviews from the food critics. It offers a fine selection of Essex produce from oysters, wet fish, shellfish, local beer and wine. The trickling water sound of oysters purifying in the corner of the dining area lends the space a special ambience while, behind the wall, one of Richard's sons, Tom (an eighth-generation oysterman), and his team are packing oysters into wooden boxes for transport.

The oysters served in 'the shed' come from the short stretch of brackish water just behind the restaurant where they have been cultivated for 2,000 years. The oysters are purified in the same building and, before I eat, I politely ask for a quick look at the set-up. Just behind the restaurant are hundreds of wooden boxes, batch labels, cultch (the mass of stones, broken shells and grit of which an oyster bed is formed) and, of course, the many oysters filtering away.

Back in the restaurant, I order half a dozen small rock oysters, some natives and a half of Mersea Island Gold 4.4 per cent. It is generally agreed that stout should be the beer of choice with oysters, but having been raised on Golden Ales from East Anglia my whole life, I encourage anyone visiting my muddy corner of the UK to get some decent bread and butter, half a dozen oysters and a Golden Ale for a true Blackwater experience. Only the one beer, mind, for those, like me, who want to get from A to B safely on their Triumph Bonneville.

Sitting with Richard Haward at one of the tables in the corner of his bustling restaurant, there is an old wrinkled poster on the wall behind our heads announcing: 'THE BLACKWATER RIVER; Oysters and Mussels Fisheries Order Confirmation Act 1879 PUBLIC NOTICE'. It is an Act of Parliament which allows the Hawards to fish oysters here. It refers to the Tollesbury & Mersea Native Oyster Fishery Company, which had been formed three years earlier on 15 December 1876. However, it was Edward the Confessor who had supposedly given West Mersea a charter in 1046 (the oldest oyster-related charter in England). In 1687, King Charles II gave the oyster beds to Charterhouse Hospital, to keep the staff and patients in nutritious local food from just seventy miles away.

In those days, over 120 oyster smacks and roughly 640 men from nearby Tollesbury and Mersea were in action fishing the native oysters here. To be an oyster dredgerman, you had to do four years' apprenticeship and you would subsequently earn ten shillings (50p) a week. One of the great things about the 'company', as it is called, was that it made a rota and selected which boats (members of the company) would go out and fish during the week in order to distribute fairly income from the fishery. All dredgermen bought into the company in a bid to protect/preserve oyster stocks and provide stability. The company was overseen by elected Jurymen who would organise the policing of the Blackwater to protect the precious oysters, as well as to take the catch to local Packing Shed Island to be packed for market.

We continue to eat our fresh seafood as Richard tells me more about the local history: 'The oyster industry here boomed in the late 1800s and continued to be fairly lucrative until the two world wars took all the fishermen to fight, meaning barbed wire was laid out to prevent poachers stealing our oysters.'

As I enjoy the extraordinary taste of the native oysters in front of me, I'm reminded of the unique characteristics associated with this precious mollusc. The native oyster (*ostrea edulis*, also known as Flat, European Flat, Plat, Edulis and Belon) is indigenous to the UK and Ireland with a global distribution along the coasts of Scandinavia down to the Mediterranean and the Black Sea. Outside Essex, the main UK stocks today are located in the rivers and flats of the Thames Estuary, the Solent, River Fal, the west coast of Scotland and Lough Foyle. They prefer highly productive estuarine and shallow coastal water habitats (like the Blackwater) but can be found in the sea over 30m deep.

Ostrea edulis translates to 'edible bones'. First present in the Miocene period (5.3–23 million years ago), it is the traditional oyster that has been eaten by humans in Europe for thousands of years and therefore any archaeological shell remains from the 1800s back to the Stone Age will be this species of oyster. The most famous native in the world is the Belon from Brittany, but Ireland's Galway, and England's Colchester and Whitstable are up there with the best of them.

The native has slightly beige-coloured meat and a brown, round or disc-like shell, hence the term 'flat oyster'. It is seasonal, meaning it can only be eaten in the colder months of the year – famously, the months with the letter 'R' in their spelling, September–April. There are a number of reasons for this – first, when water

23

temperatures rise in the summer, native oysters reproduce. This spawning process happens inside their shell (having evolved in colder waters), which makes the oyster taste extremely creamy, which is unpalatable to some, and the meat discolours, making it less attractive to serve. Rock oysters, on the other hand, expel their eggs into the sea.

Second, a closed season (May–August) allows the native stocks to replenish, a form of animal husbandry which has been practised for hundreds of years. And lastly, in the days before widespread refrigeration and oyster purification processes, eating oysters from warm waters was ill advised because of the risk of toxins and water-borne diseases.

The native is therefore highly prized because of its seasonality, its indigenous nature but also because it takes four or five years to grow to market size before it can be eaten. The taste of a native varies from bay to bay around the coasts, but in general the taste is more of iodine, zinc and game, with a nuttier finish than a rock oyster in my opinion. If a rock oyster is more like chicken, lamb or pork, then natives are closer to the stronger gaminess of rabbit, pheasant and venison. When eating a native oyster, just have it on its own or with a small squeeze of lemon and refrain from dressing or cooking it – it is a delicacy to be eaten just as mother nature intended.

Native oyster restoration is under way in many places around the UK and Ireland including Mumbles in Wales, Galway Bay in Ireland, the Solent, Humber and River Blackwater in England and the Dornoch Firth in Scotland. This is being done to restore native oyster beds to their former glory by focusing efforts on native repopulation (closing off areas to fishing and relaying native oysters in areas close together to increase the chances of successful reproduction). The native oyster numbers were severely depleted in the early twentieth century after rampant overfishing, poor water quality from increased sewage and ultimately a change in habitat through environmental pressure.

As with the marshy creeks behind the restaurant, native oysters are generally fished from the water using boats with a dredge (effectively a large metal net) on the stern which takes them from the bottom. The oysterman has a specialist knowledge of the oyster bed beneath the water, and it's an honour to sit here with the Hawards, such masters of their craft.

Richard's wife Heather started the Company Shed over twenty-five years ago, and it has become hugely successful, now run by daughter Caroline. On East Mersea, they have also opened a rustic place called Mahalah's, and at both establishments you can find the rare wine from the Mersea Island Vineyard, comprising ten acres of gently sloping, south-facing fields where, legend has it, the Romans also grew grapes.

The architecture of the Company Shed building itself is indicative of this part of the world. All around the Blackwater Estuary you can see these wooden-clad sheds, shacks and houses painted either white or black. They are not too dissimilar from those pictured in the bayous of Louisiana, except we have mud and egrets instead of swamp and alligators. Looking out to the murky water is a fine example of one of these buildings sitting proud on a half-submerged island – it is the packing shed on Packing Shed Island. This restored timber building was used during the height of the British oyster industry in the mid-1800s. Records show that 700 million oysters were consumed in London in 1864, and that is not including the rest of the isles or provinces. So grand was the oyster industry at that time that 120,000 men around the coasts of Britain were involved in fishing oysters.

I walk down the boardwalk to the very end where there is a blue-and-white boat moored called *Lady Grace*. This beautifully maintained motorboat belongs to Stacey Belbin, who captains the boat on trips round the creeks of Mersea and the River Blackwater. Stacey has been on the water since she was two years old and is a Mersea girl through and through. I clamber into the boat and, as we pull away from the jetty, we pass her sister and dad in another boat who have just returned from fishing herring in the creek. Stacey sounds the horn of the *Lady Grace* and we exchange waves. We motor over towards a heap of oyster shells on the shore where local oysterman Mike Dawson – who owns the West Mersea Oyster Bar just along the coast – sorts his oysters and has a large concrete holding pen which fills with the tides. Turning east back out into the water, we pass *Fisher Lassie*, an old oyster smack owned by the late Peter French, one of the legendary Mersea oyster family names. The boat is heavily laden with nets and oyster-related equipment. I salute silently.

Into view comes Cobmarsh Island, bang in the middle of the creek. Like me, Stacey is a bird lover and our oyster trip doubles up as a bird-watching opportunity. She points out that Cobmarsh Island is a favourite nesting ground for the rare common tern, and it serves as a paradise for many other species of waders and sea birds – there are lapwings, oystercatchers, turnstones and plovers everywhere you look. A brent goose flies over our heads and Stacey tells me of the time she saw one struggling to fly. Upon closer inspection, the goose had an oyster clamped shut on its foot, and the bird finally shook it off and flew away.

In the distance is the coastal feature of Sales Point with St Peter's on the Wall Chapel looking on to it. The chapel is the earliest building of Christian Worship in Britain still standing. It was built in AD 644 by St Cedd who sailed down the east coast from Lindisfarne to bring Christianity to the East Saxons. This area was famed for a very special oyster, too, called the Wallfleet or 'Walflete' (*ostrea edulis*), which is no longer with us. In 1594, a cartographer from Somerset by the name of John Norden surveyed a number of English counties and wrote: 'Some of the sea shore of Essex yields the best oysters in England called Walflete Oysters . . .'

The *Lady Grace* is now in open water and, at our current trajectory and with enough fuel, we might reach Amsterdam, but we spin round instead and head towards Packing Shed Island. The Packing Shed was built around 1890 (after the original blew away in a storm) and lends its name to the islet, which is no bigger than half a football pitch at low tide; at high tide, the island disappears, leaving just the packing shed standing on stilts.

At the turn of the century, the oyster boats would come in from a day's dredging and haul their catches into the shed where 50–70 fishermen would clean, grade and pack the oysters to be shipped by Thames barge to Billingsgate Fish Market in London or further afield. Between the wars, amid fears of the island being washed away, thousands of invasive slipper limpets were dredged up from the Blackwater to give the native oyster a chance to feed. The limpet shell was dumped on Packing Shed Island to bolster the island and help it accumulate sturdier foundations. Today, an annual event is held in mid-September on the island which involves a series of boats starting at 9.00 a.m. to see how many oysters they can dredge by afternoon, unload into the shed and complete their shucking before anyone else.

Stacey steers the boat back towards the harbour where we float gently past a series of willow sticks poking out of the murky water. These are called 'withy sticks' and are stuck into the muddy river beds at low tide to mark out where the oyster beds are. Willow is the chosen tree because of its ability to move with the water.

Navigating a series of dredge boats, our last stop is to pay homage to a very special boat called the *Boadicea*. She is the oldest working oyster smack in Europe and was built in 1808 in Maldon. She was launched three years after Lord Nelson's death at Trafalgar and worked these waters until 1938 when she was bought for £175 by Michael Frost. The boat has stayed in the Frost family ever since. The current owner, Reuben Frost, teaches us all a lesson when he says, 'I think she's survived so long because she's always been loved.' It is quite fitting that *Boadicea* is still here as it was Boadicea herself who attacked Colchester, the then capital of Roman Britain, in AD 60–61, completely destroying the town. It was only after this that the Romans moved the capital of their new territory to London.

With the sights, sounds and smells of Mersea Island so vivid as I disembark *Lady Grace*, I thank Stacey for her time and expertise, and prepare to follow in Boadicea's footsteps and make my own raid on Colchester – or the Colchester Oyster Fishery, to be precise. Unlike the warrior queen, I'm anticipating slightly less bloodshed and a lot more oysters.

3

Colchester

Location: *River Pyefleet and River Coln, Essex, England*
Natural habitat: *Brackish tributary/estuary*

*'The old luxorious Romans vaunts did make
of gustful oysters took in Lucrine Lake
Your Essex better hath and such perchance
as tempted Caeser first to pass thorough France.'*

A poem written by Sir Aston Cockain
in 1669 as a tribute to Essex oysters

It is a very short six-mile ride from Richard Haward's and Mike Dawson's West Mersea oyster businesses to my next destination, the world-famous Colchester Oyster Fishery at East Mersea. The short journey is a testament to the long-standing shellfish industry of this oyster-rich area. It's a joy to ride my bike through this particular part of north Essex, with the shifting corners and serpentine bends through the flat fields of Mersea Island keeping the engine purring happily as we zip past hedgerows and houses.

It's not long before a little white sign appears with a picture of an oyster boat saying 'Pyefleet Est. 1189'. Turning off the tarmac road, the tyres crunch on to an uneven country track made up of dirt and shell, and the alluring fresh smell of the Pyefleet Creek wafts ever stronger through the air. I cruise into the fishery and park on the grass next to a line of boats in various stages of repair.

I'm greeted by a very upbeat Paul Harding, the Managing Director of the Colchester Oyster Fishery, who makes me a much-needed brew which I enjoy outside in the sun. Over the sea wall, the distant sound of a tractor at the water's edge throbs in the background as it brings in an oyster haul from the water. After the tide has gone out, plovers and turnstones forage the newly exposed beach and little egrets fly overhead, with the surrounding pristine salt marsh teeming with birdlife.

It is not long before Essex oysterman Graham Larkin comes over. Walking up on to the sea wall, he points over to the sweeping Pyefleet and explains how he and the crew are the latest in a long line of oyster gatherers here. Just fifty years ago, they worked from a hut on Pewit Island on the southern side of the Blackwater – 'only reachable by boat and orders were sent by carrier pigeon'. He tells me that another of his fellow oystermen, Tiny, has worked there for forty-five years.

Graham and I head into the main building that is the fishery's HQ. The familiar noise of aquaculture pumps becomes much louder as we skirt past lobsters and thousands of oysters in their holding tanks drinking away the hours. As well as oysters, Colchester Oyster Fishery has an extensive stock of all types of shellfish, crustaceans and fish. In the early 1980s, they diversified into many different types of shellfish and seafood after oyster stocks hit worryingly low numbers.

Now that Colchester rocks are right in front of me, it's probably a good time to explain a little more about them. The rock oyster is the other main type of oyster eaten in the UK and Ireland. It is also known as 'gigas' (after the Latin name), as well as the Pacific, cupped, Japanese, Miyagi or Creuse oyster to many in Europe. It is traditionally found in the Japan/Korea area of the Pacific and was introduced on a large scale to the UK and Ireland in the 1960s and '70s for cultivation after a few years of quarantined scientific hatchery work in Conwy, Wales, which meant that farmers could rely on a more consistent stock. Prior to this mass introduction, the rock oyster has, in fact, been present in British waters for centuries, having been thought to have been linked to the movements of Portuguese merchant ships which traded with Macau.

The rock oyster is easy to tell apart from the native by its shape. First, it has a deep cupped shell if you look at it side on; and looking from the top of the shell, it is elongated like an arrow with a rough, jagged surface. The meat of the oyster is a more pale/creamy-white colour compared to the native. In terms of taste, like the native, this is totally dependent on where the oyster comes from, but the rock in general is less nutty and gamey. Regarding taste, I like to think the rock oyster is to chicken what natives are to game.

The rock is the most common oyster in the world – making up about 75 per cent of all oyster production – and is favoured by farmers for a number of reasons: it only takes 1.5–3 years to grow to market size (more or less half the time to maturity for a flat oyster). They are a hardy oyster to cultivate, meaning they are less prone to disease and more tolerant of temperature/salinity fluctuations (from brackish to full ocean salinity) compared to the native, and therefore less commercially risky. As mentioned before, in the summer, the Pacific rock oyster does become milky, just like the native, but the reproduction process happens in the water, not in the shell (because it evolved in warmer waters), and so is more palatable. It can therefore be enjoyed all year round; the 'R'-in-the-month rule need not apply. Some rock oysters do not turn milky at all in the summer – these are called triploids. My main bit of advice if you are eating milky rock oysters in the height of summer is to add mignonette to the oyster as the tart vinegar and sweet oyster go incredibly well together. Milky rock oysters are also great for cooking.

Just as native oyster restoration is of paramount importance for the good of the environment and native species survival, equally important in my eyes is the respect for the husbandry involved in hatching and farming rock oysters. Unlike the labels 'organic' (for eggs) or 'wild' (for fish) in terms of elevating food status, in the world of oysters, 'farmed' is desirable. The author Rowan Jacobsen puts it perfectly: 'Oysters spend their entire lives attached to one spot. They free range as much as broccoli.'

But why *are* farmed oysters such a wonderful product? Rock oysters do not require feed like other forms of farming (such as cattle and salmon). A farmer puts them in the water where they are turned and moved around to different parts of the farm depending on whether they are being grown or fattened/finished. While the oyster is submerged, they clean the water by removing and digesting the naturally occurring phytoplankton/algae that gathers its energy through photosynthesis. It is the very nutrients in the brackish waters from these rivers and the unspoilt salt marshes that give Pyefleet oysters their unique flavour. After the oyster has reached maturity, the farmer takes them out of the water and they are ready for plating. As farming goes, it is as low-impact as you can get.

We climb some wooden stairs and walk along a gangway that runs the length of the building at roof height, and enter a large wooden meeting room with huge windows through which daylight pours in. Graham calls me over to the panoramic window and we gaze outside to the Pyefleet Creek where the oysters are fished, although the fisheries extend way beyond this, running 9.5 miles all the way up into Colchester town itself. Graham goes on to explain that Roman vessels worked the very same stretch of water.

The Colchester Archaeological Trust has excavated tons of oyster shells in the area. In the 1970s, they discovered a large dump of oyster shell at the Balkerne Gate on the perimeter of the

Roman city walls on what was the main Roman route to London. It had been a site of a stall selling oysters, not too dissimilar from my own in London. Archaeologists have also found oyster shell dumps at the old Roman garrison, suggesting they were eaten domestically and part of army rations. The wealth of shell remains shows how much the oyster was loved and featured in everyday life; after all, they were one of the resources which the Romans invaded Britain to exploit, along with timber, wool, metals, crops, slaves and silver.

Graham and I take a moment to enjoy the fantastic view and then take a seat at one of the large wooden dining tables where Colchester Oyster Fishery hold events. He spreads out a map on the table and points to our location; his index finger starts on the right-hand side of Mersea Island in East Mersea and then defines the fishery's limits as he runs anticlockwise just above Mersea Island to the Pyefleet Creek. To the south of the island is the Blackwater Estuary, and to the east you can see the River Colne running north to south down from Colchester.

In 1189, King Richard I (or Richard the Lion Heart) gave a group of local people called the Colchester Corporation a charter to control the River Colne in return for supplying men to help build Dover Castle. It has been fiercely defended through the years with various local riverside manors and new kings trying to reassign the charter. Colchester would become very wealthy from its oyster beds and thus did very well to secure this privilege from King Richard during his first year on the English throne.

What the charter created was a closed fishery, meaning the oyster beds were not common ground, could not be fished by the public and were thus defended fiercely from outsiders, as well as those from within the town not abiding by the rules. The offence of imprisonment was bestowed on those who trespassed on the protected beds. In the Mersea, Colchester and Blackwater Estuary area, disputes over oyster dredging have been recorded since the reign of King Edward III (1327–77). Later in the 1800s, coastguards were introduced and paid in rum to keep watch and stop poaching dredgermen from stealing precious bivalves.

Disputes over oysters was a common theme as the precious natural resource became more popular in the 1800s, when the region saw the creation of private police forces or guardians. The Chesapeake Bay in the USA has its own particularly bloody history of oyster-related skirmishes, but oyster stealing was rife everywhere and Colchester was no exception. It's also true that 'inadvertent' and perfectly innocent dredging occurred from time to time, with passing boats sometimes blissfully unaware of the willow markers – the withies – that would have identified the oyster beds, and often continued their dredging in ignorance of the local restrictions.

A more positive by-product of the closed fishery saw early forms of conservation through husbandry to ensure the town's prosperity. Through due diligence, closed seasons were introduced to the area to protect stocks of oysters and the town of Colchester was the top priority when it came to its supply of oysters, even ahead of the population of London.

Today, a collective group of multi-disciplinary stakeholders have formed the Essex Native Oyster Restoration Initiative (ENORI project) which has recognised that native oysters in the area have reduced in population by an estimated 95 per cent due to 'over-harvesting, disease, competition from invasive species and predators'. To put the numbers of oysters in perspective, in the mid-1800s there were roughly 250 fishing smacks under sail, working from the River Colne alone and manned by roughly 1,000 hands with up to 500 million oysters sold a year; by the 1960s, just 8–10 million oysters were sold annually. The Colchester Oyster has been labelled as an 'ecosystem engineer' as they 'facilitate the wider conditions for nature to thrive – stabilising shorelines, filtering water and providing vital food and habitat for coastal wildlife'. By encouraging the various stakeholders to communicate and take collaborative action, the ENORI project hopes to pave the way for future conservation.

Over the other side of the Pyefleet waters, Graham points to the rival town of Brightlingsea. Although there has been no oyster fishing or farming there since the freezing winter of 1962/63, Brightlingsea played a huge part in the area's history. It was once a bustling hub of oyster fishing, just as Colchester was. A 70ft Essex smack – known as a skillinger – called the *Pioneer*, which fell into decay after a life spent dredging oysters in the North Sea, was found over there in the 1920s, and it has now been restored.

To fish the elusive deep-sea oyster, you needed a skillinger, which was the crowning glory of all Essex sail boats. They would leave these Essex waters and venture into the North Sea as far as the Netherlands, Denmark and the French coast between Dunkirk and Cherbourg, in waters of over twenty-four fathoms (around 130ft deep). It was a common sight to see skillingers return from week-long voyages with broken masts, ripped sails and crew sadly unaccounted for.

In March 1883, of the eight skillingers that had left from Brightlingsea, one returned bearing a flag in its rigging for a lost crew member, followed by four badly damaged boats; the other three boats never returned from the North Sea. In 1888, a local lady called Mrs Barber, wife of a deep-sea oysterman, lost her husband, three sons and two sons-in-law all to the full savagery of the North Sea. There were no harbours or coves for refuge out in the open sea during a storm. A Brightlingsea preacher said in 1891 to a packed church after the disappearance of a boat called the *Glance*, that he had seen 101 lives lost at sea in his eighteen years at Brightlingsea.

So why did oystermen risk their lives knowing the dangers of undertaking this line of work? Well, the answer is simple – as well as the risks, the skillingers were equally famed for bringing home record hauls of oysters and a big catch meant big money. After the Napoleonic Wars, Colchester boats sailed to the French coast of the English Channel to dredge from the rich oyster beds. In 1832, it was reported that the boats were disappointed with the lack of

British naval protection during their fishing trip with the hostile French navy trying to stop them. In 1833, a Brightlingsea boat was seized by the French and the crew were set adrift. A boat called the *Heiress* in 1886 hauled a record-breaking catch of 44,800 oysters in eighteen days and 24,000 oysters in just three days. The *Heiress'* record was broken in 1887 by the boat *Guide*, with 49,000 in nineteen days. These record hauls were not to last, though – after changes to the fishing laws and more tragedies, deep-sea oyster dredging ended after the turn of the century. It was extremely dangerous work and was the toughest and cruellest trade Essex men ever undertook.

One major difference between Colchester and Brightlingsea was that while Colchester was a closed fishery, Brightlingsea was not included in the charter of 1189 and so was deemed 'common ground'. Anybody from Brightlingsea could fish there right up until the seventeenth century. In Henry Benham's brilliant book *Essex Gold*, he tells of a man called Horace Day who re-laid 200 bushels of Portuguese oysters in Brightlingsea Creek, which were quickly dredged up by the Pyefleet Fishery as they were considered to be on disputed beds. Colchester were fierce defenders of their realm. However, Brightlingsea would always 'try it on' and their boats would range all over the east coast, bringing oysters and brood back to lay in the area.

With hindsight, the oyster industry was at least partly a victim of its own success and the fact that Brightlingsea felt it had to bring in other species of oyster meant native oysters were being overfished. By bringing in foreign stock, other unwanted species would hitch a ride and, unlike the foreign oysters, the invasive oyster drills and slipper limpets bred and flourished here, with disastrous results.

As well as Colchester, Brightlingsea (through a rich fishing history) was deemed important enough to be added to the Norman Cinque Ports, originally an Anglo-Saxon concept, but named in 1100 during the Norman era. The term encompasses five coastal towns in Kent and Sussex to protect trade routes and to be ready to support the Crown in times of threat. The original five towns were Hastings, Rye (originally New Romney), Hythe, Dover and Sandwich.

In a directory from 1890, we are informed: 'A great trade is carried on in Brightlingsea in oysters and nowhere else in the United Kingdom can such a variety and quantity be seen as every sort in cultivation can be seen here.' As well as local natives, oysters from Brittany in France, Bluepoints (*crassostrea virginica*) from east-coast America and the Portuguese (*crassostrea angulata*) were being grown in Brightlingsea. It had become an international trade, but not necessarily for a good reason. By the first half of the twentieth century, fishermen were managing over-depleted oyster fisheries all over Britain and Ireland by importing oysters to try to maintain momentum of production and demand, but there was now the additional burden of pests from imported North American stocks.

As a result, British spatfalls (the settling of young oysters to the sea-bed) became lighter and less frequent and, on top of this, cold winters and floods further reduced the precious stock levels. As the twentieth century progressed, the catch fell from 40 million oysters in 1920 to about 8 million during the 1950s. Then, after a short period of respite, the severe winter of 1962/63 virtually destroyed the east-coast beds. By the end of that decade, landings had fallen to 3 million. This is where the rock oyster and hatcheries came into their own.

Not only were oysters being enjoyed here 2,000 years ago, there are records of them being eaten at the Colchester Market which was chartered in the 1300s and it is still in operation today. The historic annual 'oyster feast' is still held with local dignitaries at Colchester Town Hall to celebrate the start of the oyster season in a tradition that goes back 700 years.

4

Deben

Location: *Ramsholt, Suffolk, England*
Natural habitat: *Tidal estuary*

Sweeping past the 2,000-year-old Roman walls of Colchester (the oldest town walls in Britain), I ease my bike on to the A12 towards Ipswich. The Essex–Suffolk border is very beautiful whatever the season – the ancient, gently rolling Dedham Vale and Stour Valley are agricultural gems, and have been dubbed 'Constable country' having been immortalised by John Constable, whose carefree childhood was spent on the banks of the Stour. I feel the same way about this corner of England – open spaces and big, ever-changing skies.

Turning north-east, the dual carriageway slices through the arable land of East Anglia and bypasses the industrial ports of Felixstowe and Harwich. The etymology of the place names around these parts of Suffolk are quintessentially Saxon (Saxmundham, in particular) and a reminder of how connected the East Anglian coast of Britain has always been to continental Europe. Ipswich is one of England's oldest towns and its port has played an important role in shaping English history. Although the Dark Ages that ensued after the Romans left Britain saw little in the way of recorded history, we know that oysters still made their way from the river to be enjoyed in the towns. In May 2016, archaeologists excavated medieval artefacts in the heart of Saxon Ipswich to find many remains, including oyster shell, in a low-status medieval settlement. It had been part of a staple diet in the late medieval period.

The road opens up after Woodbridge and leads to a quiet world of luscious, leafy hedgerows and oak-lined fields. Near the hamlet of Ramsholt, the sand creeps on to country roads almost out of nowhere and the bike starts to wobble at 40 mph. My legs spring out like stabilisers and I find both feet patting the ground like a goose on hot coals until I establish some control. It is scary for about twenty seconds but the combination of riding through the sand and easing off the gas restores my equilibrium. Sand and road tyres do not mix!

Before too long, I'm riding on gravel and rolling into a farmyard flecked with Oklahoma-style red dirt from the sand in the local area. The set-up at Deben Oysters makes a very good first impression. There appears to be plenty to explore, so I park the Triumph next to a water bowser and work my way along some outbuildings looking for Jonathan Simper's office until the last door of a black wooden-clad building is flung open and a smiling Jonathan appears, every inch the country gentleman, even down to his rather elegant flat cap. The Simpers of Suffolk have been fishing the Deben for years, having been mixed farmers in Suffolk for eleven generations. Each generation has become a little more involved with the coast, particularly over the last six generations, and now Harry, Jonathan's son, is actually a fully fledged and award-winning skipper.

There are deeds for fishing native oysters on the Deben which date back to the 1760s and there were smacks working here in the 1880s and '90s. Robert Simper started his rock oyster business in the 1980s and then concentrated on other types of farming, leaving the oysters to go wild. Recently, the oysters have taken off again. As well as wild settlement, they have racks where oysters are grown quickly in a straight channel created in the 1930s after a river wall broke through and flooded fifty acres with grey mud, and the young oysters love the nutrients in the silt. One of the greatest things about their oysters is that the Deben flushes out more than half the water in the river every twenty-four hours.

Having been invited to explore the farm after a refreshing brew, a Land Rover carries us through asparagus fields set in rich red soil until we get to the bottom of a hill. The Simpers spend most of their time and energy cultivating mussels and asparagus, and while the rock oysters are not the main income of the farming operation, they represent a very valuable natural food resource as they are the only oysters in the Deben.

Once out of the vehicle, we walk past an old wooden rowing boat and down on to the sandy beach littered with small rocks and shell. The whole area of the Deben yields fossilised remains from the London Clay, the Red Crag, Coralline and bedrock. As well as fossilised sharks' teeth and crustaceans, a wide variety of molluscs can be found here from prehistoric times.

It is this local Deben geology and the beautifully low-lying East Anglian marsh that all have an impact on the oyster's flavour. Deben oysters are particularly renowned for their distinctive salty flavour with marshy vegetal notes. And the reason for these oysters tasting so remarkably different from other varieties in other locations? Oysters filter feed on phytoplankton (suspended organic particles) and nutrients by pumping water through their gills. An individual oyster can filter up to ten litres of water per hour, although there are huge variations in the volume of water filtered according to size, variety, seasonal differences, the amount of nutrients in the water, and so on. This means the taste of an oyster is a function of its environment. Different bodies of water will naturally have different levels of minerals, nutrients, salinity and types of algae, leading to different locations lending the oysters different flavours. This can vary from bay to bay on the same stretch of coast (Maldon and Colchester, for example) but can be seen more obviously in different geographical areas.

Another important aspect to consider when talking about the taste of an oyster is time of year and rainfall. In the Deben (as well as the rest of Britain and Ireland), the oyster's year starts in January when the oysters enter the year in good condition (plump and firm) having spent the previous autumn building up reserves to get through winter. During the winter, the time will have been spent using as little energy as possible to stay alive in the cold waters, opening their shell for oxygen every now and then and living off their reserves. If it has been a mild winter, by mid-February they start to grow again, but a harsh winter will delay this until the weather and water warm up. In spring, the oysters are in prime condition, which they maintain until mid-June when it is time to reproduce. In summer, when the water temperature reaches 16°C –18°C (late July/early August), it is time to release the eggs, which is when they turn milky. After spawning, it takes the oyster 6–8 weeks to recover to full fatness, during which time they feed frantically to stock up on reserves for the forthcoming winter.

The environmental factors that make an oyster taste distinctive to its location generally stay the same (i.e., a Maldon will always be a brackish river and Achill will always have water running off the peat bogs), but the biology of an oyster's annual cycle of behaviour is predictable and will also affect the taste. Finally, increased rainfall makes a sweeter/buttery taste compared with the saltier taste after a dry summer – no rain means more seawater, while plenty of rain results in more freshwater being filtered. Needless to say, the taste of oysters is marvellous and fluctuates, but their natural environment stays the same.

The Deben estuary is roughly twelve miles long, and the Simpers work on the mussels and oysters in the river all year round, believing that their shellfish are among the freshest to reach London consumers. Their boats primarily focus on sea fishing from the beach at Aldeburgh because the mouth of the estuary can be dangerous, with a number of drownings because of its narrow width, the force of water that can sometimes be expelled, and the dangerous waves that can be generated in windy weather.

As with other shellfish farmers, the Simpers have to work with the tides, weather and lie of the land for each fishing trip and prefer to launch from the beach with an engine in the boat – not a traditional choice for most oystermen. Jonathan Simper tells me, 'Oystermen from the Blackwater have made comments about it not being traditional to have an engine in the boat . . . I always say to them, "I never see you in the Deben much lately . . ." to which they reply, "Oh no, I daren't go in the dangerous Deben!" Well . . . there is your answer!'

The Simpers head up the local oyster and seafood festival called the Woodbridge Shuck which is held in September at Whisstocks Quayside in the riverside market town of Woodbridge. Most of the activity happens around the town but the festival promotes the beauty of the surrounding area, as well as the gastronomic and artisan delights of local farmers, eateries and producers. A highlight is the possibility of finding a Deben Giant – an oyster of 150g-plus in weight, which Jonathan Simper likes to 'bung under the grill' until it pops open; he then whips the top shell off saving the liquor, adds a healthy dollop of blue cheese and puts it back under the grill until it melts. Pure heaven.

5

Butley Creek

Location: *Orford, Suffolk, England*
Natural habitat: *Tidal creek*

Ipswich has long been a prosperous town within touching distance of healthy oyster beds. Before the Normans arrived, Lenten food restrictions dominated the springtime for medieval Christians and the church also enforced fish days (usually on a Friday but sometimes Wednesday or Saturday). In addition to the religious requirement – as a tribute to Jesus who was executed on Good Friday *and* 'died for our sins, thus sacrificing his flesh for mankind' – fish days also provided for the poor and maintained the town's personal supply of seafood. It cannot be a coincidence that a correlation existed between the natural distribution of oyster beds and recorded wealth of Anglo-Saxon England in the towns of Ipswich, Southampton and Aldwych in London.

Out of reach of Ipswich and the giant River Orwell, I wind my way on towards Woodbridge. Now just shy of my destination, I park the bike and take in the wonderful surroundings. This really is one of the best places to experience the majesty of East Anglia.

In fact, just outside Woodbridge is one of the most important archaeological finds in England, Sutton Hoo, a site that rivals Stonehenge in significance.

The lush Suffolk countryside starts to transform into red-brick homesteads and the scenery becomes quite residential. I ride off the tarmac and on to a half-mile dirt track, navigating the ruts and welts, weaving round the potholes, before arriving at Butley Creek HQ to be greeted by Bill Pinney.

The Butley Creek river remains unspoilt, with Bill observing that it looks like it did a hundred years ago. The surrounding marshland is home to a thriving biodiversity of British birds and mammals, with seals often seen gliding through the water and oystercatchers flying overhead. It is a calm and quiet backwater that time has forgotten and the tranquillity makes it a perfect environment for oyster growing.

The Pinneys farm the area throughout the year in harmony with the changing seasons. In summer, the oysters grow and the fishing boat will catch lobster, crab and sole, while in winter the oysters concentrate on survival and the day boat will bring in cod and skate.

Butley Creek oysters are always high on my list when it comes to buying shellfish for London and, despite their proximity to the capital, they are quite rare due to the small stretch of river they inhabit. The Pinneys have farmed oysters here since the late 1950s, when Richard Pinney left London to look for a quieter life in the Suffolk countryside. Once settled, he decided to restore the old oyster beds in the creek next to his cottage. He imported oysters from Portugal to see if they would grow as a potential business and they loved their new home. Today, Bill and his family run the operation along with Irene, all working in different parts of the business – a world-class smokehouse, a shop, a busy wholesale set-up, day-boat fishing, oyster farming and a top-quality restaurant.

The rock oysters are grown initially in small blue mushroom boxes suspended from homemade rafts (five mushroom boxes stacked one on top of the other under a floating wooden board) anchored to the bed of the river. The homemade set-up is ingenious, one that Bill Pinney has made almost entirely from recycled materials. Once the oysters grow big enough, they are transferred to standard mesh bags and submerged again to feed on the nutrients suspended in the water. Once they reach a certain size, the oysters are then scattered on to the bottom of the river where the shell grows stronger and the oyster sits filtering happily until it is fished and rowed to shore.

There are on-site purification facilities that take a minimum of 42 hours to complete before the oysters are washed, hand graded and lovingly packed for market. From tide to table, the entire production process takes about 2–3 years and causes virtually no negative impact on the environment.

Bill's approach, which embraces sustainable, low- or no-impact animal husbandry, is a shining example of how oyster farming serves as a great model for good food acquisition. Mankind over the past 200 years or so has become increasingly more careless when it comes to the environment, and Bill has many stories – and warnings – about the negative effects of man's impact on biodiversity around the south-eastern coastline, which becomes a persistent theme for all sustainable farmers for whom the purity and cleanliness of the natural world is paramount. Bill had been aware of the potential problem with plastics for thirty years or so, but 'it always fell on deaf ears', he told me, until it was picked up by Sir David Attenborough, beamed into people's living rooms on a Sunday night, and instantly became a top priority for government and local authorities.

Bill is a man who knows and understands the waters around his region, and is in tune with the effects of tiny changes in the ecosystem around him. These tiny changes are warning signs of bigger, more critical impacts, and we need to listen to Bill and others like him to ensure we are doing all we can to protect the treasures that the natural world has given us. Livelihoods depend on it – as well as the health and wellbeing of humankind who operate at the top end of the food chain. Destroy one part of that chain, and the entire network will fall apart.

I'm now standing at the side of this crystal-clear, gently flowing creek, as Bill pops open a couple of medium-sized, market-ready oysters, typical of the ones I use at my oyster cart. It is one of the most special experiences standing right next to the place of origin of your food. The essence of the creek and this location is embodied in the taste of this oyster. The flavour has a hint of sweetness in the meat that varies throughout the seasons, tasting best in the autumn and spring. The Butley Creek environment gives the flesh and liquor a vegetable, grassy note with a slight cucumber finish that reflects its East Anglian environment. There is no overbearing salty flavour, as the oyster is from a river where it takes on the constant flow of nutrients coming downstream from the river's source in the Rendelsham Forest, through Bill Pinney's patch and on to the North Sea.

Walking back up the beach and over the sea wall, there before me is the legendary smokehouse – a standalone wooden building beside a cornfield puffing oak smoke out of a soot-stained chimney. We saunter over to the building past an impressive stack of heavy oak wood logs and pull the door open to the outhouse, which comprises working rooms for the blockman, storage spaces and, of course, the smoker itself. The beauty of the smoking at Butley Creek is the simplicity of the process. It is an art form that I truly believe the giants of the fish-smoking industry would never be able to rival. One key factor (and it is no secret) is that, after being salted, the smoking of the fish is done right through the meat. Although this sounds ridiculously simple, you would be surprised how many people these days are just imbuing the product with a hint of smoke for flavour, and not taking the trouble to reduce the water content. Of course, they do this to keep the weight up and so make more money. At Pinney's of Orford, it is the simple and honest process that is the foundation for their success as smokers.

Having successfully refrained from devouring all the smoked fish hanging in the smokehouse, I head back to Orford to the Pinneys' celebrated restaurant – Butley Creek Oysterage. The red-brick restaurant sits comfortably opposite Pump Street Chocolate in the market square of Orford, a couple of miles away from the oyster fishery. Overlooking the town is a Norman castle built in 1165 by Henry II, while quaint Suffolk houses flank the quiet roads that radiate from the square.

Legend has it that, in 1167, a group of men went fishing from Orford Ness and their nets became tangled on what they thought was a dolphin or seal, but it turned out to be a hairy, shaggy-bearded merman. The fishermen brought him ashore, fed him and tortured him. The merman remained silent throughout his time on land, and was eventually allowed to return to the waters at Orford, still tethered by three lines of nets; he eventually escaped and was never seen again. The Butley Creek Oysterage uses the Merman of Orford as its logo and there is a memorial to him hanging in the Orford market square.

The town of Orford straddles the River Alde that, in turn, flows through Orford Ness Nature Reserve. Since the 1100s, Orford established itself as a port when the surrounding marshes were drained and although it used to be a smuggler's haven, it now attracts people throughout the year to its muddy shores. Customs and search officers from nearby Aldeburgh in the 1800s used to patrol the Orford waters twice a week to try and catch the smugglers out.

There is no doubt that the restaurant is one of the main attractions of the town. It has remained relatively unchanged since it opened in the 1950s. It has a daily chalked menu on the wall of British classics that celebrate Pinney's entire range of products. It is here that one can find a traditional Suffolk feast of seasonal and locally caught seafood that gives visitors an insight into what has been eaten here for hundreds of years.

There are many local favourites on the menu, with my preference being the heavenly Angels on Horseback, the best smoked cod roe you will ever find and a pint of local Suffolk beer or a glass of East Anglian wine. There is also the option of a seafood platter that will leave you extraordinarily satisfied. A wonderfully deep-tasting smoked cod roe and mackerel landed on my wooden table, flanked by rock oysters, a golden local 3.3 per cent ale and some butter and crusty bread. That will see me nicely through to Norfolk.

6

Brancaster

Location: *Norfolk, England*
Natural habitat: *Salt marsh and sandy shingle
channel with freshwater springs*

Fifty miles to the north of Orford lies the old Roman fort of Caister, just on the outskirts of Great Yarmouth. It was built around AD 200 as part of a chain of forts that ran from the Wash clockwise along the beaches down to the south coast which the Romans dubbed the 'Saxon Shore'. The string of sea defences were thought to have been in constant anticipation of Saxon raiders arriving from continental Europe.

Another significant historical fact about this region dating back to the Roman invasion is the rich oyster culture. The brackish waters of the rivers Waveny, Yare, Bure and Ant formed a complex network of waterways that acted as a key to unlock the passage into East Anglia from the North Sea; they would also have provided the same ideal conditions for oyster production as we have seen in Essex. As well as the usual Roman artefacts, over 10,000 oyster shells were excavated at the fort along with bones from ducks, foxes, hares, badgers and cows.

Going even further back in time, in the nearby Nar Valley of Norfolk and also Woodston in neighbouring Cambridgeshire, evidence has been uncovered of ancient oysters from marine deposits that date to over 300,000 years ago. There are similar records from raised beach deposits on the south coast in Sussex going back at least 200,000 years. It's therefore safe to say that *ostrea edulis* has been a part of the north-west European marine mollusc fauna for the last million years at least. Not only has the estuary-rich south-eastern corner of Britain been a hub of oyster culture during recent history, but these records show that there is hard evidence for the bivalve's presence long before modern humans came to Britain 40,000 years ago.

Elsewhere in Europe at the same time, Neanderthals were the first to start using marine resources in any kind of extensive way. While there is no solid evidence of this yet in Britain, there are clear signs of shellfish exploitation in continental Europe (Italy and Gibraltar) from the last 40,000 years, which suggests a general acceptance that British and Irish populations would have been doing the same thing. But if this is the case, why have we not found any evidence of Neanderthals eating oysters in Britain at the same time? Essentially, we lost most of our shell middens when the seas rose in the Holocene, the current geological epoch that started around 11,700 years ago.

The stunning rural scenery of Norfolk is relatively unchanged since the agricultural revolution of the 1700s, as though it's been daubed with every conceivable shade of green and yellow. It is exhilarating to ride a motorbike through this sun-dappled landscape, carving my way through the warmth of the day.

Shortly after Fakenham and climbing to higher ground, the road eventually tilts gently downwards revealing a breathtaking view of the sea and the temperature suddenly drops a few degrees with the stiff onshore breeze. The sun is still out, but the raw energy of the sea's north-easterly wind tugs at my jeans. The cooling influence of the sea has given this part of Norfolk a deserved reputation for growing and then malting barley for brewing over the last 2,000 years and north Norfolk barley is desirable worldwide to this day.

I reduce the speed as I arrive at Brancaster. All the more traditional residential properties in this area have made good use of the local materials in their construction. The villages of Docking and Brancaster have classic examples of brick-and-flint houses made from local worked flint and clay. It is truly indicative of north Norfolk's wonderful rural charm, with many buildings standing largely unchanged since Horatio Nelson would frequent the Hoste pub – then called the Pitt Arms – to receive his dispatches during a period of unemployment in nearby Burnham Market in the late 1700s.

Turning east along the main village road in the direction of the town of Cromer, famous for its crabs, it is the neighbouring village of Brancaster Staithe that I'm aiming for. After just a minute, I pull into the The White Horse pub and guest house. This was my planned destination for lunch before meeting up with oyster farmers Richard Loose and Ben Sutherland at the Fish Shed at low tide, which I'd been told will be at 3.00 p.m.

The sprawling forest-green salt marsh and mocha-coloured mudflats offer a welcome sight, while I breathe in the familiar scent of sea-salted vegetation. I switch the engine off and sit back momentarily. Perched on the sea wall below the pub, the curvilinear, flint-speckled, moss-topped holiday rentals that snake away from the main pub building remind me of fantasy hobbit dwellings. I make a mental note to return here one day.

Walking into The White Horse, I settle myself in front of the panoramic windows for a spot of lunch. Paying homage to the north Norfolk brewing tradition, I order a half of Lucky Lobster, a 4.2 per cent pale ale produced by Brancaster Brewery. It is made using local Norfolk Maris Otter barley with Mistral hops for bitterness and aroma. My first sip of crisp British ale conjures up images of brightly coloured marram grass and sand dunes, and is enjoyed looking over the salt marsh, the oyster/mussel beds and the mysterious Scolt Head. It is the perfect reward for my bike journey.

I then tuck into six Brancaster rock oysters on the half shell and a crab sandwich on brown bread for good measure. My first Brancaster oyster is a fantastic meaty mouthful, large in size (about 110g) and full of firm flesh with a sweet finish. This is perhaps because the tidal channels where the oysters are grown are not only influenced by the sea but also some freshwater springs which pop up near the oyster farm. The oysters are served with a home-made mignonette of samphire, diced shallots and apple cider vinegar, half a teaspoon of which on the raw oyster gives a sweet taste of pickle that reminds me of rollmops. As someone who works predominantly with red wine vinegar, apple cider vinegar is a welcome change and very fitting for the orchard-rich county of Norfolk.

After a delicious lunch, I saddle up and prepare for the shortest journey I may ever have made – The White Horse to the Fish Shed is a distance of about 40m across the road.

A little early, I walk into the Fish Shed and have a quick chat with Mrs Bocking who tells me she is Ben Sutherland's aunt. She started the Fish Shed in 1989 with her husband from the back of their house just selling local fresh fish and shellfish; they now also sell local meat, game, pies, fruit and vegetables. The Fish Shed, along with two outlets of Gurney's Fish Shop in Thornham and Burnham Market, is a direct link back to the proud history of the coastal industry in north Norfolk. Mussel and oyster pits dating from the medieval period to the nineteenth century have been excavated, indicating a long-standing shellfish industry on this coast. Although Brancaster is the only place producing oysters now, the cold waters of the former smuggler harbours of Thornham, Blakeney and Brancaster are peppered with shallow, salty tidal marshes, bays and inlets – ideal for oyster beds, both natural and farmed. Historically, Brancaster was heavily involved in native oyster dredging in the nineteenth century, with the smacks regularly forging out into the bay and bringing the natives back to the harbour for market. Then came the mussel and whelk industries and, ultimately, the gigas oyster after the natives decreased in number.

The son of local shellfish farmer Cyril Sutherland, Ben and I gear up in waders for a jaunt across the sandy channel to the oyster beds. Ben's father Cyril used to spend his time whelking and potting in the summer and producing oysters in the winter. He then focused on the mussels, but always made sure he nursed a stock of oysters even when he wasn't intent on selling them; he was, in fact, the first in this harbour to have the rock oyster.

Another Brancaster oyster farmer, Richard Loose, was originally a carpenter by trade but moved into oysters and, by focusing solely on this one precious resource, he became the most successful oysterman in Brancaster. When Ben came home to help his father, he soon discovered that he enjoyed the oysters more than mussels; he also realised that oyster production would offer a much more stable living than that of crabs, lobsters or mussels, and it tended to be much less impacted by restrictions and regulatory changes.

The Sutherlands and Richard Loose lease their oyster grounds in the Norton Creek from the Brancaster Fishermen's Society which, in turn, leases the ground from the National Trust. That secures their sole rights to fish these grounds.

Brancaster Staithe Harbour was once a far busier port with ships laden with coal and grain. Trade declined in the 1800s but, today, a thriving fishing industry survives, and the harbour bustles with pleasure craft. We stand by some old oyster holding pits where they had once been landed, giving the oysters time to purge their stomachs before market. They look like muddy 10ft swimming pools with bricked walls and were a precursor to the purification process of today. Ben tells me about a sunken oyster smack which supposedly has a gold sovereign buried beneath its mast. He then points to a boat called the *Laura May*, which his friend Jon owns and runs as Branta Cruises. Jon operates tours along the north Norfolk coastline all year following the ever-changing wild-life of grey seals and shore birds. Again, something else to return for.

Richard approaches along the harbour with his working gear in a mesh sack and together the three of us walk a barely visible foot-path through the samphire and stonecrop-scattered salt marsh until we arrive at the sandy gravel channel. We follow the channel out of the harbour in a north-easterly direction towards Scolt Head, chatting all the way. The sun is glistening off the water as we wade through it, knee-deep in some areas. The two oyster farmers have an encyclopaedic knowledge of this stretch of land, and regularly point out quicksand and sudden drops in the under-water terrain to save me from any nasty surprises. It's a privilege to spend time with working people so in tune with their environ-ment. Once we near the oyster farms, the mussel reefs start to appear and the ground turns black with shells crackling underfoot.

We stop now at Richard's farm where he has been working his oysters flat out since the mid-1970s, after having tried oyster seed on his father's mussel beds. And as if it was all perfectly planned, Richard is now slowly cutting back on his workload as he looks towards retirement, while Ben is building up production on his farm half a mile away. Richard claims that one of the reasons he has been able to enjoy such success with the business is because of the great communication between local fishermen and the National Trust. They've had the same person in charge of dealing with shell fishermen for a long time, someone who really understands the importance of the longshore economy – oyster and mussel farm-ing, whelking, samphire picking, cockles – all the different trades living cheek-by-jowl in the harbour. We all agree on the impor-tance of mutual understanding, and preserving the naturalness of the harbour and the livelihoods of the local people.

Even the wildlife seems relaxed – an egret gently touches down to join us among Richard's trestles. 'She comes here all the time,' he tells us. 'She likes to fish in between the trestles while I'm working,' he says, looking at the bird like she is an old friend. 'She takes no notice of us at all. If we find a broken oyster, we throw it to the birds and they love it. When we move the trestles around, the shore crabs scatter and the gulls come straight in.' Long may the longshore industries continue to collaborate with their natural surroundings and flourish.

Ben and I leave Richard to get on with some work, and the pair of us wade to the Sutherlands' farm a little way up the channel. Ben grows his oysters in open boxes, much like the brown plastic bread boxes you see in the supermarket and restaurant kitchens. He is pretty relaxed about not having them in bags like Richard, and both systems seem to work. Between them, they supply all the main eateries along the north Norfolk coast from King's Lynn to Cromer, including Titchwell Manor, Caesar's at Wells, Rocky Bottoms at West Runton and, of course, Brancaster's White Horse. 'A decent product always sells,' says Ben. 'It is quality not the quantity that will reap rewards.' Ben tips out a mesh bag of giant rock oysters, which must weigh in at 200g each and which he saves especially for a Chinese customer.

Although the sun is still bright, it has arced beyond its zenith and Richard has work to do before the tide stops him for the day. Ben and I wade to higher ground and begin making our way back to Brancaster Staithe harbour along the faint salt marsh track. For the whole time I have been here, I have been acutely aware of the presence of Scolt Head, an island of sand dunes, marram grass and rare birds. It has been in clear view from every point on our trip across the salt marsh, and the fact that it's a perfectly natural, desolate and unpopulated environment makes it awe-inspiring; it touches a primal nerve in me in some ways, perhaps reminding us of a time when we were wild, too.

7

Lindisfarne

Location: *Northumberland, England*
Natural habitat: *Sheltered North Sea bay*

In the past, it was customary for monks at Lindisfarne to send oysters, fish and lobsters to Durham Cathedral as a Christmas gift; in the 1700s, they have been recorded as having sent hundreds of live lobsters and thousands of oysters. The fish would have come from Beadnell just down the coast from Lindisfarne, which has been a centre for the fishing industry since the 1300s. If you walk out on to the rocks at Beadnell near the harbour today, you can still see the 'brat holes' – a manmade depression carved into the rock which acted as holding pens for fish before being sent to market.

Lindisfarne Oysters are the only oyster fishery on the English east coast north of Norfolk. The ride between Norfolk and Northumberland is the longest distance between any two fisheries on my tour of our most precious oyster farms – along with Scotland to the Bristol Channel – and a wake-up call to me having decided to do the whole trip on a motorcycle. But as we embark on this mammoth 300-mile journey north, there are still plenty of places along the way that bear the mark of the oyster's presence in our lives throughout history.

Leaving the quiet, unassuming and ancient villages of Norfolk that surround the eastern flank of the Wash Estuary, I ride south to the market town of King's Lynn, a famed twelfth-century sea port. The name is believed to have derived from the Celtic word 'lin' for lake or pool, referring to the expansive intertidal waters of the Wash; it's probably no surprise that it was Henry VIII who decreed that the word 'King' should be inserted in front of it.

The seafood-rich town of characterful Tudor houses, smooth cobbles and ancient brickwork slips past me as I ride out on to the A17 into Lincolnshire. The Triumph and I have entered the Fens, a unique geographical feature of the eastern counties of England. The creating of the Fens was important in helping to prevent devastating flooding to what essentially has always been England's 'bread basket'– the grain- and vegetable-producing flat fields of eastern England. This land was originally wetlands that were then artificially drained – as ordained by King Charles I in the 1630s – to create a dry agricultural landscape with organised drainage channels, pumping stations and sea walls to control flooding. The area I am currently riding through is known as South Holland, a part of southern Lincolnshire that owes its name to the Dutch 'adventurers' who were tasked with draining the Fens. Riding away from the coast through the flattest of flat landscapes with big skies and roads just above sea level, I join the A1 – the Great North Road.

The A1 takes me away from the soggy Fens slicing through the rest of Lincolnshire and the gently sloping Wolds. Before leaving the county, fifty miles directly east and just south of the mighty River Humber are the coastal towns of Grimsby and Cleethorpes. There are no oyster beds here any more, but both places are synonymous with the fishing industry. Grimsby Town Football Club are nicknamed 'the Mariners' and have three fish in their black-and-white crest, and Grimsby was once home to the largest fishing fleet in the world in the 1950s.

Grimsby's long fishing tradition was based on the trawler where nets are dragged along the bottom of the sea-bed in the North Sea. With over 25,000 fish species in the world, 200 are generally caught for eating from the North Sea – cod and haddock being the most sought after. However, the oyster industry also once thrived here and, at time of writing, restoration efforts are beginning in the Humber.

I recall being in Scarborough with my brother Mike and marvelling at the fish trailer on the seaside near all the arcades. Mike asked the elderly lady peering down at us from behind the counter if he could buy an oyster, and I asked where it had come from. She replied, 'Grimsby, where else?'

Not wishing to appear a know-it-all, I carefully suggested that I didn't think that there were any active oyster beds between Norfolk and Northumberland. It therefore couldn't have come from Grimsby.

'These oysters come from Grimsby!' she repeated indignantly. And she looked back at my brother as if to shut me up. 'Do you want lemon with that, love?'

I held my tongue. Mike nodded, and she pulled out a green bottle of processed Jif lemon juice and squeezed half the bottle all over the oyster and gave it to him. With donkey rides and fake lemon juice it felt as though Scarborough was locked in a time warp, and the power of Grimsby's fishing reputation was right there before my eyes. It also shows, perhaps, how the last two or three generations in the UK haven't really placed much importance on food provenance. In the first half of the twentieth century, oysters would have been much more abundant and available, and thus people would have been much more aware of where they'd come from. The lady in the fish trailer on Scarborough beach had grown up in a different era; despite that, and despite the Jif lemon, Mike said he'd enjoyed the oyster!

It has been said that Cleethorpes was built on the oyster industry. In the *White's Directory* of 1826, of the 42 tradesmen recorded,

12 were fishermen and oyster dealers. The oystermen would fish the baby oysters in the North Sea and re-lay them in the beds off the coast. By 1854, 24 smacks were employed with four crew each to maintain the 300 acres of oyster beds around Cleethorpes. The mature oysters were sent to the markets of Hull, Sheffield, York, Leeds and Scarborough, with bushel numbers increasing when the railway reached Cleethorpes in 1863.

Records show that Joseph Grant was the first to set up an oyster stall on Cleethorpes beach in 1839. The oyster business was so good that he then went into business with a partner renting out bathing machines while seaside holidays were all the rage with townsfolk wanting a break from the industrialised areas. Oysters and swimming – the man was clearly entrepreneurial. On one particular day – 24 November 1852 – it is recorded that the Lord Mayor of Cleethorpes bought 2,000 small and 800 large native oysters from Joseph's stall. This shows that Joseph's oyster business was still going strong eleven years later, and that it was respected and popular enough for a local man of power to want to invest in such large quantities for what could have only been a banquet to impress.

Spurred on by rampant supply and demand, by the 1870s native oysters were becoming scarce and the industry started to wobble. However, to try and ease the strain, a shipment of over one million American oysters were laid in the beds at Cleethorpes in 1872 to fatten up for market, which boosted the industry once again. This was an initiative taken by a local fisherman's son called Thomas Leesing, who had been taking regular trips from Liverpool to New York in February and March while bringing back oysters with him. He had been travelling to Northport Bay, Long Island, in New York State, which was a globally recognised producer of oysters – principally the Bluepoint. Leesing's efforts encouraged an industry boom and put Cleethorpes oysters on the map again. However, in 1902, an outbreak of typhoid in Sheffield and Doncaster was blamed solely on Cleethorpes oysters and the oyster beds were found to be polluted and the oysters declared unfit for human consumption. By 1904, the beds were closed and that was the final nail in the coffin for the local oyster industry. This became a recurring theme at the end of the nineteenth and the beginning of the twentieth centuries, and helped to put people off oysters for a very long time.

Continuing north along the A1, I power into South Yorkshire passing Doncaster, Leeds and Sheffield. With York to the east, I recall the visit to the Jorvik Viking Centre in the middle of the city a few years ago. In one of the many cabinets, one can see a pile of native oyster shells still very much recognisable and intact from the eighth and ninth centuries. They had been excavated from Coppergate, a thriving central part of Viking York where trade would have been bustling.

The welcoming arms of Antony Gormley's iconic Angel of the North statue in Gateshead greet me as I skirt the Metro Centre and glide into the city of Newcastle-upon-Tyne. The unique cultural identity of this city and its inhabitants has played a huge part in my life through my father's side of the family. Once on the north side of the River Tyne, I turn right, down between the beautiful stone buildings and on to cobbled streets, then finally arriving at the historic quayside.

Having put in a huge shift on the bike today, I schedule a well-earned reviver at the Broad Chare Restaurant and Pub by the river. It is a renowned ale house with great beer and seasonal, hearty Geordie food. The pub is named after the street outside, just a stone's throw from the Tyne in the old industrial buildings. The word 'chare' is an old north-east dialect word for a medieval narrow lane, so the name literally means the 'broad narrow lane'. The pub's timber frames and stone floors feel timeless and very homely. The menu printed on cream card rotates produce with the seasons, including traditional, old-style favourites such as braised oxtail, ham shank, pease pudding and, of course, Lindisfarne oysters. The farm is just 40 miles to the north in the wild and beautiful county of Northumberland.

I order six oysters, a hot scotch egg, croquettes and deep-fried monkfish cheeks, all washed down with a bottle of Newcastle Brown Ale with a half-pint glass to lengthen the enjoyment.

My stomach filled, I ease the bike along the Broad Chare away from the Quayside and up the hill. Breaking free of the city, past the Town Moor, I join the A1 to continue northwards. The houses and factories slowly peter out before surrendering to the eerie undulating landscape of Northumberland. This stretch of road between Newcastle and Edinburgh is one of the most beautiful in Britain, peppered with castles like Alnwick and Warkworth with the North Sea on one side and the rural rugged fields on the other. I zip past Bedlington, Amble, Alnwick, Craster, the quaint fishing village of Seahouses, beautiful Bamburgh (the final resting place of lifeboat heroine Grace Darling) and, finally, into the beautifully wild Lindisfarne National Nature Reserve.

The Lindisfarne Oysters signage sits perched on the edge of a farmyard, leading to a grey breeze-block outhouse with a white door and a small white sign bearing the company name. I can just make out the familiar sound of trickling water and pumps, just like that of the Company Shed in Essex. Surrounded by bags of cultch, I clamber into a marsh-green Land Rover Defender to scramble across Christopher and Helen Sutherland's land to their oyster beds. Rumbling over cattle grids through fields, I hop out four times to open and close gates and we arrive at the psammosere (an ecological succession of plant life that began on newly exposed coastal sand) and its signature sand dunes and marram grass. The Land Rover turns away from the pristine dunes along a sandy track flanked by purple-and-pink salt-loving plants and on towards the oyster racks. We alight and set to work emptying the trailer of oyster bags and strapping them to the racks.

This location is absolutely beautiful; facing inwards, the long sweeping bay is sheltered from the North Sea and Christopher explains how the shallow waters maintain the water temperature which, in turn, creates a sweet and creamy oyster. The oysters are set in the intertidal waters just off the mainland within the nature reserve, equidistant from Bamburgh Castle and its sprawling sand dunes and Holy Island itself.

The Sutherland family have been farming the Pacific rock oyster here since the 1970s on restored oyster beds which date back to 1381, and the fantastic quality of the oyster shows just how good they are at their husbandry. All Lindisfarne oysters I have ever shucked and tasted have had a sweet creamy flavour profile which is extremely distinctive. The Sutherlands cultivate them on a site established by the monks of the Lindisfarne Priory, which I can see in all its proud majesty in the distance, jutting out of the sea.

The Holy Island of Lindisfarne is considered by many to be a most sacred place, dating back to Anglo-Saxon times. Lindisfarne is most famous for being the site of the first Viking raids on Britain in the Dark Ages; the monks of the monastery on Lindisfarne were brutally murdered by marauding Norsemen in AD 793, and the invaders would go on to rule in the north of Britain under Danelaw until 1066.

The Lindisfarne Gospels, the famously intricate and exquisite manuscripts illuminated by the monks, were created using inks on vellum (animal skin, usually cowhide) and painted by candlelight in a fusion of Celtic, Mediterranean and Saxon styles around AD 715–720, making it the most important book of its time. It was very common for oyster and mussel shells to be used as vessels for the paints and the white colours in the book were most likely created from calcium carbonate, which could be found in chalk or ground-up seashells or eggshell. This practice is also celebrated in the Medeltids Museum in Stockholm, where the use of bivalve shells (mussels, in this case) is highlighted in an exhibition about Stockholm's medieval church painters and how they carried out their mural work using dry plaster colour pigments held in shells. And from around the fifteenth and sixteenth centuries in the north-eastern woodlands of the USA, the Lenape tribe native to the New York region famously used oyster shells as cutting tools. So not only was the little bivalve seen as a commodity and a food source, it was also an intrinsic element in mankind's cultural heritage and literally incorporated into our most celebrated arts and crafts.

While working on the oyster racks, I can hear a rhythmic moaning sound in the distance. I stop to focus on it, and at first think it is the drone of the North Sea just over the sand dunes. I eventually work out where it's coming from – a grey-looking island just north of us. I then realise it is not an island at all – it's a colony of seals.

The wildlife here is breathtaking; there are thousands of migrating birds, too, nesting in the dunes. They come and go as they please and all these diverse species seem to co-exist in a finely balanced harmony, something Christopher tells me he has witnessed throughout his time in this part of Northumberland. Living and working in these sorts of environments, the oysterman tends to be more in tune with the rhythms of nature than many of us in society today, living as we do in towns and cities where contact with the natural world is minimal.

The following morning, I head to Riley's Fish Shack for breakfast. I ride through Cullercoats – my granny's birthplace – and park the bike on a cliff overlooking the North Sea in Tynemouth. This renowned Fish Shack is nestled between the sea cliffs on King Edward's Bay offering fantastic local seafood in a converted shipping container. Lindisfarne Oysters are on the menu, as well as other high-quality, locally sourced produce, all listed on an ever-changing, black-slatted specials board. The shack is a first-come, first-served marvel that has queues before midday and I am lucky to have bagged a table before the rush.

Head chef/owner Adam Riley cooks up my order and I sit gazing out to sea. Adam serves up a piping-hot oyster Rockefeller fresh from his clay oven and creates a dressed oyster comprising sea herbs, North Sea seabass crudo, ceviche and a fennel mignonette comprised of diced banana shallot and apple with a dash of Hepple Gin from the juniper bushes growing on the remote moors of Northumberland to add fruity summer notes. It is refreshing, unique and all from the natural coastal environment in front of me, a world away from the bustle of daily life.

Adam Riley is a huge fan of langoustines, and is perfectly positioned to take advantage of their abundance with nearby North Shields being England's largest prawn/langoustine landing port. In 2017, over 1,000 tons were landed here and it is estimated that over 90 per cent were sent overseas – and we wonder why the rest of the world does not know about our seafood!

Riley's Fish Shack is a perfect place for sampling oysters and seafood, and for getting to know the local people of Tynemouth. Most importantly, it has a proprietor in Adam who leads by example without fanfare or fuss. This kind of establishment is important for the future of oysters and seafood in the north-east. Imagine if we had more shacks and stalls like Riley's for people to enjoy the freshest daily catch: the local economies would benefit enormously. It is so simple, and there's every chance eateries like Adam's will become even more prevalent and popular in the years to come.

8

Loch Ryan (*Loch Rìoghaine*)

Location: *Stranraer, Scotland*
Natural habitat: *Native oyster fishery grown
on submarine beds of Loch Ryan*

Upon entering Scotland after Berwick-upon-Tweed, I head north towards Edinburgh following the coast as it pinches in at the Firth of the Forth. This location was once home to a famous native-oyster fishery, which fed the pubs and oyster houses of Edinburgh. What is less well known is that the oysters of this region helped to inform Charles Darwin's Theory of Evolution and change humanity's understanding of our origins. Darwin attended the University of Edinburgh at the age of sixteen with his brother to study Medicine. Having more of an interest in natural history, he became distracted from his primary studies and found inspiration in the oysters growing along the nearby shoreline. During the winter when oysters were in season, Darwin wandered along the shores of the Firth of Forth with the zoologist Robert Grant, and sailed with the oystermen of Newhaven to gather specimens to study. While at Edinburgh, the greatest naturalist ever to have lived gave his first scientific presentation on his observations of seashore animals.

Native oysters are no longer a force to be reckoned with in the Forth, which makes Loch Ryan a very special place as it only produces highly prized native oysters, and no other varieties. The native is the oyster-lover's oyster – it has a dense, slightly metallic and complex flavour, and evokes images of misty Breton shores, despite us being on the south-western tip of Scotland. The oysters from Loch Ryan are wonderfully satisfying and will be worth travelling all this way for.

Arriving in Cairnryan, I'm mindful that I've only ever previously experienced Scotland as a younger man when travelling to gigs in a handful of cities – Aberdeen, Dundee, Edinburgh and Glasgow. I have never taken the time to fully appreciate the raw natural beauty that Scotland has in abundance beyond its larger conurbations.

I turn south on the A77 to the home of the Wallace family on the eastern shore of Loch Ryan – the most southerly of all Scotland's sea lochs – where I've arranged to meet them before the festivities of the Stranraer Oyster Festival kick off later this evening. I gently coax the Triumph down a long pea-shingle drive towards a beautiful old white house. As I park up, the door is flung open and out step Ben and Malcolm Wallace (son and father respectively), who instantly take an interest in my bike, and eventually invite me in for tea. The whole family is here, and the charm of their welcome is particularly heartwarming. The tea, biscuits and cakes they ply me with all add to the general sense of bonhomie.

The oyster beds here were granted by Royal Charter to the Wallace family in 1701 by King William III, meaning that the family have exclusive rights to the beds and do not need to renew the licence to fish. A local called Tristan Hugh-Jones and his father were asked by the Wallace family to come and help run the oyster fishery in 1996 because of their vast experience in working with native oysters in County Cork, Ireland.

The beds are located on the eastern side of this relatively sheltered loch, almost equidistant from Cairnryan port and the town of Stranraer, with the Wallace family home overlooking them. Loch Ryan itself is roughly 7.5 miles long and 2.5 miles wide, making it a manageable fishery by the two fishing boats – *Vital Spark* and the *Haematopus* – the latter of which I am about to set sail in with Tristan and his crew.

To reach the boat, I mount the bike and ride south for a few minutes with the loch on my right and open fields on my left; I pass dozens of wading birds foraging by the water and perhaps hundreds of curlew and oystercatchers sitting in one of the fields, an extraordinary and rare sight. Loch Ryan is well known for its bird watching and is one of the most important wildlife sites in the UK. However, it is not just birds and oyster farmers who have harvested the shellfish here – in caves surrounding the loch at Cairnryan and at the head of the loch in Stranraer, archaeologists have discovered prehistoric oysters, along with flint and hammer stones. This shows that, for thousands of years, Loch Ryan was used as a pit stop on the main west coast sea route, and it's the shortest distance for a sea trip across to Ireland from Cairnryan to Belfast.

I consider the centuries-old oyster cultivation as I ride into the town past a big white marquee where twenty-first century folk will be eating the native oyster this weekend as part of the festival. They are most likely to have had their oysters shucked with a knife, though, rather than flint or stone.

Arriving in Stranraer town, I leave my bike by the harbour, where costermongers and oyster girls over 100 years ago would have lined the harbour walls selling oysters from the fishery. I clamber down on to the sea-worn red fishing boat which is moored in the harbour to join the waiting crew: Neil the oysterman, skipper Rab, John, Tristan and Shaun. We then set sail for a part of the loch called Lefnoll Point, which has a hard sea-bed providing an ideal growing surface for the native oysters. Our catch will then be ceremoniously brought to shore for the opening of the oyster festival this evening. The boat presses on through the water, and I lean in to talk with Rab while watching his depth gauge register deepening waters.

In the thirteenth century, the native oyster fishery of the Forth covered over 50 square miles and was one of the most commercially important in Scotland. Now, this is a self-sufficient native oyster bed, the only commercially harvested one in Scotland. By harvesting the oysters slowly, and replacing the small oysters in the beds, the hope is to build a larger population, which will then breed more, leading in turn to more product to take to market. Oysters from here are also sent up to the Dornoch Firth to support the oyster restoration project up there (the Dornoch Environmental Enhancement Project – also known as DEEP).

The boat carves through the gentle waves as gannets arrow into the sea like airborne missiles. As we approach the eastern side of the loch, the water movement is much greater with more nutrients for the Loch Ryan natives to eat and, in turn, grow faster. We are very close to the caves in the cliffs used by prehistoric oyster gatherers; like them, the innate knowledge of the local environment and the natural feel that my fellow crew members have for the right location of the oyster beds is very impressive, this insight being intrinsic to all those who have historically worked this stretch of Loch Ryan.

When Rab is happy with our location, the winch creaks as it unwinds, dropping the dredge to the bottom of the sea loch. The boat advances gently in a zigzag pattern to work the ground efficiently in ways that only these oystermen can really understand. After five minutes or so, the winch cranks into action and the dredge is wound back up towards the stern of the boat before rising out of the water with the catch. It is a wonderful sight; it swings above our heads and is grabbed by the oyster boys in their yellow oilskins to stabilise it. With a mallet, John smacks open the latch holding the metal dredge together and out tumbles a shimmering catch of oysters, along with a few crabs and sea squirts which are returned to the water.

To achieve the desired catch of 2,000 market oysters, the crew has to sift through 40,000 or so specimens that are usually too small, which will form part of future stock. The benefit of re-laying the oysters close together is that they are near to each other, so that in the summer months when they breed, there is much more chance that the male will be able to fertilise the female oysters' eggs. As we all begin to hand-grade the oysters on the stern of the boat, it is clear that through some careful management, by harvesting only the very largest for market, the fishermen have been able to re-lay plenty of oysters for future years. These oysters will grow and also be brood stock for about another five years or so until they are harvested. The oysters here grow at a rate of about 11g per year – they are much slower growing than the rock oyster – so by the time people eat Loch Ryan native oysters, they will be about eight years old.

With our orange baskets full of natives, the discarded specimens – the bycatch – is gently put back in the sea unharmed, save for a few starfish and crabs which the fishermen will show to the kids of Stranraer this weekend to teach them about the sea. We make our way back to the harbour in a south-eastern trajectory just as flecks of rain start to speckle the deck.

Once docked, we heave the baskets up the steps on to the pier and the oysters are taken directly into the marquee for the Stranraer Oyster Festival. The festival promotes the fabulous oysters from Loch Ryan, but also brings the community together for a party with shucking competitions, beer, a festival market, local food and seafood recipes. My favourite recipe on their list is Cullen Skink, a staple Scottish soup much like a smoky chowder with the main ingredients being haddock, potato and onions. It is typical in the north-east of the country and is named after the Scottish town of Cullen with the word 'skink' deriving from the Germanic word 'schenke' meaning ham, skin or knuckle.

While we've been out on the loch, the harbour has come alive and the festivities have begun. The oystermen throw on their smocks and take stock of the catch while hopeful competitors in the Scottish Oyster Shucking Championship held here each year sharpen their knives.

9

Loch Fyne (*Loch Fìne*)

Location: *Cairndow, Argyll, Scotland*
Natural habitat: *Fjordic tidal sea loch/
brackish waters at oyster farm*

As I push on northwards, the trees lining the A83 are auburn-leaved with toffee-blushed bracken carpeting the base of their trunks. I reach and then bypass Glasgow and its outlying districts, and become aware of my proximity to the Roman Balmuildy fort on the Antonine Wall, where archaeologists discovered Roman oyster shells from the mid-second century. The Antonine Wall was the north-west frontier of the Roman Empire, running from Clyde in the west to Forth in the east, and was built around AD 142. It was part of a 3,000-mile network of frontiers that spanned three continents.

The daylight is fading and my potential enjoyment of the extraordinary beauty of Loch Lomond and the Trossachs National Park is unfortunately superseded by an effort to stay alive on the wet roads in gathering gloom with nothing but the warmth and rhythmic throb of the engine for comfort.

The wet weather has been almost biblical in the latter stages of my trip today and, eventually, the perfect antidote is provided by a cosy room in an enchanting bed and breakfast, with steaming soup and smoked haddock for supper. The shower in my room is tinglingly hot and the radiators are cranked up to the max to dry out my drenched gear. Feeling like a weary journeyman of old who has taken refuge in a mountain bothy, I go to bed physically drained, with a full stomach and a heart warmed by a Scottish home.

My breakfast table the next morning is set facing the vast expanse of Loch Fyne, the longest sea loch in Scotland at 40 miles long, running from Clachan to the Sound of Bute. It can reach a maximum depth of 600ft in parts, and can accommodate humpback whales as well as naval submarines, whose sonar technology was tested here during the Cold War.

I finish my breakfast, hop back on the bike – in my now dry kit – and take the A83 north past Auchindrain and Inveraray, surging over stone bridges with the morning sun spraying shafts of light between the birch and pine trees. I reach the small village of Clachan, which faces Cairndow at the head of Loch Fyne, where the River Fyne enters the loch. Clachan is famously where the flagship Loch Fyne Oyster restaurant opened in 1988 and, along with the oysters it harvests, it still remains under the control of the oyster farm. All the other Loch Fyne restaurants – more than twenty of them now, scattered the length of the UK between Edinburgh and Portsmouth – were bought by Suffolk-based Greene King Brewery in 2007 for £68 million.

The Loch Fyne story starts in 1978 with a local landowner Johnny Noble and a marine biologist called Andy Lane who, together, found native oyster shells on the foreshore of Loch Fyne indicating that the area had favourable growing conditions for oysters. They started selling from a small timber shack on a layby in Cairndow off the A83 and, as they acquired a reputation for great quality shellfish, they took over some local farm buildings and turned them into their first restaurant. The oyster farm was developed in the upper reaches of the loch where the oysters bene-fited from the freshwater nutrients from the River Fyne which, in turn, is nourished with tributary run-off from the surrounding alpine vegetation.

The Loch Fyne area has a very special feel to it – standing here at sea level looking up through the glen and the steep mountain sides imbues you with a sense of humility. I am standing in Campbell Clan territory, and the blue-and-green hues of the hill-sides are evocative of the Campbell tartan. Cairndow translates as 'the black cairn' – a cairn being a pile of stones to mark a memo-rial or boundary – a fitting name, as it was just down the road in Kilmartin Glen where over 350 prehistoric and historic monu-ments have been recorded within just a six-mile radius.

Just off the coast, beyond the Isle of Mull, is the historic and spiritual Iona Island, another of this region's natural wonders and a sacred place to many. There is an old Gaelic saying: '*Nach Urramach an Cuan*', which translates literally as 'How worthy of honour is the sea', and that is the Loch Fyne philosophy which is painted on the wall of the Loch Fyne Oyster Bar. This concept, married with the values of growing high-grade shellfish in the fertile waters of Loch Fyne, have made this oyster company a household name.

As I gently roll to a halt in the farm, in front of me there is the Loch Fyne Oysters signage depicting an eighteenth- or nineteenth-century woman with a headscarf and a striped, full skirt carrying a basket of fish on her back, which would have held oysters in times gone by. Walking up to a cabin, I find Iain MacKay – the grandly titled Aquaculture Manager – who invites me in. It is the morning tea time, just like back in Maldon, and it wouldn't surprise me if oyster farmers do this the world over, to the minute!

A friendly fellow called Andre takes me out to the plant and starts a tour of the set-up. The grading machine has oyster sizes from 65g to 150g. Andre says that in recent times there has been a shift in preferred oyster sizes by restaurants, a change with which

I am perfectly familiar. When I was serving oysters in Maldon's Promenade Park in 2006, it was the norm then that market-sized oysters would be 80g–110g, but now some customers prefer the smaller grades. 'Our top sellers are 65g–75g and 75g–90g now, where it used to be 90g–105g,' Andre tells me.

I'm aware that the Asian market loves a large oyster, both on the half shell and for making oyster sauce, but it does seem that the Western markets have moved towards a smaller oyster. This might be because more and more people are interested in the shellfish and want to start small, or perhaps oysters are more accepted as part of a meal – before starters, for instance – so people do not want to fill up before their main course.

Walking round the plant, Andre points to the different oysters in the various purification tanks. The waters here are classified as grade A, but they continue to purify the oysters with UV-treated loch water as an additional precaution for a minimum of 42 hours to ensure the oysters reach the table in the best possible condition. And as well as farming their own oysters in the loch, Loch Fyne work with 10–15 partner growers including Arisaig, Ailot, Gigha, Kyle of Tongue, Islay, Colonsay, Lismore, Barra in the Outer Hebrides and Morecambe Bay, all working together and supporting each other. Right now, one of the staff is packing a selection box for the Loch Fyne Restaurants all over the UK so diners can sample the different types of Scottish oysters. These little Scottish gems are then dispatched across the length and breadth of our island nation in beautiful wooden oyster boxes bearing the blue Loch Fyne logo of the lady carrying the fish, a symbol that certifies the quality and provenance of the oysters.

Walking down past the old Ardkinglas House, I wade out into the crystal-clear water of the loch to speak with Iain MacKay. As I feel the icy cold water seeping into my boot through a hole in the rubber, Iain points to the head of the loch where the river brings freshwater, lending the oysters their brackish crisp taste. There is no sub-tidal growing here; right now we are both standing on the low-tide mark where Loch Fyne likes to farm. In these conditions, the oyster grows at a steady rate, has a good quality meat and becomes a very robust mature specimen, with a good shelf life of around nine days. This enables them to be exported as far afield as Singapore and Dubai while still retaining their distinctive qualities in top condition, a testament to the knowledge and expertise of the Loch Fyne team.

I start helping Iain hang his swinging baskets from the trestles and we chat away. Iain tells me about the proximity he has to the natural world in all its forms as he works on the oyster farm, and he reels off various encounters with wildlife with a mixture of day-job mundanity and awed reverence. He was out in the boat one day when a pilot whale breached near him, and he's been visited by porpoises and seals in the water, and golden eagles, buzzards and sparrowhawks in the skies. It is a wonderful privilege to experience the beauty of this place with him, and to see his oysters growing here, knowing that the area has a long history of both shellfish and fish consumption. Just up the road, more evidence of ancient oyster consumption has been found in the form of an ancient shell midden at the River Add and Inveraray.

We continue with the work for another ten minutes and start to head up the beach when a brightly coloured rainbow spans the loch painting a perfect reflection in the water. Iain looks at me with a smile that says, 'What a send-off.'

Leaving the farm, I ride back up the track and turn north on the A83 following the rainbow back towards Clachan, passing the creel fishermen still working on their catch in the waters beside me, and heading towards the River Fyne at the head of the loch, where it appears one end of the rainbow is firmly rooted within the Loch Fyne restaurant. I can't very well ignore this sign from above and its guaranteed pot of gold, so I am soon propped up at the counter sampling some of the oysters.

It is a culinary experience not to be missed. This state-of-the-art restaurant is a perfect example of an establishment that has received constant love, care and attention for the last thirty years in stark contrast to other well-known but nondescript 'chains' which seem to have sprung up everywhere. During the sale of the company, founder Andrew Lane looked for a buyer who was interested in 'a philosophy, not just a brand'. This pioneering restaurant has preserved all that is wonderful about Scottish gastronomy, and celebrates the best aspects of local cuisine in a wholly authentic way. As producers, purveyors and smokers of shellfish, fish, venison, organic meat and beverages, they could not be better placed to represent all that is good about Scotland and its gourmet fare.

As I leave the restaurant, I have even more appreciation now of the stewardship of the oyster farmers at Loch Fyne, enabling the harvesting of quality local produce and working hand-in-hand with third-party producers; such a philosophy is driving the success of the business, today and for the years to come.

10

Loch Creran (*Loch Criathrain*)

Location: *Loch Creran, Argyll, Scotland*
Natural habitat: *Tidal sea loch*

Leaving Cairndow and Inveraray, I press on up into the hills heading north towards Oban. The weather becomes more changeable and, when the heavens open, I dive under cover to sit out the rain and ride on when it brightens up. Intermittently, as the clouds scud across the vast skies, the sun bathes the landscape in a golden glow, and I'm treated to a series of rainbows, one after the other, spanning the glens and lochs. I have never experienced such a concentration of rainbows before, and it almost feels as though I am riding through and under them. I have to pull over near Kilchurn Castle on the A819 to take a moment to appreciate the shimmering, translucent hues in the evening sky.

I continue on the A85 circumnavigating Loch Awe, Loch Etive, the glens and snowy hills, pass through Benderloch and arrive at Caledonian Oysters on the quiet banks of Loch Creran. Turning off the tarmac road on to a pebbly track, some fallow deer break cover, startled, and disappear into the woods beyond.

The rutted track continues and my suspension is hammered on the way down to the water's edge, where I am greeted by the smiling face of oyster farmer Judith Vajk, in her yellow oilskins and waders, waving me over to the oyster-grading machine. It is midway through the working day and she and her crew are busy grading, purifying and working the oysters.

'Beautiful deer just up the road!' I say as I greet Judith.

'Oh yes, they're lovely, aren't they? We get four types of deer in Scotland – red, roe, fallow and sika – but red and roe are the native species. Just here on the loch we get otters playing in the water, too!'

Standing in a working grading shed out of the spitting rain, I gaze at the rock oysters in the tanks and ask if I might try one. Judith has two at the ready and allows me to shuck them for us both to eat. What a beautiful taste! Sweet and briny, but not overly salty, considering the dry summer we have had. The long finish on the oyster conjures up images of Loch Creran – a tidal sea loch – a stone's throw from where I am standing now. It is not quite the Highlands here, but the whole area was carved by glaciers and you can see the famous Glen Coe just a little further north.

The waters of Loch Creran are influenced by the sea with tides twice a day flooding in from the south-west beyond the Isle of Lismore and there are three rivers in the north-east of the loch that bring the cool freshwater from the hills; it's a huge advantage for the oysters to benefit from the best of both worlds in the middle of this geographical wonderland. The oyster's backnotes are lingering on my palate and I still can just make out the sweet, creamy hints of the summer. It is a beautiful sensation.

Judith chuckles that some of her customers at Perth Farmers' Market in Perth, Scone Game Fair and in local restaurants say the oysters have floral notes. With Oban being the nearest main town, I ask Judith why she travels 2.5 hours across Loch Tay or Loch Earn to trade at Perth?

'I am from over that way and it gives me a chance to see my family,' she explains.

For many, family is always a good enough reason to do anything. I guess, too, farming oysters on the west coast and selling them on the east really puts the 'Caledonia' into Caledonian Oysters, the name deriving from the Roman name for the whole of modern Scotland.

Judith tells me about the history of the oyster farm, explaining that she met her husband Hugo in France while he was working for SATMAR, the French oyster hatchery. They wanted to start their own farm but could not find a suitable location in France, so they tried both Jersey and Guernsey, but to no avail. Eventually, still within the Channel Islands, they ended up on the tiny island of Herm, where they trialled several hundred oysters in the mid-1980s and ended up staying there for ten years. They were married and had their children there, and then returned to Judith's native Scotland and bought the very oyster farm I am at today.

We take a walk through the shed and Judith suddenly says, 'Do you know what a serpulid is?'

I draw a blank and shake my head.

'Loch Creran is a Special Site of Scientific Interest (SSSI) and a Marine Protected Area because it has the largest marine tubeworm reefs in Scotland,' she says, holding up a beautiful white coral-like clump of reef. 'It is special because the serpulid or organ-pipe worms rarely form reefs together.' Just like kelp, these reefs provide homes for other sea creatures, such as spider crabs, urchins and lobsters.

We wander out of the shed and down to the water. It is calm and glass-like as it mirrors the clearing sky. The rain has subsided for now and it feels as though I should probably take full advantage of the drier weather to continue onwards. I thank Judith and her team and wish them well. And as I climb back on to my bike, I thank my lucky stars that I've been able to experience a tiny snapshot of the love story that led to the creation of Caledonian Oysters, and the beauty of the produce that is still driven by that love story today.

I head for Oban town, and a room at the Royal Hotel on Argyle Square. Judith kindly offers to meet me in a local restaurant on the seafront called Cuan Mor, meaning 'big ocean' in Gaelic. We catch up again over my 'ham and haddie' (gammon and smoked haddock on a bed of mash with a cheesy sauce) and her fish and chips. Caledonian oysters are not on the menu here, but they are at Cuan Mor's sister restaurant called the Waterfront on the pier, and also in the brilliantly named Ee-usk (meaning 'fish') restaurant at the other end of Oban Bay. For seafood lovers, Oban is a joy – it is known as the seafood capital of Scotland, and for good reason. I'm in gastronomic heaven, and will be sorry to have to leave this special place as I continue on my journey.

11

Colonsay, Islay and Mull
(*Colbhasa, Ìle agus Muile*)

Location: *Inner Hebrides, Scotland*
Natural habitat: *Sea strait*

The charming island of Colonsay is loved by everybody I have spoken to about it. The ferry trip from Oban takes just over two hours and carries you into the middle of the pure Scottish sea waters, fifteen miles south of Mull. To the south of Colonsay itself are the islands of Islay and Jura where, on a clear day, you can see Ireland's northernmost county, Donegal, with the Atlantic Ocean beyond. With just over a hundred inhabitants on Colonsay, this small isle in the middle of the sea is home to one of Britain's remotest communities.

These islands have welcomed intrepid visitors for thousands of years. On the even smaller tidal island of neighbouring Oronsay, huge shell middens dating from 4100 BC and 3400 BC have been found. These finds suggested that, over a 700-year period, visitors would have enjoyed a mixed diet of marine and terrestrial protein, suggesting seasonal visits and varying patterns of site occupation.

Both Colonsay and Oronsay have provided a great deal of evidence of prehistoric human activity, including the early shell mounds, three cairns, eight standing stones, eight hut circles, five ancient field systems, nine forts and a medieval priory. The middens also serve as proof of a highly active and healthy biodiversity, over and above all the shell remnants – remains of cormorant, shag, goose, shelduck, water rail, ringed plover, tern, gull, razorbill, guillemot, gannet, seal, otter, red deer, pig, dolphin and red-breasted merganser have all been found here at one time or another. And most exciting of all, eight bones of the now extinct Great Auk – the celebrated, docile, flightless seabird that so charmed sailors in the eighteenth and nineteenth centuries – were found here, too.

Andrew Abrahams farms his oysters on the island having arrived here in 1977. At that time, Andrew initially looked at growing mussels, but knew that native oysters had been grown here successfully in 1910. He took up rock oyster farming in the salty Atlantic coastal waters and sold his first oysters to Poole and Loch Fyne – and the rest is history. The Colonsay oyster can be sampled on the island itself and all over Scotland through Loch Fyne's distribution network where the oyster's 'merroir' – the characteristic taste of an oyster from a specific location – is well known for its strong salinity, derived from its Atlantic home.

It is not just oysters that Andrew is known for – he makes critically acclaimed honey from the rare European black bee (*apis mellifera mellifera*). Much like the *edulis* oyster, the European black bee (sometimes called the dark bee) numbers have diminished drastically over the last century and it was thought to have been almost extinct in Britain. Upon discovering some disused hives in a derelict barn, Andrew visited the Scottish east coast for a couple of summers to learn the craft of beekeeping, and he was following in a noble tradition – in the 1940s and '50s, a man called Niall McNeill reared his own queen bees on Colonsay, and was instrumental in maintaining a thriving beekeeping community and sharing his skills and knowledge in this tiny island region. Rearing bees in an island environment helps to ensure large, healthy colonies, as the virgin queens prefer to roam up to five miles to mate, something they cannot do in these isolated communities.

In a similar way to the native oyster in its wildly natural habitat, the European black bee has been the dominant honeybee here since the last Ice Age, but is now restricted to just a few isolated pockets on the fringes of rural areas in countries including Ireland, Scotland, Denmark, Norway and Switzerland. Vulnerable to viruses, the bee population has been decimated in recent times, although a small number of colonies have survived. Their resilience is impressive, despite these challenges, and they are capable of surviving the harshest of northern European climates; they can fly in wet weather and in temperatures as low as 2°C while producing sufficient honey to enable them to see out the winter. They are our native species of bee and we should cherish and protect them as we do the native oyster.

Tasting the deeply golden, intensely sweet honey is a joy – the flavour is intensely floral, aromatic and wonderfully rounded, making it a unique and complex taste experience. Over 50 per cent of all British wildflower species grow on Colonsay and Oronsay, which accounts for the complexity of the flavour – the bees collect pollen from thousands of different plant and wildflower species from spring to autumn, and they do so flying up to two to three miles from their hives. The pollen from heathers normally makes up about 60–70 per cent of the honey, but the colour and taste of Colonsay honey will vary hugely depending on the season and the weather. In spring, the honey tends to taste more of sycamore and bluebell; in summer, more of bramble or clover; in autumn, the predominant flavour will be heather.

Andrew has protected the Colonsay black bees by having won a campaign to make it illegal to import non-native bees to the island. Because man has commercialised bees, we have tipped the balance away from natural selection (much like the rampant overfishing of native oysters in the late 1800s/early 1900s). On top of this, the industrialisation of farmland destroyed the natural bee wildflower habitat in most of Britain. Grasslands were fertilised by nitrogen, hedgerows uprooted for fields and insecticide was introduced. The parallels with the native oyster are obvious.

The fact that Andrew is involved in both industries is extremely rare, too – he should be lauded for continuing the age-old traditions of oyster and bee husbandry – both onshore and off it – on a wind-swept Celtic island in the middle of the sea. And it doesn't go unnoticed – he is rightly revered by his peers and his customers alike.

It is a short ferry ride from Colonsay to Islay, a wildlife paradise with seals, dolphins and basking sharks circling its 130-mile coastline and 200 different species of bird, including the puffin, festooning the cliffs.

Islay oysters are grown at the head of a tidal sea loch called Loch Gruinart, which has also been the primary roost for the thousands of protected Greenland barnacle geese that arrive on Islay each year. The oysters' saltiness is balanced by a discernible sweetness – the heavily saline waters of the Atlantic sweep in and out of the estuary twice a day, resulting in the oysters' adductor muscles having to work extremely hard. And they are meaty all year round as the water temperature does not drop too low in winter, ensuring that they never become very lean; in summer, the temperature doesn't rise enough for them to spawn. Some locals still remember eating wild native oysters but no wild beds exist in the area any more, so the Islay oyster farmers – Craig and Petra Archibald – solely cultivate the Pacific rocks.

The Celtic island of Islay is also known as the Queen of the Hebrides, and one of its most famous exports is a distinctively peaty, smoky whisky. It is believed that monks from Ireland first brought whisky distilling to Islay, now boasting eight working distilleries. The combination of pure freshwater, fertile lands for growing barley and the presence of the peat bogs lend the local whisky its signature taste. The peat is rich in decaying mosses, heather and lichen, all often shrouded in a fine sea spray, which adds a very distinctive character when compared with the peat found on the mainland. And on Islay, peat is also used as a fuel for the kilns in which the malt barley is dried, thereby adding another layer of unique flavour to the highly prized product.

Another unique characteristic of Islay's distilleries is that the storage facilities are next to the sea and, because wood is porous, the marine environment in the form of airborne particles gradually penetrates the barrels, leaving its coastal signature on the character of the end product. Islay whisky can therefore have a saltiness to it, as well as the peat and smoke.

Given the proximity of oyster and whisky production on Islay, it's natural to think about how these high-quality products might be paired together – indeed, whether they should be at all. There's a prevailing myth that whisky and oysters simply don't go together – but just one taste will prove how perfect the marriage can be. At the whisky festival here in May, the two whiskies that are used most with Islay oysters are a sixteen-year-old, peaty Lagavulin or a smooth, easy-drinking Bunnahabhain.

Whisky and oysters also both take on the characteristics of the environment that surrounds them – informing their terroir and merroir – meaning both food and drink have a connection through place of origin and water. And the salinity in the shellfish from the north coast of Islay is beautifully paired with the local whisky's smoky notes.

Other wonderful flavour and texture combinations are possible if we look beyond the Islay region. Salty oysters might be successfully paired with Douglas Laing's Rock Oyster whisky, a rich, smoky spirit of maritime character made from blended malt based on whiskies from Jura, Islay, Arran and Orkney. Another option as an entry-level tasting experience might be pairing a sweeter, lighter, leaner oyster with a light and sweet lowland grain whisky such as Haig Club from the Cameronbridge distillery, or perhaps trying a native oyster from the Dornoch Firth in the Scottish Highlands with a wee dram of Glenmorangie.

Once you have paired up your preferred whisky with a suitable oyster, it's advisable first to sip the briny oyster liquor from the shell to prepare your palate; then take a sip of the whisky and let the flavours marry in your mouth; then eat the oyster; lastly, pour a little of the whisky into the empty shell to enable the salt of the oyster liquor to reduce the alcohol content, and then drink the whisky from the shell.

Over 100 miles due north of Islay lies the Isle of Mull, the third-largest island in Scotland and the second-largest in the Inner Hebrides. It measures 30 miles from east to west and 27 miles north to south, and has a munro – a mountain rising to 914.4m (over 3,000ft) above sea level – called Ben More.

Mull can easily lay claim to be the pearl of the Hebrides. The prevailing landscape is beautifully verdant with woodland and hills swathed in all shades of green, much loved by Scottish writers Robert Louis Stevenson and Walter Scott, as well as England's Keats, Wordsworth and painter Turner. And as I ride through the rain-spattered countryside, the thought of oysters, pearls and their transluscent shells is not very far away in the light that catches the water droplets dancing and shimmering all around me, and the iridescent hues of the wet road ahead.

Loch Ba lies at the feet of Ben More to my left, where one of the island's most powerful witches, Cailleach Bheur, called home. Legend has it that on the dawn of every hundredth year, she would bathe in the loch at dawn before any other creature had woken. The waters of the loch were her life-giving elixir for centuries until a shepherd's dog barked one morning, breaking the spell. Just further south are the Lochbuie standing stones, a reminder of times long past when megaliths were erected for rituals, a clear sign of the spiritual heritage and distinctive energy of this unique island.

I continue on down to Calgary, the town that lent the city in Alberta, Canada, its name; in 1875, Colonel James Macleod was asked to come up with a name for the original fort that stood where the city is today and, having visited his wife's family in

Calgary on the Isle of Mull, he was inspired to use the name, thinking that it meant 'pure running waters' in Gaelic; in fact, it actually means 'bay farm', which perhaps wasn't quite so suitable for the Canadian city that would develop over time. And as another reminder of the rich historical heritage of this place, on the north shore of Calgary Bay you can still see remnants of a stone pier from which the residents boarded boats bound for the New World.

The Mull oyster farm is situated on the exposed north-west coast of the island just near Calgary. Nick Turnbull lives just above the oyster farm and, having been a fisherman for crabs, lobsters and prawns, he diversified into oysters in 1990 with his fishing partner George Martin. Now his son Kenny runs the fishing side and Gordon runs the oysters, with Nick occasionally helping out after having taken retirement.

Isle of Mull oysters were first harvested in 1993, and they then joined the Scottish Shellfish Marketing Group (SSMG) in 1995, which gave them access to the shelves of UK supermarkets. Today, a number of the biggest UK retailers stock Isle of Mull oysters, and the SSMG has Scottish produce in over 7,000 supermarkets around UK and Europe – an incredible achievement.

The Turnbulls' oysters are grown in a narrow sea loch that is exposed to the Atlantic Sea at one end. The oysters are located in the middle of the loch, at the head of which fresh, clear nutrient-rich water enters from the nearby mountains. Although the oysters are facing the sea, their position in the loch lends them a less salty taste than those grown at Colonsay because of the freshwater running down from an inner loch on the Bellart River. This entirely natural set of conditions gives a really clean shell, unlike the muddy oyster shells from my native Essex.

The farm's location on Mull is stunningly beautiful – the oyster-men and women can see over to the islands of Rúm, Eigg, Coll, Tiree and Staffa as they work the bags, and sometimes as far afield as Barra and Uist. And if they're lucky, they'll catch a glimpse of whales, dolphins, basking sharks and the island's famed white-tailed sea eagles. The Mull oyster farmers love their job, particularly when they are on the beach on a sunny day but, as Gordon admits, life as an oyster farmer doesn't always live up to the pastoral idyll it's sometimes painted – he chuckles darkly as he tells me that conditions don't get much worse than working outdoors in a northerly gale.

A clue as to how long oysters have been eaten in this area comes from the island of Guna, lying to the north-west of Mull, where both Iron and Bronze Age shell middens have been found. And on a nearby island called Ulva, nestled in the western hollow of Mull, the archaeological discovery of shell remains in a cave show the presence of humans 7,000 years ago. What makes this discovery so special, though, is the positioning of the shells; they are lying horizontally on midden deposits with the outer side of the shell pointing downward, suggesting that they had been used as some form of container.

At the northern point of Mull is Tobermory, a pretty harbour town famed for its brightly coloured houses which adorn Scottish postcards. The town also has a well-established production facility called the Tobermory Distillery, founded in 1798, which produces a very highly regarded range of whiskies. So as I spend the last few hours on these shores, following the coastal path among the hooded crows and gulls, I look forward to raising a glass or two to the craggy, wildly majestic isles of the Hebrides, their pristine waters and delicious oysters on the outer edge of Western Europe.

Oyster harvesting in the early
1900s. Image courtesy of
Whitstable Oyster Fishery.

Eating the first haul of the season,
1940s. Image courtesy of Rosemary
Williams and family (Prep That Fish).

Boadicea, the oyster smack built in 1808
that now rests in Mersea Island, Essex.

The packing shed, Mersea Island, Essex.

A shucked native oyster (note the disc-like shape and brown colour).

Native oysters from Loch Ryan, Scotland.

A dressed rock oyster from Lindisfarne, Northumberland.

A rock oyster (note the deep cupped shell and arrow-like shape).

Fossilised Jurassic bivalve shells
at Portland Bill, Dorset.

An exposed oyster
midden in Sligo Bay.

A giant fossilised native oyster
from the Swale Estuary, Kent.

Thousands of discarded oyster shells are found
amongst brick, bone and clay pipe on the
Thames riverbed in London at low tide today.

Fishing for natives in Loch Ryan, Scotland.

Kian Louët-Feisser growing rock oysters in a swinging basket.

Trestles of oysters amid an Atlantic storm in Achill.

Baby rock oysters in the nursey at Walney Island, Cumbria.

Kelsey Thompson of Morecombe Bay Hatchery in Cumbria.

A rock oyster that has settled on a clay pipe at Lees Court Oysters, Kent.

Cultch in Sligo.

An oyster filter feeding in a
purification tank, River Teign, Devon.

The Maldon Oyster Farm on the River Blackwater in Essex at sunrise.

The large sweeping bay of Irish Premium Oysters farm in Donegal, Ireland.

The creeks and marshes of the River Crouch, Essex.

The harsh landscape of Ireland's Atlantic coast means that working conditions are often tough.

Rack-and-bag trestle farming at Lindisfarne, Northumberland is environmentally friendly.

Intertidal farming at Achill Oysters on the west coast of Ireland. Image courtesy of Achill Oysters.

12

Ockran

Location: *Wester Ross, the Highlands, Scotland*
Natural habitat: *Tidal sea loch*

In 2012, a giant oyster weighing in at over 1.3kg and 201mm in diameter was fished from the staggering depth of 400ft just 27 miles off the Shetland island of Bressay; the monster was then taken to the North Atlantic Fisheries College Marine Centre for closer examination. Later, it was confirmed that the Bressay specimen was the largest UK native oyster on record, knocking the previous record holder from Cornwall off the top spot.

While the Shetland Islands remain a tantalising destination, the furthest north I'll be travelling on this trip is to Ockran Oysters in the Highland town of Ullapool. It will be the perfect place to gain a deeper understanding of what makes the waters so pure in the ecosystem feeding the oysters in this stunning part of the British Isles.

Leaving Oban, my ride takes me north-east of Loch Creran and Oban, passing by and through many lochs and glens. I am following in the tracks of General Wade, the British engineer who masterminded the military roadbuilding programme through the Highlands and Grampians to allow the English army to quash any Jacobite flare-ups in the late eighteenth century. As the daylight starts to fade, I fuel up in Fort William beneath towering Ben Nevis, the highest peak in Britain. Ben Nevis translates literally as 'malicious' or 'venomous' mountain in Gaelic, and right now it does look very ominous indeed, with a gathering mist shrouding the peak. All I can see above the lamps of the petrol station is a sheer black wall of rock soaring into the darkly purpling sky.

While paying for fuel at the kiosk, among the usual symbols of Scottish heritage – the Loch Ness monster, bagpipes, a tartan kilt – a postcard catches my eye. On the front is a picture of what looks like a sweet little tabby house cat in a woodland. I ask the lady behind the counter about it. She tells me that it's a picture of a Scottish wildcat, and that this pure breed of wildcat is fast dying out. Their numbers were decimated by the Victorians, as well as the prevalence of interbreeding with domestic species, but they are still seen from time to time. It is a native species to Britain, and there was a time when the Highlands were simply called 'Cat' because of the abundant little feline and its fearsome personality. They have been known to fight to the death for their freedom; for many, they epitomise what it takes to be truly free, and I am struck by what a perfect emblem the wildcat is to have on a postcard representing Scotland. And if I meet one on my travels, however sweet it looks, I probably won't try to stroke it.

After a challenging ride north-west along one of General Wade's original roadways, I break free from settlements and streetlights and become enveloped by the wilder, unrelenting Highlands. The undulating A835 from Inverness to Ullapool has many warning signs bearing images of rockfalls, ice, sheep and deer in the road. Despite the snow on the mountain summits and the chilly night-time temperatures, icy roads do not seem to be a threat just yet. I have yet to see a rockfall and the sheep have kept their distance – it is the deer that give me real concern. The Bonneville and I are punching our way northwards with nothing but the starry night sky and the serried ranks of Scots pine for company . . . until the road becomes lined with red deer, Britain's largest wild animal. These spectral shapes are the hinds and stags who have come down from the cold hills to eat grasses, sedges and heathers in the lower reaches of this fertile landscape. I have counted at least eighty of these majestic creatures as I ease past them, having slowed so as not to spook them. They are so close to the road it feels as though they might bolt at any moment – either into the tree line or into my path – and the consequences don't bear thinking about. I am relieved when I eventually see the sign for Ullapool, and the soft glow of the town's outskirts, with the promise of a warm supper and some rest, hoves into view.

The home of Ailsa McLellan and Joe Hayes, the owners of Ockran Oysters, is a self-built timber-framed house with furniture skilfully made by Joe, and housing a wood-burning stove with two grey lurchers sprawling beside it. Their neighbours have one of the most northerly straw bale houses in the British Isles. There is wine and beer being offered as I put my motorbike gloves and boots next to the fire to thaw out.

Aisla tells me that the Ockran oyster farm is just five miles north of Ullapool, the pretty little fishing village that was originally built to service the herring industry. The oysters are at the head of Loch Kannaird near the point at which the River Kannaird flows into the sea and, in turn, the 1 square mile area of the farm forms part of the inner section of Loch Broom on the north-west coast of Scotland. The North Atlantic circulation brings warm water to this part of west Scotland, improving the climate by warming the prevailing westerly airflow. Simultaneously, the Scottish Coastal Current flowing northwards carries water through the minches (the straits between the Scottish Highlands and northern Inner Hebrides from Lewis and Harris in the Outer Hebrides) and around the Outer Hebrides and then flows into the northern North Sea, which, in effect, constantly refreshes this virtually landlocked ecosystem with nutrient-rich oceanic water. This inevitably has an effect on the oyster's taste, which is also influenced by the freshwater flowing in from the river.

Ailsa tells me that they named their oyster business after their house, 'Ockran', which is a Norse name for an area of land in North Maven on the Shetland Islands which Ailsa's distant family had to abandon during the clearances in the nineteenth century, when many of the islanders were forcibly evicted from their crofts to make way for sheep. Almost all of the rock oysters farmed by Joe and Ailsa go to the Isle of Skye (also known as the Misty Isle), Scotland's second-largest island. Ockran oysters are served predominantly in the Oyster Shed, but can be eaten in other seafood restaurants as well.

Ockran make a point of saving roughly 1,000 oysters a week for the Ullapool area. Their local trade development is deemed important for both oyster farm and Ullapool as a way of promoting the world-class produce from the area. The oysters here benefit hugely from the loch marine environments, with ancient Caledonian forest lining the water's edge. Wester Ross itself is remote, unspoilt and breathtakingly wild, with the purity of the landscape being perfectly mirrored in the crisp quality of the oysters, who obligingly filter the loch water until it is crystal clear.

Although there are local fishing fleets of prawn creelers and a couple of small prawn trawlers, Spanish and French boats also land white fish here, although it is immediately exported to the continent – a common occurrence with British seafood. A great deal of brown crab is landed in Ullapool, too, some of which is shipped live to China. In 2009, for example, the Scottish Government's statistics show that 69 per cent of the total brown crab landed (around 7,400 tonnes) came from four main landing areas in Scotland – the Hebrides, Sule, South Minch and Orkney – not far from here. However, the majority was exported to 'live markets', leaving it almost impossible for someone to go to places like Ullapool and eat the local brown crab.

Ailsa has a licence to hand pick and farm seaweed in this beautiful part of the world, too. The marine superfood is rich in iodine, calcium and minerals and is a great source of natural antioxidants and amino acids. The seaweed grows naturally in Scottish waters, particularly in and around the Ockran oyster farm, which creates a wonderful micro habitat for other marine life. By hand picking the seaweed, Ailsa and Joe are only taking what they need in a low-impact manner, unlike a recent proposal for an environmentally damaging, industrial-sized kelp dredging operation that has recently been submitted and against which Ockran Oysters are petitioning. The kelp is a keystone species, a cornerstone of the natural environment, without which the entire ecosystem would change irreparably or collapse. Much like an oyster reef, kelp (also called Cuvie or Tangle) provides nurseries and shelter for fish and invertebrates including our precious cod, pollock, European lobster, velvet swimming crab and spider crabs. Ailsa is passionate about protecting this particular part of her native Scotland, and points out that it has already been designated a 'Marine Protected Area', which led to a ban on scallop dredging a couple of years ago; she is determined not to let the natural environment suffer in the same way as the original oyster industry here 100 years ago.

Kelp is also one of the few living organisms known to prevent and reverse increasing ocean acidity. The world's oceans are absorbing carbon dioxide from fossil fuels at an unprecedented rate and the resulting acidification is destroying marine ecosystems. All shellfish stocks are now being affected, with oysters being inhibited from making a strong shell suitable for protecting it against predators. Without a resilient shell, there will be fewer oysters, which means less filtered water, increased marine nitrogen and fewer healthy ecosystems for aquatic fauna and flora. You don't need a Masters in biochemistry to appreciate the precarious state of our natural world, the current threat that global warming presents, and the need for robust protection of wild natural resources in the face of ever-growing commercialism and greed.

Ailsa and Joe are doing all they can to nurture and protect their livelihood and, as a wider aim, the natural world that surrounds them for generations to come.

After a delicious lasagne, I am thawing out very happily, relaxing into the warmth of their welcome and beguiled by the energy they have for the work that they clearly love. To add to the sense of wellbeing, Joe digs out three bottles of malt whisky and Ailsa brings some dried seaweed flakes to the table for us to nibble on while we sip our drams of Scotch. The seaweed is peppery and is a perfect accompaniment to the floral notes of the whisky.

The following day, I wander outside and have to squint in the brilliant morning light as the sun sparkles off Loch Broom. Joe, the lurchers and I then wander along an old postman's track, through the golden wisps of grass and mauve heather in the glen of the River Kannaird, which delivers Highland nutrients to the oyster farm. It is not long before we reach a huge slab of rock the size of a small truck up-ended at a 75° angle. Scrambling on to a boulder, we shimmy under the huge slab and crawl inside to a cave-like shelter. The dogs watch on as I squeeze ungracefully into the hole and crouch on the moist, muddy surface.

It is by no means a deep cave, quite the opposite in fact, but it does have the feel of a primeval shelter of sorts, despite the damp underfoot. Joe, also squatting, reaches under a rock behind him and then shows me what is in his hands. He is cradling a native oyster shell, as well as the shell of winkle, mussel and limpet. We are crouching within a midden, and it is a wonderful moment. Neither of us has an idea of the age of the shells due to the wet environment and the fact that they are not embedded in an exposed layer, but someone – many hundreds or maybe even thousands of years ago – will have brought these 'precious' shells up here from the nearby loch to eat while being protected from the wind and rain.

It is sobering to think that the earliest settlers of this area arrived over 8,000 years ago and left us shell middens to remember them by, and that the shellfish-eating Vikings arrived on the west coast of Scotland at the end of the eighth century; today, Joe and I are connecting with those ancient consumers of exactly the same product that Ockran Oysters is now farming only a stone's throw from here. It's amazing to think that the heritage of our ancient hunter-gatherers can be seen, touched, felt and tasted if you know where to look.

13

Morecambe Bay

Location: *Walney, Morecambe Bay, Cumbria, England*
Natural habitat: *Sweeping tidal sandy bay*

Crossing back over the Scottish–English border on my Triumph, I enter Cumbria and feel an emotional surge as I return to my home country. In times gone by, I would be crossing the counties of Cumberland and then Westmorland, but they have now been amalgamated into one area under the administration of Cumbria. The county's coastline stretches from the Solway Firth right down to Morecambe Bay.

Skirting the edge of the Lake District and continuing down into Morecambe Bay, I glide along the Furness Peninsula that juts out into the Irish Sea. It has been inhabited for the last 3,000 years with archaeology dating from Druid, Roman and Viking cultures and, in later years, the discovery of iron ore and steelworks from the 1880s were the largest in the world of their kind. Riding through Ulverston and Barrow-in-Furness, I cross the short, black-and-gold Jubilee bridge and roll on to Walney Island, an eleven-mile island created by glaciers 10,000 years ago. I trundle through

Vickerstown past Powerful Street and Himalaya Street, named after the ships that were built in the nearby Vickers shipyard.

Soon I am on the southern fringes of Walney with sandy Morecambe Bay and its salt marsh on my left and grassy dunes on my right with the bluest of skies overhead. I ride over what seems like an endless array of cattle grids, the sun glinting off the chrome of my bike, until my tyres start to bite into gravel for about half a mile. Eventually, I arrive at the tip of Walney Island, and the Morecambe Bay Hatchery.

Hatcheries are a concept from the mid-twentieth century, providing oyster farmers with a reliable source of oysters each year. This was spurred on by harsh winters which would wipe out the natural settlement of spat/baby oysters in the wild.

Oysters are hermaphroditic bivalves that spawn in warmer water temperatures and are capable of spawning within their first year of life. After environmental cues – changes in temperature, salinity, food availability, and so on – and a few months of gonad development, the oyster will be ready to spawn. When the water temperature in the hatchery reaches between 20°C and 30°C (74°F to 86°F) the oyster will release its egg or sperm to be fertilised (assuming it has enough food). Amazingly, adult females can release millions of eggs at a time, with rock oysters being more prolific than natives. Once we have a fertilised egg, this will become a larva after undergoing cell division; it then swims freely for roughly two weeks (in the wild they can last for longer). The hatchery team monitor the baby oysters and look out for a dark-coloured spot. Once this develops they tend to stop swimming and sink to the bottom where they develop a foot and look to settle. In the wild, when the oyster becomes heavy enough to sink to the sea or river bottom it will attach itself on to the substrate known as cultch – rock, shell fragments or other oyster – for the rest of its sessile life, ingesting water to gain nutrients from the phytoplankton. At this point, the larvae take on a more familiar oyster shape and are called 'spat'. As generation after generation of spat grow into adult oysters, they form compact clusters known as oyster reefs or beds. In a hatchery, this process is done in a controlled environment to ensure a steady and secure supply of oysters to the farmers and fishermen and, of course, all the restaurants.

On first impression, the hatchery looks very high-tech and other-worldly, in direct contrast with the feel of the untamed intertidal mudflats and sand dunes of the surrounding area. There are huge clear sacks of different-coloured algae bubbling away next to a warehouse and some geometrically regular, manmade ponds of different sizes. The hatchery is surrounded by sand dunes towards the sea and a pebble beach towards the bay, with post-apocalyptic slabs of concrete strewn about the site.

As I pull into the driveway, I am greeted by my host Kelsey Thompson, one of the most respected men in UK oysters and a protégé of oyster hatchery mastermind John Bayes. He was born on Walney Island and both he and his wife drive cars with the registration plates 'MOLLUSC' and 'OYSTER'. There's no doubt I'm in the right place.

After the obligatory offering of tea and a quick chat, Kelsey takes me on a tour of his set-up. We start in a small room where they breed clams, native oysters and rock oysters. They are minuscule, smaller than a grain of sand, and could be mistaken for the sludgy leftovers of finely ground coffee in a cafetière. Most hatching is done in winter because the water quality is optimal.

We move into another room where the oyster seed is a little larger and then another where the oysters and clams are bigger still. They are grown in controlled conditions to increase their chances of survival and to avoid having the spat washed away by the unpredictable elements in the outside world. Here at Walney, Kelsey produces different varieties of algae (phytoplankton) according to the needs of the different oysters, feeding them both inside and outside in the ponds.

Once large enough, the oyster graduates from the hatchery to the nursery, which uses seawater taken from Morecambe Bay which travels round the 40 acres of nutrient-rich ponds. The ponds fill from run-off from the surrounding sand hills where they are fertilised with nitrates and phosphates, which is a costly process but highly controlled, and allows oysters to grow very rapidly – in the past, they would have been fertilised by thousands of herring gulls. When the spat has grown to 4–5mm in length, they are large enough to survive outside in warmed nursery tanks; the seed is then acclimatised in three tanks, which become successively colder with the last tank matching the outside temperature. This is done to avoid shocking the oyster and to allow enzymes to digest food in colder temperatures.

We walk out on to a large wooden raft which acts as a vast outdoor floating nursery. It is about a quarter of a football pitch in size. Kelsey produces rock oysters here for many of the farmers I've visited on my tour of the UK so far. He picks up a long wooden pole the length of an oar with a bucket on the end, and plunges it into a huge tub the size of a jacuzzi and scoops out some young oysters, far more recognisable than the coffee-grain-sized ones earlier. The shells of the oyster seed here are quite dark, even verging on black, despite being washed weekly. This is caused by the high density of algae in the ponds but this gradually disappears when the seed is in the sea. Most Morecambe Bay oysters I have shucked have a sandy greyish colour and a wonderfully hardy, thick shell.

Once oysters reach 15–20mm, large enough to survive in mesh bags in the sea, they are taken two miles offshore where they are graded after six weeks and farmed until they are market ready or 'part-grown' for other oyster farms – unless the oystercatchers get to them first. Kelsey now uses bags with a mesh no bigger than 9mm as the birds were getting their beaks in through larger holes and taking all the stock.

Kelsey and his hatchery team are the perfect example of people who have learnt their skills in a pragmatic, hands-on way. Kelsey has also learnt from one of the most respected characters in British oysters, John Bayes of Seasalter Hatchery in Kent. John was a pioneer of oyster hatching in Whitstable in the 1960s. When he first started out, he simply placed oyster seed in the sea in Kent, Essex and Dorset with mixed results, until he took on the lease at Walney in the late 1970s and early '80s; Kelsey joined the operation in 1982. After John had set up Walney, he left Kelsey to run the Morecambe Bay Hatchery.

John Bayes' legacy has been felt by pretty much every oyster farmer in Britain and, further afield, most of the methods and equipment in the French and US mega hatcheries have DNA from John's original inventions and designs. He was the father of the oyster hatchery and the associated algal production techniques and has installed kit in hatcheries in sixteen countries all over the world. Without him, there is no question that Britain's oyster industry would not be in the good state it is in today. Those of us who work in the industry, or simply enjoy eating oysters, owe a great deal to John's ingenuity and passion for the little bivalve.

During the early days of the hatchery, Kelsey lived with John in Whitstable during the winter months and would commute back and forth doing whatever it took to make the business a success. After Conwy and eventually John Bayes' Seasalter hatchery closed down, Walney became the only mainland hatchery in operation, in addition to those in Guernsey and Ireland.

The Morecambe Bay oyster farm is on the north side of the bay, while Morecambe town sits on the other southern edge, with Fleetwood and Blackpool running south along the coast. In Blackpool, there is a seafood stall called Robert's Oyster Bar, one of the oldest buildings on the Promenade. The building was previously a barber shop, tripe shop and a milliner's, before being transformed into an oyster bar by an oyster dealer called J. Roberts in the late nineteenth century. The working classes and seaside holiday makers used to get a pint of beer from the Mitre pub around the corner and eat a seafood meal in those rooms for around a century, and the large 'Robert's Oyster Rooms' signage is still visible today; now, though, it is a takeaway spot for pots of prepped seafood and oysters.

Riding back to Ulverston from Walney via the coast road, I spy the oyster racks in the sweeping golden sands of Morecambe Bay. These shifting sands can sometimes engulf the oyster beds, and reminds me of the mineral-rich tidal water being filtered by Kelsey's oysters twice a day.

Majestic Morecambe Bay slips away as I crawl into the quaint but busy town of Ulverston with tractors rumbling through the high street. I can feel the town slowly switching down through the gears from the bustle of work to a more leisurely evening wind-down in the pubs, restaurants and family homes around kitchen tables. After a quick chat with Kelsey's lovely family, he and I walk to the local pub for a Cumberland sausage and a local beer.

At the western tip of Morecambe Bay, just off Walney Island, is a small fifty-acre island called Piel only accessible via a small ferry. It is in clear view of the hatchery and one of the first landmarks I saw riding towards Kelsey's set-up earlier in the day. The island has a small medieval castle which was built to protect Furness from pirates and Scottish raiders, a few eighteenth-century houses and a pub called the Ship Inn, where every landlord is crowned the King of Piel in a tradition harking back to the time when a usurping pretender to the English throne called Lambert Simnel landed there with an army of 8,000 rebels on his doomed quest to wrest the throne from Henry VII in 1487. In a ceremony most likely derived from a mocking homage to Simnel, each new landlord sits on a throne wearing a helmet and holding a sword, while residents (his loyal Knights) pour alcohol over the new monarch. Kelsey's father had been an engineer in the shipyard, retiring early to work in the hatchery, and he has been a Knight of Piel for around twenty-five years. His cousin used to be the King of Piel when Kelsey was growing up, and Kelsey himself is a virtual King of Oysters in these parts – so I am humbled to be drinking with north-west royalty.

14

Menai (*Afon Menai*)

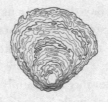

Location: *Anglesey, Wales*
Natural habitat: *Tidal strait*

As I cut through the glorious, undulating hillsides southbound from Morecambe Bay, I sail past Blackpool and approach the powerhouses of the north-west – Liverpool and Manchester.

It was in 1845 that oysters were introduced to Sinclair's Oyster Bar in the medieval shambles district of Manchester which has since been relocated brick by brick, timber by timber, just 300m from its original site after the IRA bombing of 1996, despite surviving the blitz in the Second World War. Now a Sam Smith's pub with the biggest beer garden in Manchester city centre, you can be sure that on a hot summer's day the garden will be heaving with beer-drinking Mancunians and, on a cold winter's evening, patrons will be tucked away in the nooks and crannies of the cosy 1720s building, warming their cockles with oyster-related dishes such as carpetbagger steak and the angels and devils on horseback.

It's interesting that one of the very last remaining medieval buildings in Manchester, in one of England's most important cities, is an oyster house, the people's drinking hole. And not far away in Preston, between 1771 and 1841, author Drew Smith points out that there was a gentleman's club of thirteen locals from the middle classes called the 'Oyster and Parched Pea Club', where the men would meet up and gossip over oysters, port and peas. Now that's a combination that is surely worth trying at least once.

I turn west at the Roman city of Chester to join the A55 which runs all the way to the northern Welsh port of Holyhead in Anglesey. The A55 – or the North Wales Expressway – is a great road; not only does it bridge two countries, it divides the beautiful North Wales coastline from the mystical Snowdonia National Park, and reveals castles, follies and Amalfi coast-style cliff-cut tunnels along the way.

In the middle of the North Wales coast is the medieval, walled market town of Conwy. I decide to make a quick pit-stop here to pay homage to its rich shellfish history. As I approach, the first thing I notice are the turrets of Conwy Castle, which was built between 1283 and 1289 by those loyal to Edward I of England to defend the 12-mile stretch of the Conwy River estuary. It is hugely impressive. Edging closer to the castle, I click down through the gears and advance slowly over the nineteenth-century Conwy Suspension Bridge, descending to the harbourside in search of the Mussel Museum. Mussels have been harvested for hundreds of years in the River Conwy and the beds today are found half a mile downstream in the mouth of the river. It is generally thought that the success of the industry here has been down to the fishermen honouring traditional methods (raking the beds using the 30ft rake off a small boat called a dory). Just across the way from the castle used to be the Conwy Marine Research Laboratory, which was at the forefront of shellfish research and purification within the UK and which contained the first lobster hatchery, but has since closed. Many farmed oysters in the UK are descended from original brood stock bred in Conwy.

A towering, shiny black public sculpture of giant mussels in the harbour car park testifies to the importance of the shellfish in this town, and all along the promenade are kids with crabbing nets and buckets brimming with excitement as they bait their hooks for an afternoon of crabbing. It reminds me of North Fambridge and Maldon with my family when I was that age, and brings a smile to my face that kids are still crabbing despite the ever-present distraction of twenty-first-century technology.

Turning towards the town, I spot a building next to the RNLI shop which looks to fit the description of the Mussel Museum I want to see. However, upon closer inspection, it appears the museum no longer exists and the building has become a seafood shack and a vendor of crabbing paraphernalia. While I am slightly disappointed not to be able to learn more about the local mussel industry, as compensation, I learn two shellfish-related facts from the shopkeeper that I'd never heard before: there is a pearl from a Conwy mussel as part of the Crown Jewels in the Tower of London; and Lewis Carroll's brother Robert Dodgson was the inventor of the first chlorination purifying technique for mussels in Conwy. My visit to the town has not been wasted after all!

Pressing on to Anglesey, the North Wales Expressway guides me to the Menai Strait, a narrow channel of the Irish Sea which runs from south-west to north-east for some fifteen miles. This stretch of water separating Anglesey from the Welsh mainland was carved by glaciers 20,000 years ago and sits on a tectonic fault line which was highly active about 500 million years ago. Today, the Menai Strait area is still subject to seismic activity, being the most seismically active area in Wales and one of the most active in the UK. The last recorded earthquake was in 1984 with a magnitude of 5.4 on the Richter Scale, the quake originating at a depth of approximately 15 miles below the Earth's crust.

I ride on to the Britannia Bridge, over the famous tidal currents of the strait known locally as the Swellies, and on to Anglesey. The Menai Strait is of particular environmental interest as it is sheltered from the Irish Sea waves but subject to fast tidal flows which can reach speeds of 4m per second during spring tides. The abundance of suspended nutrients in the water creates ideal conditions for filter feeders – oysters and mussels.

Now off the main road and winding my way through hedgerows and fields, it is only ten minutes before I arrive at Menai Oysters HQ on a farm in the southern part of the island. I'm warmly greeted by oyster farmer Shaun Krijnen and his father. After a few minutes' introduction, and a little chat over our mutual love of Triumphs and biking, Shaun and I head over to the oyster plant where two lads are working on the mussel haul for the day's shipping. The grading and washing machine is clanking away as the shellfish are processed at lightning speed and the yard is busy with frequent visitors and lorries coming to collect the fresh mussels and oysters.

Shaun and I head into the packing room, dominated by the purification tanks in which oysters and mussels are kept separately. Shaun's mum pops in with a handful of batch tickets for us to complete the packing of some rock oysters and offers us a cup of tea. Never one to refuse, it's a welcome start to my working life at Menai Oysters.

As we crack on with packing the rocks, Shaun and I compare packing techniques and how you can best fit fifty oysters in a box. Having bought Menai oysters over the years, I soon notice that Shaun has switched from polystyrene boxes to wooden; he tells me that he is tired of using plastic and polystyrene, and hates the fact that unless it is reused it just goes to landfill. There – away from light and potential chemical breakdown – polystyrene has been estimated to take at least 500 years to break down, if it will at all.

This sustainable philosophy at Menai Oysters extends from relying on wooden boxes throughout their operation to using paper tape for the oysters and cotton netting for mussel bags. And if a particularly large shipment of mussels needs to be packed, then the cotton bags go into large white sacks which look like they are made of plastic but are, in fact, made from potato starch. This way, if the bags and boxes find their way into the ground or the sea, it won't take long for them to decompose.

After we have finished filling the boxes with oysters, and the last batch ticket has been slipped in and the lid strapped down, Shaun offers me one of the oysters to taste. I can only see a pair of scissors nearby to shuck it with so, with a bit of bravado, I take a risk and use the scissors. Fortunately, the shell parts beautifully, and I waste no time in sucking the gorgeous meat into my mouth and savouring the burst of flavour – a fabulous mix of salinity, sweetness and freshness. Images of Snowdonia and the rushing water of the Menai Straits are immediately evoked; the oysters from here are truly first class.

Once the day's packing is done, Shaun leads me to an outhouse and unlocks the wooden door to reveal a uniquely precious treasure. As the door opens wider and allows the sun to spill into the building, it illuminates one of the most beautiful green wooden barrows I have ever seen. It is one of Menai Oysters' hand-built, oak oyster barrows, harking back to the 1800s when oyster sellers were commonplace on every street providing people from all walks of life with sustenance. On the side of the barrow is an ornate wooden carving by Shaun's father, with which he 'blessed' each cart. On the axle of the cart's wheel, Shaun has reused a metal cylinder from an old ammunition shell which fits perfectly at the centre of the spokes. This particular cart is wheeled out to food events in Wales and beyond, and has bespoke shucking blocks, drawers for crushed ice and a display for the shellfish protected by an awning. London's legendary 275-year-old oyster restaurant Wiltons in Jermyn Street is also the proud owner of one of these beautiful Menai barrows; theirs is in dark green livery.

We take our cups of tea out to the garden by the farmhouse and enjoy some shortbread biscuits under the warm sun, while blue tits dart on and off a nearby bird feeder. As we sip our tea, Shaun tells me about 48 early medieval graves that were excavated at the top of the beach near the oyster farm, including a Roman brooch. Under normal circumstances, 1,500-year-old skeletons do not normally survive in the acidic soil of north-west Wales, but here the excavated bones remained intact in the local limestone bedrock. The Druids on Anglesey – known back then as Mona Insula – were harshly treated by the Romans; the ferocity of the attack on the Druid tribes and their sacred sites in AD 60 was one of the bloodiest campaigns undertaken by the Romans in Britain, Anglesey having become the last outpost of the Druids. The force of such annihilation suggests that Anglesey was not only a site of strong resistance to the Roman invasion of Britain, and that the Celts needed punishing, but that the island was particularly sacred to the ancient peoples of Britain.

Nobody knows exactly where the Romans crossed the Menai Strait, but we know that the cavalry swam their horses over, while flat-bottomed boats carried the infantry probably somewhere near the location of today's oyster farm and not far from natural native oyster beds in the strait. Once the Romans settled North Wales, the soldiers who retired from their duties at the fort of Segontium, just on the outskirts of modern-day Caernarfon, would retire to Anglesey. This practice wasn't too dissimilar from the habits of retirees and visitors today – people flock to Anglesey for rest, recuperation and to enjoy its breathtaking natural bounty and, as we have seen in many other shellfish-rich locations on this tour, the Romans have always loved their oysters.

I finish my tea and biscuits, thank Shaun and his warmly welcoming family and head over to the bike as a huge lorry announces its arrival with a hiss of air brakes to collect another load of oysters and mussels.

Turning left out of the farm, I head for the oyster beds a couple of miles away. A few miles further south is a restaurant called Marram Grass, which Shaun supplies with seafood. They have also instituted something called a 'crop exchange', where local people can bring their home-grown produce in exchange for a voucher to dine at the restaurant. It is a trade-off that allows the restaurant access to some of the freshest seasonal produce, while building up a fantastic relationship with their locals.

Following in the footsteps of the Roman legions and Celtic tribes, I ease the bike down on to the small coast road that is barely wide enough for two cars and see the immense green swathe of the Snowdonia National Park, an extraordinarily beautiful backdrop for an oyster and mussel farm. Pulling the bike up along the edge of the beach, the vista is stunning. It is as if an abstract painter has interwoven horizontal lines of colour and texture in perfect synchronicity from top to bottom: road, beach, Menai Strait, coast, mountains and sky. The oysters here are protected from wave action but benefit from rapid tidal flows and freshwater run-off from glacier-carved hills. Occasionally, during the months of June and July there are bioluminescent plankton in the strait which produce a mesmeric blue radiance from a biochemical reaction.

Having taken in the fresh sea air and the beautiful landscape, I decide to head for the mountains before the daylight fades completely. My final destination is a small town called Trefriw in Snowdonia on the west bank of the River Conwy. In the valley, there is a hotel called the Princes Arms where I have been visiting every other summer since I was a child. And apart from the nostalgia, I decided before making this trip to North Wales that I wanted to spend some time within Snowdonia itself.

The ride is about forty minutes through the Snowdonia National Park along the A5, an extension of the Roman arterial road of Watling Street. Having got back on the Triumph, I leave the bewitching isle of Anglesey via the Britannia Bridge with a view of the beautiful Menai Suspension Bridge to my left, and with the mellowing taste still in my mouth of that Menai rock oyster I ate an hour ago in Shaun's packing room. I pick up speed past Bangor and a few outlying villages as the Triumph and I escape the flanking brickwork to be released into the deep, deep green of the valleys.

The Snowdonia National Park is unlike any other landscape I have experienced before. This part of Wales is mystically wild and beautifully unrelenting. As a non-Welsh speaker, the Welsh place names also add to this feeling of mystical other-worldliness. I ride over fairytale stone bridges, through steep mountain passes, and past fern-covered gates, ancient, moss-covered dry stone walls and babbling freshwater brooks feeding ice-cold lakes.

The daylight begins to fail as I cut through the warm evening breeze alongside the lush hills, imbuing me with a spiritual connection to this natural environment that takes me by surprise. Overhead, I can see a buzzard keeping watch on a craggy rock while rooks and jackdaws flit from tree to post prior to settling on a roost for the night. To the side of me, sheep docilely graze the verdant hillsides, scattered here and there among huge boulders; some think that these boulders were left here as a result of glacial erosion, but it's just as likely that, in this magical landscape, they were thrown here by the giants believed to have roamed these hillsides.

I power on as the darkness presses in around me, keeping an eye out for flying boulders.

15

Hook Head (*Rinn Duáin*)

Location: *Bannow Bay, County Wexford, Ireland*
Natural habitat: *Ria estuary flowing into the sea*

Before arriving in Ireland, I pass the south Welsh coast from Mumbles to Fishguard along the A40, a road which starts its life 262 miles to the east in London. Its official name is 'The London to Fishguard Trunk Road', and I'm very familiar with a short stretch of tarmac at its London end near Baker Street Station – there, it is called the Marylebone Road, just off which I spend most of my days shucking oysters in Chiltern Street.

As I count down the miles to the ferry waiting for me at Fishguard, I'm reminded of this area's rich oyster-production heritage – just south of me, the oyster beds of South Wales were once described as the most prolific in Britain in 1684. The stretch of coast from Swansea to the Gower includes the aptly named village of Oystermouth, where we're told almost the entire community was involved in oyster production; husbands would fish for oysters, their wives would sell the catch from carts along the promenade and the children would build oyster grottos from discarded shells on the beach. The famed oysters from this area were shipped to London and Europe but, as happened all over Britain, the advent of the railway spelt disaster for the oysters and overfishing ensued, depleting the stocks and destroying local livelihoods.

Once through the ferry ticket booth, I gently ease the Triumph up the ramp into the cavernous hull and ratchet it to the floor. Quickly escaping the noxious fumes of the parking deck, I'm soon up and out into the fresh Welsh sea air, my last chance to bid farewell to this enchanting and proud nation. There's quite a swell just off the Welsh coast, so I retire to a more sheltered seating area to settle in for the three-hour crossing.

It is not long before we're entering the stretch of water between Fishguard, Wales, and Rosslaire, Ireland, known as St George's Channel – it is where the saint supposedly landed in Britain after travelling from the modern-day Turkey to slay a dragon in Uffington, Berkshire.

Peering out of the window, the jagged coastline of County Wexford gradually becomes more distinct, and I am excited at the prospect of learning more about this ancient and fabled land. And cliché or not, I am struck by the sheer *greenness* of the hills. The Emerald Isle – a phrase first coined by the Belfast poet William Drennan in 1795 – is truly living up to its name as it benefits from the warm winds of the southerly Gulf Stream, providing a stable climate which has furnished the whole of Ireland's flora with an infinite variety of green hues, enjoyed by visitors ever since our early ancestors voyaged here 9,000 years ago.

I soon return to the bike and disembark, picking my way carefully down the unloading ramp and on to Irish soil under a sunny blue sky. The weather has vastly improved since leaving Wales and, riding out of Rosslaire past many garish pink Wexford Fruit roadside shacks, it is not long before I join the N25 and head towards my next destination – Hook Head Oysters.

It's interesting to note that Ireland is significantly better known for the oysters it produces than Britain. The UK is very much on a journey of rediscovery compared with the strides made by Ireland in recent times. The main reason for this – much like the management of shellfish in France – is because there was national regulation and management of the oyster industry in Ireland by its nineteenth-century English oppressors. This was not entirely because England saw the intrinsic value of oyster production, but more as one of many ways of exerting control over such an independent nation. The Irish Fisheries Act of 1842 gave the British Government-appointed commissioners and inspectors absolute authority to enforce regulations on all kinds of fishing in Ireland. All the while, Britain left her own oyster beds to be decimated in a vast unregulated free-for-all, relegating Britain to the bottom of the league of oyster bed management in the nineteenth century. Today, Ireland enjoys an international reputation for the quality and consistency of its shellfish, and I am now often asked in London for Irish oysters – the days of British oppression and Irish subjugation in the oyster trade are long gone.

I soon cross the Corock River at Wellingtonbridge and snake my way down to the water's edge at St Kieran's on the west bank of Bannow Bay. Bouncing over a slipway and jetty, I squint through the dazzling sunlight to see the silhouette of a man walking along the beach towards me – he introduces himself as Tommy Hickey of Hook Head Oysters and he's clutching live rock oysters from his farm.

Settling myself down on a sunny, sea-facing wooden bench, we are joined by Jodie, the other half of Hook Head Oysters, while Tommy shows me some plump, meaty 70g–80g specimens he has just collected from the farm. Tommy learnt his trade in the 1980s after taking an aquaculture course in Tralee, County Kerry. After graduating, he borrowed his dad's car for a tour of the west coast of Ireland before settling in Lissadell, County Sligo. Initially, he worked for little money, lived in a caravan and eventually took his wages in oyster seed. Looking for a way back to his home county of Wexford, he took the seed and started his first farm in the aptly named Oyster Point, not far from where I am sitting right now. Thirty years of graft and commitment from Tommy, and technological knowhow and marketing prowess from Jodie, the farm now produces a well-established and highly prized product.

The Hook Head Oysters farm is cradled within a natural harbour, sheltered from the Celtic Sea by Bannow Island, and stretches along the bay where native oysters once flourished. Although the native oyster occurs naturally here, they were also introduced from Wales and fished by a chap called Caesar Colclough between 1766 and 1842. Colclough, whose family lived at the local Tintern Abbey, thought the richness of the soil would enhance the size and taste of the oysters and, judging by Tommy's crop here, it is true. The first recorded transplanting of oysters into Ireland was from Milford Haven, Wales, to here in Bannow Bay, by Sir Thomas Colclough in 1614. At the end of the seventeenth century, estates were being looked at for commercial development and it was said of the oyster growing conditions in this part of Wexford that 'where the soil proved so natural to them that they grew much bigger and better tasted than those now of Milford Haven . . .' (Robert Leigh, 1684).

It was the Normans who formed counties and rough country borders, and they also recognised long-established oyster beds as commercially valuable to humanity; as a result, the husbandry of beds developed very successfully. And as with many items of value, it would not take long for the upper echelons in society (religious, royal and governmental leaders) to find a way of introducing taxation. Records show that the first recorded taxation on oysters in Ireland was at Wexford Harbour in 1281, proving the theory that oysters have not only been an important food source to both the British and Irish, but that the different national governments were talking to each other about the little bivalve and this modest staple food was important enough to be taxed by the government of the day.

The taste of the Hook Head Oyster is the result of growing in a sheltered area where the oyster can be continually turned until it is of market size. The turning and turning of the bags tumbles the rock oyster which becomes rounded with a deep cup allowing the oyster muscle to grow and fill the shell with sweet meat. The farm is surrounded by rural fields to the north, salt marsh and salt meadow to the south, the Celtic Sea to the west and freshwater influx from the Bannow River to the east. These favourable conditions for oyster growing today owe their existence to a glacial legacy as the area is known geographically as a ria or drowned river valley. It was created during the last Ice Age by glacial waters flowing south from the ice sheets that once covered Ireland, which formed the extraordinarily deep and wide Bannow Bay River valley. When the glaciers retreated and the meltwater stopped flowing here, the area silted. With the ice sheets retreating, the sea levels then rose, which added marine sediment to the silt, leading to the creation of sprawling Celtic salt marsh and mudflats that I can see across the water from where I am sitting. The action of silting has happened since the Norman Conquest, too, and local legend says that the Lost Norman city of Bannow sank beneath the waves and survives intact, buried in sand beneath the sea-bed.

The history of oysters in this region is also evidenced in the number of prehistoric middens all around this area. A digger preparing groundwork in the fields near here at St Kieran's thought it had struck a rock, only to discover a huge midden of oyster shells. There are middens in Bannow Island, Cocklestrand and Clare Island off Bannow, rich in shell, animal bones and burnt stones. Tommy points west across the bay to Fethard-on-Sea where his family live; I can just make out a brown field of barley also owned by Tommy, and even there they have found a midden full of oyster, mussel and cockle shell. Ancient shells are strewn all over the surrounding land here and it testifies to the reliance the local population had on seafood.

Other significant oyster shell deposits have been found at Skara Brae in Scotland (3100–2450 BC) and at New Grange in Ireland (3200 BC), while an island in Sligo Bay in Ireland has been named Midden Island because of plentiful oyster and periwinkle remains dating back to the Mesolithic period, which in some parts was in use right up until post-medieval times. The dense distribution of shell middens along the Irish coasts link the shore with a domestic economy – after all, why risk the danger of the seas when the fruits of the shore are so abundant?

Today, Tommy and Jodie Hickey grow their oysters to an optimum weight after a great deal of bag turning to create teardrop-shaped, deep-cupped oysters which are almost entirely sold to France. However, you can eat oysters in County Wexford at Wild and Native in Rosslare and Silver Fox at Kilmore Quay.

Apart from the highly prized oysters drawing well-deserved attention to the local area, I also learn that the lighthouse at Hook Head is the oldest working lighthouse in the world. It would be rude not to pay my respects to this grand old protector of ancient and modern seafarers, so it's not long before I'm pulling into the lighthouse car park and picking my through a coachload of Americans on a quest for their ancestral roots. The sun is high in the bluest of skies while the Celtic Sea is lapping at the exposed rocks flecked with ancient sea urchin and brachiopod fossils that must be over 200 million years old.

Like oysters, brachiopods have a pair of shells that open to filter water for food, but they are more symmetrical in shape, similar to a classic sea shell that you'd find on a beach. These hardy creatures, the ancestors of the bivalves we'd recognise today, used to dominate the sea floor 500 million years ago, but now only thirty species survive in the colder seas from the tropics to the Arctic and Antarctic. At around the time of the late Triassic period – approximately 200 million years ago – the more recognisable forms of oysters appeared, which would become increasingly more abundant through the Jurassic and Cretaceous periods.

In Britain and Ireland, evidence of this ancient oyster species is all around us today in the form of fossils. Fossil remains of the brachiopod have been preserved and are still visible in many stone-based structures – from stately buildings to stone benches – that were built or carved using the late Jurassic Portland limestone. This material is often packed with the fossils of forgotten sea creatures, such as the famous ammonite with its mesmerising logarithmic spiral. It is also very common to see the fossil oyster *liostrea expansa* and an ancient relative of the modern-day cockle *protocardia dissimilis*. And for anyone travelling through London's Euston Station, it's worth walking outside into the station plaza where there are four large, horizontal stone 'Time Benches' sculpted by Paul de Monchaux. These geological marvels are made from stone dating as far back as 280 million years, with the 'youngest' of the benches being made from 150-million-year-old Portland Roach stone, which contains oyster fossils visible to the naked eye.

The presence of all these reminders of ancient creatures in fossil form prompts me to take a moment to reflect as I look out over the Celtic Sea at the base of this historic lighthouse. I am eating a scone with a cup of tea while standing on 320-million-year-old rocks at the southern tip of Hook Head Peninsula, with the soft green grass around us being gently ruffled by the warm breeze; occasionally, I can just make out the burble of the American visitors' accents and the warmly musical Irish brogue of their hosts.

Sometimes, despite the relentless march of all those millions of years and their impact on the very stone beneath my feet, time really does stand still . . . when you give it a chance.

16

Dungarvan (*Dún Garbhán*)

Location: *Dungarvan Bay, County Waterford*
Natural habitat: *Colligan River estuary and Celtic Sea*

After the deepest of sleeps in the Ferrycarrig Hotel on the banks of the River Slaney, I venture downstairs in search of my first full Irish breakfast. It is just a couple hours after dawn and Wexford Town is gently stirring – the wading birds are out in force as the tide gradually recedes from the harbour. In the very same waters of Wexford Harbour, St Patrick fled Ireland to escape slavery in the fifth century; unlike St Patrick, it's a struggle for me to tear myself away from the breakfast buffet and make my own escape, but I eventually saddle up the Triumph Bonneville and build speed as I join the N25 towards the Ballyhack Ferry on the western tip of Wexford.

No one need worry about taking their seasickness pills on the ferry across the River Barrow to County Waterford – it only takes about ten minutes. The Vikings founded the city of Waterford in AD 914, using the Norse word '*Veðrafjorðr*', meaning 'windy fjord'. And this part of Ireland has cemented its place in the English

117

language after Oliver Cromwell coined the phrase 'by hook or by crook' when describing how he'd take Waterford by any means necessary, landing in either Hook, Wexford, or Crooke, Waterford.

The toy-sized car ferry sails to Passage East just north of Crooke and the Viking town of Woodstown where the Barlow family run one of the largest oyster aquaculture operations in Ireland with most of the stock produced for export. But this is not my destination today.

I wind my way back to the N25 and ride westwards past Curraghmore House, the historic home of the Ninth Marquis of Waterford, where there is a 250-year-old decorative house built out of shells, including oysters. Then I cruise along the Copper Coast of Ireland's ancient eastern seaboard, passing through the Viking town of Dungarvan, where I find my next port of call – Dungarvan Shellfish run by Joe Harty and his family.

The bike's suspension is tested as I bobble along a country track down to a cattle farm set within vividly green hills overlooking Dungarvan Bay. Between stacks of aquaculture bags and metal trestles, I am met by Joe Harty, who has an instantly likeable personality. His down-to-earth, authentic style is present in his Ireland rugby top, faded working jeans and his unruly hairstyle. 'Welcome to Harty's oyster farm,' says a welcoming Joe with a twinkle in his eye and his arms open wide. 'I wear my heart on my sleeve and I use my hands to farm oysters.' He's my kind of oysterman!

Joe shows me to Harty's HQ where his siblings – Ita, Shay and Ray – and his colleague Catriona are working in the office, and he introduces me to the army of dedicated workers busy grading thousands of rock oysters. The Harty family have been farmers here since 1835; originally cattle farmers, Joe's father Jim diversified into oysters in 1985, designing the entire set-up. In 1995, he teamed up with celebrated French oyster farmer Yves Tafforret, as well as working with North American oyster giants Taylor Shellfish – testament to the high quality of Dungarvan oysters. Thirty years later, the strength of this collaboration has seen Joe recently on the Great Wall of China opening oysters competitively at the 'Shuck Off' festival standing alongside his partner, Taylor Shellfish. And despite the no-alcohol rule on the global landmark, Joe will have had a Guinness nearby. He is a true maverick.

It was the Duke of Devonshire of Lismore Castle who brought oysters here before the famine of 1845. In fact, oysters kept people alive during the famine, as most other foods were rationed or banned. The Duke recognised that Dungarvan Bay was perfect for shellfish growing because of the geography of the area, and now the Hartys farm 40 million oysters annually on their 140 hectares.

An oyster produced in these waters imparts a sweetness derived from the freshwater run-off from the twelve Comeragh Mountains. Dungarvan oysters are high in salinity from the Celtic Sea and furnished by nutrients from the Colligan River – optimal growing conditions. The Hartys put the younger oysters near the river then move them to the deeper salty water for finishing, where they acquire their oceanic citrusy notes; this comes from the eelgrass which grows in and around the trestles and is another reminder that oysters, like wine, take on the key characteristics of their environment and differ in taste from bay to bay. As well as adding to the flavour of Dungarvan oysters, the eelgrass is loved by brent geese that migrate here from Canada during the colder weather; the geese then eat the eelgrass off the oyster bags, which saves the farmers from having to turn them. After noticing this, the Hartys built a bird corridor for the geese to live in during the few months they stay in the area. This arrangement of bed and board for the geese is clearly mutually beneficial – everyone gets something out of it.

We head back out into the yard and wander over to the nursery, where Joe pulls a mysterious-looking wooden cube out from an outdoor water tank. It is roughly three shoe boxes in height with a mesh bottom fashioned out of recycled oyster bags. Joe points to the periwinkles in amongst the baby oysters; they are cohabiting with the oyster seed in this hatchery and effectively clean and turn the oysters. Periwinkles are a gastropod, one of the other classes of mollusc; instead of filter feeding, they graze on seaweed and algae which means they will latch on to just about anything to feast on the rich green nutrients. He submerges the oysters again and takes me to a reserve tank sunk into the ground for holding oysters in recirculated seawater. Joe tells me that there is an otter who has claimed this area as his home, and takes care of anything that preys on the oysters. Everything here is designed to work symbiotically with nature. 'The only problem,' Joe chuckles, 'is my pug fell in the other day and I had to scoop him out.'

Dungarvan Shellfish is a highly successful business, operating in many countries on a large scale but preserving the integrity of the family heritage throughout the production process. The Hartys' business was the first Origin Green Company, an initiative promoting the provenance of Irish produce and preventing the oysters from losing their direct link back to the waters they come from. They use solely wooden boxes for oyster packing and work closely with BIM (Ireland's Food Development Agency) to eradicate polystyrene boxes from the supply chain.

After gazing across the bay and taking in the sheer scale of this hugely impressive oyster farm, Joe and I finish our tour of the set-up and Joe asks me if I have had lunch yet. Having had a really great breakfast, I had brought along some honey sandwiches, thinking that a light snack would probably suffice. Joe has other ideas: 'Leave your sandwiches, mate, and have some of our top-grade, special number 2 oysters. They are full of meat and, more importantly, why have cotton when you can have silk?'

He has a point. We ride up to Joe's house on the hill overlooking the farm and Dungarvan Bay and, as I stop in the driveway, I notice that my bike is parked next to a whale skull which Joe found on the farm. There is another one around the corner, apparently, and Joe, his eyes twinkling with disarming humour and just a touch of mischief, says, 'I will ship it over to London, my man . . . just let me know!'

It is not every day you're given the chance to own a whale cranium, so I immediately accept his generous offer, unsure if he is serious; he is, he assures me. I've no idea where I'll put it, but I'll worry about that later. We seal the deal with two cans of Guinness and set up camp on the wooden garden furniture with the awe-inspiring Waterford scenery rolling out and away from us. Meanwhile, Joe's hyperactive pug makes a nuisance of himself, trying to attract our attention; I placate him while Joe deftly shucks some rock oysters. There is something magical about being here today in this gorgeous landscape and with Joe preparing these beautiful, fresh oysters. He offers me one and, as I taste my first mouthful, it's as though I'm being enveloped by the very landscape itself – an authentic reminder of the oyster's surroundings and its place of origin. As Joe tells me, his oysters score highly in their salinity, sweetness and texture. There's a meatiness and a tenderness to them, so much so that some have described them as a 'dessert' oyster. And in addition to that lovely citrusy note, there's a faint cucumber finish. I'm in heaven.

Joe shucks . . . slurps . . . and smiles. The Hartys know how to live. He points across Dungarvan Bay to the Comeragh Mountain range and tells me a few stories about the 'magic' inhabiting this part of Ireland. It's not hard to be drawn into Joe's world of tall tales and mystical happenings. We sit there as the dusk starts to paint ever deepening pink streaks across the sky, both of us shucking oysters, sipping Guinness and trying to get the pug to calm down. Now *that* would be magic.

Today, Dungarvan oysters can be eaten in the Cliffhouse Hotel in Waterford and the Tannery in Dungarvan, and I make a note to visit them if at all possible as I ride away from Dungarvan Bay, through Dungarvan itself and on to Waterford, where I've booked a room for the night. I make a pilgrimage down to the quayside to a building called the Reginald Tower, known locally as 'the Reg', the oldest civic building in Ireland. It has been in continuous use for over 800 years and sits proudly overlooking the River Suir. I walk round the tower and explore the 'Viking Triangle' – the historic and cultural centre of Waterford – past the famous crystal factory and back to a local tavern and a pint of the black stuff. There are plenty of choices of authentic, local establishments for a decent drink in Waterford, but it could possibly have been the oysters laid out at the front by the imposing sculpture of a Viking longboat that magically drew me to this one.

Sláinte, Joe, and Dungarvan oysters!

17

Rossmore (*An Ros Mór*)

Location: *North Channel of Cork Harbour, Cork, Ireland*
Natural habitat: *Sheltered natural harbour*

After a relaxing morning, I reacquaint the Bonneville with the N25, leave County Waterford and plough on into County Cork, Ireland's largest county. Passing the town of Midleton where Jameson whiskey is distilled, I turn south and ride up a small road past a collection of manmade ponds and arrive at some extraordinarily beautiful country cottages on the water's edge of Cork Harbour. I am here to meet Tristan Hugh-Jones of Rossmore Oysters, who we met earlier in the trip at Loch Ryan, where he works in partnership with the Wallace family. Rossmore Oysters farms both native and rock oysters as well as being a successful wholesaler. The rock oyster business is in another part of Cork Harbour but I have come to visit the native fishery. The fishery here has been closed for some years, but at one time they were one of the biggest native oyster suppliers to London. I have come here to see what I can learn about water stewardship and to understand more about how the oyster can raise alarm bells when water quality deteriorates, just like it did at the start of the twentieth century.

As I park up, Tristan appears with a warm greeting and a wonderful positive energy. After a bit of bike chat, we step into his ancient cottage where he has lived all his life, and Tristan pours two cups of steaming tea and carves some slices from an industrial-sized slab of fresh shortbread. I'm struck, yet again, at how time is not always a constant, irresistible force – here we are, sitting at a handsome wooden table bearing all the dints and knocks of family life over many years, next to an ancient stone fireplace under wonderfully crooked beams. Half-burnt candles sit slumped in bronze holders and an upright piano stands proudly against the white cobb walls on the flagstone floor. Tristan's home has an undeniable, timeless charm, reflecting the warmth and generosity of its residents over many generations.

As I sip my tea, I ask Tristan why Rossmore native oysters stopped being harvested from the waters here, having been a dominant force in the oyster markets of the 1980s and '90s. Tristan leans back in his wooden chair, looks up to the ceiling and begins to explain that his father, David Hugh-Jones, wanted to be a farmer after completing an agriculture course in Cambridge around the early 1960s. Once he had graduated, he looked around for oyster beds in East Anglia but none were available. After the infamous winter in 1963 when the entire oyster harvest was lost, he travelled west, away from the harsh winters of the east coast and settled in Ireland in 1969, where he gained knowledge from BIM (the Irish Seafood Development agency) in Galway while learning his trade. One day, he went diving in County Cork and found some very native-friendly bottom ground and, along with the evidence from the local middens, he suspected it would be able to sustain an oyster population. An initial attempt near Hook Head in Wexford had washed away in a storm, so the Hugh-Jones family decided to settle here.

It was around this time that a precious oyster fishery order was given to the Hugh-Joneses which enabled them to fish oysters here for life, as opposed to a licence which would need renewing. The large ponds outside the cottage were built in the early 1970s by Tristan's parents as a way of breeding oysters. This practice had been pioneered after the Second World War, when the science of breeding shellfish really came to the fore, with successful operations appearing at that time in Seasalter in Kent and Conwy in Wales. It is believed that it was in Conwy originally where native oysters had been left in a tank over the summer, and that when the tank was eventually cleaned out, the workers noticed all the healthy baby oysters on the side of the tank wall; this showed that if you leave oysters in the tank over summer, there's a chance that they might breed.

The Hugh-Jones family, though, wanted to go back a step and encourage an entirely natural process, so they built a large pond outside the cottage in the early 1970s and relied on the warm climate to encourage spawning. The only drawback now was that you only get one chance for spawning with an outside pond as opposed to the controlled conditions of an indoor hatchery, so they received an EU grant to build twenty-one ponds. This allowed them to experiment on brood stock from Galway and Tralee in a number of ponds, which, in turn, gave them over forty years' worth of experience in just two years simply by scaling up the number of different conditions in different ponds. It was a very clever way of doing an enormous amount of research in a very short space of time.

By the late 1970s, the Rossmore operation was ready to start producing for the commercial market, and sent two tea chests full of oysters to two prominent sellers at Billingsgate in London. The first was to Bill Potter, who described them as 'the worst oysters he'd ever seen', and the second chest went to Bill Bentley who said, 'These are brilliant ... crack on!' With that encouragement, Rossmore Oysters took on the entire London market and dominated it by the 1980s and '90s. Food critic Charles Campion once said in the *Evening Standard* that there wasn't one of the top twenty London restaurants that did not have Rossmore oysters on the menu.

In 1994, they sold 80–100 tons of native and 200 tons of rock oysters – business was genuinely booming. Then in 1996, the local authority responsible for Cork and the surrounding area undertook some 'sewage works improvement' which immediately polluted the waters. It meant Rossmore went from purifying oysters in two days to the process lasting two months in an effort to make them suitable for human consumption. The council at the time vowed to solve the problem by the year 2000 but, after Rossmore unwittingly sold a contaminated consignment to a Hong Kong purchaser, despite the most rigorous due diligence, many consumers became ill, and bad news travelled fast. The result was that the Irish authorities closed down the Rossmore operation in 2002, and not a single oyster has been sold from here since.

Tristan is still clearly bearing the emotional scars of this devastating situation, and I share his pain on hearing the story. There's very little that can be said to find anything positive from what I've heard, so we lighten the mood as I venture out to the shore with Tristan to look at the pond set-up and see the baby oysters growing on the cultch. The warm summer has encouraged prolific breeding; Tristan scoops up some mussel and old oyster shell and shows me fingernail-sized circles of baby oyster clinging to their chosen substrates. No matter the manmade commercial, legal and political turmoil going on around them – nature and the oysters simply persist.

The fresh, ozone-laden breeze tugs at our clothing as we step down on to a ramshackle pier and board Tristan's skiff boat. We then motor out to the red metal dredging boat to fish up some native oysters from these closed beds. Hopping aboard the dredger, Tristan quickly submerges the dredge and works the ground, carving serpentine curves with the boat. When the winch is started, the metal dredge is raised out of the water until it is above our heads. I grab it with one hand to steady it and Tristan yanks the latch open to release the glistening abundance of Cork natives on to the sorting deck.

There are a huge number of oysters of market size in among the crabs, sponges and squirts. We sort through the catch and Tristan sends the dredge plunging back down into the depths for more. He is illustrating a point that here at Rossmore they have 2,000 acres of Cork Harbour, 8 miles of trestles, a variety of ponds, rights to a foreshore and the infrastructure to run a fantastic oyster fishery and farm – they are 100 per cent ready to restart commercial production, as long as the water quality is of a sufficient standard, something that Rossmore is passionate about. And declaring the fishery open would also boost the local economy and bring more employment to the local area. Irish Water have 'promised' to ensure that waters are clean by 2021, and Rossmore are cautiously optimistic, so much so that Tristan confirms they are now starting to breed natives again and aim to hit the ground running. One hopes that the future is bright for Tristan and his team, and that whatever needs to be done to ensure the return of pure, clear waters to Cork Harbour, is done.

As we glide through the millpond-calm surface of the channel at dusk, with white egrets in the treetops and the occasional vigilant heron on the river bank, it is not long before we find ourselves right in the middle of one of the largest natural harbours in the world. Tristan brings the boat to a stop and points to some choice native oysters we dredged from his fishery that were bred three years ago in the onshore ponds.

'Go on then, pop them open!' he says. Assured by his knowledge and years of wisdom in the industry, I locate a small knife – given to me by Joe Harty in Dungarvan – and shuck. Tristan is keen to show me the oysters are good here now and he is ready for action. We clink shells to former and future Rossmore glory, and I taste a plump and meaty oyster with a vaguely firm and succulent texture. It is a privilege eating oysters on a boat and I count myself lucky to be doing so in Tristan's company.

We tie up alongside the pier of Lower Aghada and head into the cosy Pepperstack Pub for my first pint of Beamish Irish Stout, brewed in Cork. Beamish goes perfectly with the natives; it has a slightly syrupier finish than Guinness and perhaps a blacker malt.

Tristan and I tuck into some short rib and he tells me that a few popular oyster spots in the area are the Metropole Hotel, the English Market in Cork and the Blue Haven in Kinsale.

As the evening slips into night, Tristan's experience and influence in the oyster trade shines through. Now helping to run Loch Ryan in Scotland and the Helford in Cornwall, Tristan tells me a bit about some of the colourful characters he's come across, and the unusual business practices that helped make the oyster trade tick. For example, in the 1990s, all the delivery drivers from different businesses used to meet outside Wiltons Restaurant in London with their bunches of keys to get into the various loading bays and kitchens of all their main customers. You'd see Colchester, West Mersea and Rossmore all trying to deliver to the same twenty restaurants. The drivers would then shuffle all the orders around so that Colchester would do the city, Mersea the east and Rossmore would handle the west. Sometimes, one of the oyster companies would have a new restaurant manager ringing up to ask why on earth they'd been delivering someone else's oysters. Tristan laughs at the memory, and says, 'Sometimes, I would even give them to the milkman to deliver on Berkeley Square.'

I ask him about whether competition between the producers ever affected this ingenious scheme, to which Tristan replies, 'If you wanted to do it alone, then fine, but you'd be in London a lot longer than if you helped each other. It was better for everyone.'

We settle up, wander back to the boat, and head back across the harbour under a stout-coloured midnight sky.

18

Sherkin Island (*Inis Arcáin*)

Location: *Sherkin Island, County Cork, Ireland*
Natural habitat: *Tidal estuary/Atlantic Ocean*

Today is very special – my destination is the Irish-speaking Sherkin Island, a Celtic outcrop of windswept wild beaches and jagged peninsulas in the south-western corner of County Cork. It juts out into the Atlantic with neighbouring islands Cape Clear, Heir, Long Island and a handful of uninhabited islands only reachable by boat. The Sherkin ferry runs from the port of Baltimore just 9 miles south of Skibbereen. Sherkin measures 3 miles long by 1.5 miles wide and has a population of roughly ninety people, of which one of the families are the Murphys. My hosts today will be Michael and Robbie Murphy, the farmers of Sherkin Island Oysters.

After passing Oysterhaven, a town richly associated over the years with bivalve production, I arrive at the small fishing town of Baltimore and carefully work my way down to the harbour. Once there, I try to negotiate with the captain over allowing me to take my bike on the ferry without being charged a king's ransom. He's having none of it, as it would involve him putting down a huge ramp and the 'inconvenience' would need to be paid for. I decide to back off and let the ferry leave at 8.00 a.m.; I'll park the bike and wait to catch the 8.30 a.m. to Sherkin, thereby avoiding having to take out a small mortgage.

Just twenty minutes later the ferry arrives and a handful of islanders disembark, including some schoolchildren with their parents, some fishermen and a lady holding a flat car tyre; this is obviously the morning commute and school run from Sherkin to Baltimore. Once the boat is empty, I walk down some large stone steps to sea level and heave my bag on to the red metal deck. I then run back up the steps to help a man load up the boat with bottles of semi-skimmed milk which, like me, are bound for Sherkin. I pay the captain of the ferry and enjoy the breezy ten-minute crossing.

As we cross the short stretch of water, the sight of Sherkin Island is truly breathtaking. The soft grey stonework of the medieval Franciscan monastery just on the edge of the coast, nestled in among grasses, shrubs and low-lying hills is very beautiful, having been built in AD 1460 by Fineen O'Driscoll. He was a trouble-maker – an 'alleged' smuggler, pirate and raider – from the local O'Driscoll family who originated from this area and many of whom are buried in the monastery. One story has it that, in 1537, four ships carrying 100 tuns of wine (there were typically about 250 gallons in a tun) from Lisbon to Waterford took shelter from a storm in Baltimore Harbour, where the O'Driscolls invited the crew ashore for hospitality in Baltimore Castle. Chieftain of Sherkin, Conoghure O'Driscoll, apparently imprisoned the Portuguese sailors and stole 75 tuns of wine for the local people. Later, Waterford retaliated by raiding Sherkin and recovering the stolen cargo.

After docking at the short jetty in the harbour, I walk up the stone steps to a hand waving out of a black car bearing all the hallmarks of oyster-related mud splatters on the wheels. As I greet the driver – Michael Murphy – and hand over a token 'thank-you' of a packet of biscuits, Michael asks me, 'Did you see my wife . . . she was carrying a car tyre?'

I confirm the sighting of a woman with a tyre, and he grins as we head straight to his oyster farm. Perhaps that's the way to transport vehicles on the ferries round here without having to pay the earth – break them down into their component parts and smuggle them across bit by bit.

The roads on Sherkin are a driver's dream; there is a main ring road circling the island connecting all the beaches to the harbour with countless tributary tracks branching off the tarmac to secluded bays, crofts and homesteads. I point to a grassy track sloping down from the road towards the sea and ask Michael, 'Is that a boreen?'

'It is indeed,' he tells me. 'There are many on the island.' I've been aware of the word from some Irish song lyrics, but I've never seen one before. A boreen is a country trackway which translates to 'little road'. Boreens are a clue to Ireland's historical dependence on coastal sustenance as they were bygone work trails made by the indigenous population, carved into the earth through natural erosion by the feet of man and animal. Michael slows to allow me a moment to gaze at this minor marvel, and we drive on along undulating roads flanked by egrets, seaweed and dry stone walls.

Pulling over at a small jetty on the other side of the island, we leave the car and clamber over gently rising soft ground to a natural coastal viewpoint. The craggy coastline snakes its way around us and Michael points down to a gorge between us and another headland where one of his Sherkin Island oyster farms sits nestled beautifully between the weathered rocks. This has to be one of the most picture-postcard oyster farms I have ever seen; it is a perfect example of man working with and around nature. The seawater has submerged the trestles in the crystal-clear water, leaving shimmering hues of green, blue, grey and seaweed brown. This part of south-west Ireland was extensively subject to glacial erosion during the last Ice Age up until about 10,000 years ago, with the rocks all around us showing signs of being shaped by ice as well as by the sheer power of the Atlantic Ocean's buffeting waves.

The oysters grow quickly here from 2g to 40g in a year, and live in highly salinated waters; the river is tidal for 9 miles all the way up to Skibbereen. This year, because of the dry summer, there has been very little freshwater flowing downstream. Michael tells me that he was out in his boat recently and was able to see about 25ft down to the sea floor through the crystal-clear waters, whereas usually at the mouth of the river visibility is limited to only about 1ft.

We branch off the roadway on to a gravel track, descending to a small beach where Michael introduces me to his brother Robbie. They tell me that they have about 8,000 oysters to grade before 1.30 p.m., and suggest that if I want to go for a walk along the coast they will be finished soon. As attractive as it is to wander along an unexplored coastline, especially in this picturesque part of the world, I'm more than happy to help where oysters are concerned, so I pull on some waders and gloves and take my place at the counting end of the production line.

During grading, I notice that the oysters seem to be of a very decent weight, and Michael confirms that it has been a good crop. He then adds that you can never take that for granted. 'Oysters can break your heart if you find out, after a year of hard work, there is high mortality.' It is a sobering thought, one we should all remember every time we carelessly indulge in the most wonderful and apparently plentiful seafood in restaurants; those precious resources represent an extraordinary expense of blood, sweat and tears by farmers and fishermen struggling through all weathers to bring their catch to the table.

I am handed a few Sherkin oysters to try from the pristine marine waters. The taste is a perfect marriage of the chilled Atlantic visiting the wild shores of Sherkin with a crisp slick finish. A dry white wine would go sublimely with high salinity.

Once the haul has all been bagged up, Michael and I break off and leave Robbie to organise the oysters' onward journey to Glenbeigh, County Kerry, and the fishmongers in Skibbereen and Baltimore eateries. I'm rewarded with a ham and cheese sandwich and a cup of tea in one of the Murphy family homes up a nearby hill. Michael's house overlooks the Gaelic-speaking Cape Clear Island which has the only petrol station for the islands, and beyond that the vast expanse of the Atlantic Ocean. The West Cork islands are circled by a huge variety of marine creatures, including blue whales, humpback whales and dolphins; many of these majestic creatures patrolling Sherkin's waters have been beautifully photographed by Robbie Murphy when not oyster farming with his brother, exhibiting his photographs all over Ireland.

Our work now done, Michael kindly offers to drive me round the whole island before I return to my bike in Baltimore. As we lace our boots in his hallway, Michael points to a framed map of the area on his wall and points out the various trestle sites that make up Sherkin Island Oysters. He indicates how the specific ecosystems of the different bays lend the oysters very different flavour profiles. He points to the stretch of open sea just south of Sherkin and north-west of Cape Clear, telling me how dangerous it is to work these waters without a really sound knowledge of the local area.

As we drive around the stunning Horseshoe Harbour, the natural harbour that gives Sherkin its horseshoe shape, the sun is slowly sinking towards the horizon; Michael then pulls over to let me explore another boreen. Our next stop is the beach of Cow Strand, where sand martins soar down from the grassy clifftops towards the shards of 350-million-year-old sandstone strewn across the white sand high-water mark.

Leaving Sherkin and the Murphys, I know I will return. The people are warm and open and in perfect tune with the natural rhythms of island life. For me, coming from Essex, the most populous county of England and living and working in London, one of

Europe's most densely populated cities, spending time on Sherkin Island has been a breath of fresh air. A wild Celtic gem of an island set like a precious jewel in a shimmering, silvery sea. And out of all the places I've visited so far, the oysters from this island must be among the most difficult to get hold of and to savour.

19

Tralee to Moyasta (*Trá Lí go Maigh Sheasta*)

Location: *Tralee Bay, County Kerry and
Kilrush, County Clare, Ireland*
Natural habitat: *Sheltered bay fed by River
Shannon and Atlantic Ocean*

The air is heavy with moisture and the forecast suggests rain. Venturing north on my two-hour trip, I pick out a route that takes me towards Bantry Bay. I pull over briefly to marvel at the rocky Bantry coastline before continuing on towards my stop-off destination of Tralee and the Dingle Peninsula, finishing with a night in Killarney. I'll then push on to Moyasta Oysters on Poulnasherry Bay in County Clare.

I cross from County Cork to Kerry through Turner's Rock Tunnel. It is both a brilliant physical and psychological landmark to ride through – a hand-hewn tunnel on the boundary of two historic counties. If I were travelling the other way (north to south), the view would be incredible, emerging into Cork with the stunning vista of Barley Lake and Bantry Bay laid out before you. I pull to the side of the road and look back over my shoulder; it is beautiful but, as in life, one must not spend too long looking back in order to go forward. I press on.

The Emerald Isle has already more than lived up to its name on frequent occasions on this trip, and I didn't think it was possible to go beyond the maximum 'greenness' in intensity and variety that I've already witnessed; but believe me when I say that I have never seen grass fields as green as those growing between the lush woodlands flanking the N71 from Skibbereen to Killarney. It is such a bright hue it almost seems manufactured, as if a lurid yellow and green had been mixed on a watercolour palette. It's the colour equivalent of the sound being turned up to 11!

Now well within the Ring of Kerry, I'm enjoying the challenge of this ride – the luscious, dense foliage all round me, and the snaking, angled turns of the road, all of which have been successfully navigated while the weather's remained fine. But as I reach Upper Lake in Killarney National Park, the sky's overcast tone gradually gives way to even thicker dark clouds. A downpour is imminent.

The west coast of Ireland gets rain for up to 225 days per year versus the east coast's 150 days. My visor starts to become crazed with rivulets of water and I switch the Bonneville into rain mode to gain more traction on the road. Within five minutes, I'm immersed in a virtual Niagara Falls of rainwater. I grit my teeth and decide to continue on as safely as I can to Killarney.

Once in the town, I make straight for my hotel and set about drying my gear and warming up. Having showered and changed, I head for Quinlan's Seafood Bar in the high street for some wholesome Valentia Harbour Chowder and soda bread to warm my cockles.

The following day, I am up with the sparrows to take advantage of the dry weather. Fully breakfasted on white pudding, tomatoes and bacon, I gear up and head towards Dingle for lunch. This part of Ireland is rich in seafood culture with many oyster farms in the coves and estuaries. One of the richest shellfish grounds in Europe is Castlemaine Harbour, where you can get hold of the famous Cromane Mussels as sold by wholesalers Glenbeigh Shellfish based between Cromane and Rossbeigh on the Ring of Kerry. However, most notable is the historic Tralee native oyster fishery on the northern side of the Dingle Peninsula, which I will ride past today.

As I pass Castlemaine Harbour, to my left I have stunning views of the Atlantic Ocean and to my right are steep grassy hillsides. The sky is clear and brilliantly blue, and the surfers are out on their boards waiting for the perfect breaker just off Inch Beach.

I arrive in the bustling town of Dingle, a picturesque place that is an obvious attraction for every tourist within a 50-mile radius. I park the bike and walk up the steep-sloped high street, resisting being seduced by the many trinket shops and boutiques, having been recommended to try the oysters in Adam's Bar halfway up Main Street. I find the down-to-earth bar and nestle into a four-person wooden booth anticipating the salty sweetness of some Kerry oysters. I order a cup of tea and some water and give my order to the waitress. I settle in, enjoying the homely feel of this place, when the waitress returns with the worst five words in the English language: 'Sorry . . . we're out of oysters.'

I try to remain philosophical – at least they have a chowder on the menu, which is another of my all-time favourites, so I order that instead, along with the obligatory soda bread. The majority of Irish seafood chowders I have eaten have generally all contained smoked haddock as the main fish (with variants of hake and salmon), and the shellfish is usually mussels. It reminds me of the famous clam chowders of New England and Manhattan in North America; after all, the Dingle Peninsula is Europe's most western point. Like oysters, chowder was a food of the poor and oysters would often be thrown into the mix with just about anything that was available, depending on the season or what the boats had managed to bring in.

I settle up and return to the Bonneville. I decide to take the mountain road running from the south-west to the north-west through the Dingle Peninsula – the Conor Pass. It's a route that motorcyclists dream about – twisty and turny, with knuckle-whitening drops at the edge of the road, and stunning views of verdant glacial valleys and lakes around virtually every terrifying bend. It is quite simply the best ride I have ever had.

Descending the mountain on the northern side, the road narrows to barely a single lane with sheer rock cliff on the right and a vertiginous drop on the left. It's single-file traffic here, so I pull to the side to take in the northerly view towards County Clare and, in the distance, I can just make out the Aran Islands off County Galway. I'm soon back on the bike and circumnavigating the mountain lakes down to Castlegregory, the site of Tralee Bay Hatchery.

Tralee Bay is historically one of the primary breeding grounds for the flat oyster with its pristine marine environment. The hatchery here was set up in 2012 by Denis Shea, who has over thirty years' experience in the oyster game and has been responsible for turning native oyster production in the area from 6.75 tonnes in 1986 to 310 tonnes in 2009. The aim of the hatchery was to focus on producing seed oysters, clams, sea urchin and scallops for farmers and, in recent years, it has reignited the focus on boosting the numbers of native oysters. Tralee is one of the few native oyster beds with natural reproduction in Western Europe. It even has Stone Age middens flanking the bay. In the harbour, there are 78 boats with over 200 fishermen and women working the waters fishing for oysters. In the last few years, though, native oyster settlement (baby oysters attaching themselves on to a substrate, such as mussel or oyster shell) has been far too low to keep the fishery alive. However, people of County Kerry are proud that the principal fisheries for native oysters in Ireland are here in Tralee Bay (and to much lesser extents in inner Galway Bay, Lough Foyle, Lough Swilly, Kilkieran Bay and, infrequently, in Blacksod Bay and Clew Bay).

I ride on round the historic county town of Tralee, a maritime settlement which oversaw the growth of one of Ireland's great native oyster fisheries. It is the combination of rivers draining into the sheltered bay which created the perfect native oyster conditions for reproduction.

Despite not being able to see any production facilities today, I can at least sample the delights of this oyster-rich area, so I head west to The Oyster Tavern in Tralee for six native oysters plucked from virtually outside the front door in Tralee Bay, and then I cross over the road to Spa Seafoods and eat six Kerry rocks served on a bed of Tralee Bay pebbles. On the decking facing south, I can just make out the aroma from a fish smokehouse as I sit admiring the sun-dappled mountains. The best oysters in the most picturesque setting – life doesn't get much better than this.

After a short ride north from Tralee, I arrive at the Tarbert ferry terminal, and wait in line with two French bikers and a small line of cars. It's dry and bright today with clear visibility, and it's not long before we spy the red-and-white ferry advancing across the estuary towards us. Once docked, I nudge the bike up the loading ramp – it's always been a particular pleasure of mine to board these local ferries – and we're soon sailing north across the River Shannon, crossing over the border of three counties with Kerry to the south, Limerick to the east, Clare to the north and, of course, the Atlantic Ocean to the west.

After a twenty-minute crossing, we dock on the north bank of the Shannon at the small town of Killimer, County Clare. My journey will now take me north-west along the N67 passing through the towns of Kilrush, Leadmore and Moyasta (named after the Moyasta River) which perches on the southern bank of Poulnasherry Bay. I am now in the heart of West Clare. I circumvent the indented bay towards the seaside town of Kilkee, eventually leaving the tarmac and forging a path down a rough farmer's track which slopes down to the sea, where I am greeted by Thomas and Hannah Galvin by the water's edge. As I come to a stop, the rain begins, so we step into one of the farm buildings to take shelter and, to my absolute delight, I am welcomed with the antidote to my

139

lunchtime disappointment – nine of the sweetest words in the English language: 'Would you like to try some of our oysters?' The Galvins have prepared some Moyasta rocks for me, and I couldn't be happier or feel more warmly welcomed.

Guzzling down a few plump 70g–80g rock oysters, it is clear that the Galvins produce a high-quality bivalve, suffused with a richly herbaceous and sweet taste and a plump, meaty texture. I'm also struck by the shape of the oyster – the deep teardrop cup of the shell comes from freely swinging on trestles in baskets within the swirling mix of river and ocean water within the bay.

Having gulped down six oysters, the distinctive taste really excites me. First, the oysters filter the pure Grade A waters of the bay, but this part of West Clare is also particularly rich with peat bogs. Having ridden from Moyasta, I passed many of these bogs which were formed from ancient lakes and forests that now drain into Poulnasherry Bay through the rivers and streams. There used to be thirteen turf boats operating out of the bay taking peat to Limerick docks, and all the particular characteristics and nutrients contained within the peat will have naturally been imparted in some way into the oysters.

In addition to the effect of the peaty turf, the local oysters are also benefiting from the River Shannon circulating around the bay and, of course, the salty splendour of the Atlantic Ocean. Onshore, we are surrounded by rice grass and reeds which add vegetal notes to the oyster's flavour, giving it a long finish. It is a fantastic mix.

We are joined by Thomas's father, Michael Galvin, who started the oyster farm over twenty-eight years ago after seeing a trestle being carried down to the water while Michael was dairy farming. He handed the farm over to Thomas in 2012, and his brother Bernard acts as farm manager. Together, the Galvin family have elevated Moyasta Oysters to become one of the foremost Irish oyster brands in quality and quantity.

The history of the oyster in this part of the world, though, goes back to much earlier times. Poulnasherry means 'hole of the oyster', quite literally; the entire bay was a large native oyster site at one time and had been so for millennia, but stocks were damaged by a huge algal bloom called 'red tide'. When Michael bought the land here, they used to come down to the water and find huge piles of old native oyster shell. The whole bay was full of them and it is a stark reminder, as we have seen elsewhere on this trip, that Ireland's oyster industry was significantly more thriving in the twentieth century than Britain's.

The rain eventually subsides and we walk out into the yard and down to the shore. The Galvins keep natives in one area to encourage breeding, and I'm allowed to shuck a few more oysters and share them with the Galvin family by the water's edge. They tell me that we are standing on the site of the former home of a local legend – a blacksmith and champion boxer named Matthew Curran who fought in the early 1900s.

Bernard mentions that an order is ready for shipping and Michael springs into action, explaining that the oysters are going to a hotel in the local town of Ballyvaughan in the Burren, just north of here and where I will be going next. Sadly, much as I'd like to deliver it myself, the order is too large to fit on the bike. He tells us that the hotel ordered five dozen in the first week, and three weeks later they were taking thirty dozen. Having tasted their oysters, it's not hard to see why they'd be in ever-increasing demand. Moyasta do very well servicing the local area and are part of the Taste the Atlantic programme, which aims to tie in seafood dining with the Wild Atlantic Way coast road from Donegal down to Kerry.

The Galvins are also developing a visitor centre at their farm which will encourage locals and tourists to come down and learn about the oysters of Poulnasherry Bay in a hands-on way. This philosophy of opening their doors to all-comers, and encouraging them to give the shellfish a try, is inevitably going to result in more sales, and more converts from suspicion and ignorance to oyster lovers. To prove his point, Michael says that they were exhibiting with other food producers at a local festival recently, and found themselves pitched next to a cake seller who had a steady stream of customers. There were queues for the cakes in the morning, with people looking vaguely disgusted at the oysters on the Moyasta stand. Michael smiles as he remembers deciding to let people try the oysters and, by lunchtime, they were rushed off their feet shucking as fast as they could. By the end of the day, Moyasta were sold out. It's not rocket science, is it – enable people to try something wonderful, and they'll be converts for life.

It is the end of the working day and Moyasta Oysters needs to close up for the night. I've been well looked after and I've had my fill of the most wonderful produce; it's a pleasant evening, and I say farewell before winding my way back up the track to the main road. One last look at the bay with that lingering vegetal earthy note still on my tongue, I click up through the gears and ride north through County Clare towards the Flaggy Shore.

20

Flaggy Shore (*Na Leacacha*)

Location: *Flaggy Shore, North Clare, Ireland*
Natural habitat: *Atlantic Ocean*

I am bound for Flaggy Shore Oysters of North Clare. Continuing north along the Wild Atlantic Way coast road, I power on, leaning into the many curves and bends along this dream of a route. It is impossible not to steal a quick look out to sea on the straights, while the twists and turns take all my concentration.

I pass through Kilkee, Doonbeg and Spanish Point, where over 1,000 men are buried after the Spanish Armada ships were wrecked along the west coast of Ireland in 1588. I am making good progress, sweeping past the majestic Cliffs of Moher and the Aran Islands and then on through Doolin. The road then cuts inland and passes through the spa town of Lisdoonvarna, which is famous now for its annual September matchmaking festival, and on towards Ballyvaughan.

The famous Burren limestone starts to assert itself as I travel further north, becoming more prominent among the low-lying plants on the grassy hillsides. It is a beautiful ride, one that is clearly popular with plenty of other bikers and motorists who regularly pull over to take in the views. 'Burren' comes from the Irish word '*boírean*' meaning 'a rocky place', an extremely apt description of the environment with the grey-white hues of the rocky surface projecting out from beneath the wind-blown flora. This landscape was formed during the lower carboniferous period as part of a tropical seabed 350 million years ago, and you can still see the evidence of this pre-existing marine habitat in the fossils of various sea creatures, such as sea urchin, ammonite and coral. The sweeping hills and valleys on my right are a clear sign that this area was originally covered by huge glaciers during the last Ice Age.

Turning left off the Wild Atlantic Way, I pass Linnane's, the famous seafood restaurant on the outskirts of Kinvara in the foothills of the Burren. I have eaten in Linnane's before and it has rightly become a world-renowned institution. There are few frills here – it simply serves the freshest lobster, crab and oysters caught metres away from your table at the right price with great beer on tap.

Working my way round the back of the restaurant, there's an unremarkable, Scandinavian-style red building which houses the Redbank Food Company, the legendary owner of Flaggy Shore Oysters, where I am greeted by siblings Lorcan and Ciara. The building sits right on the harbour and faces the Flaggy Shore itself, a stunningly wild section of western Ireland's coastline, with Galway Bay to the north and the open Atlantic to the west. The area has continually inspired some of Ireland's most famous literary masters, with James Joyce's *Ulysses* referencing the oysters of Redbank, and Seamus Heaney extolling the virtues of this rugged landscape in his poem 'Postscript':

> '*And some time make the time to drive out west*
> *Into County Clare, along the Flaggy Shore,*
> *In September or October, when the wind*
> *And the light are working off each other . . .*'

Gerry O'Halloran, a tall, bearded man with a shock of white hair and a wide grin, walks into the building and greets me warmly. He is a very well-respected man in the industry, a marine biologist by profession, and the founder of Redbank Food Company and father of Ciara and Lorcan, who now run Flaggy Shore Oysters. In Gerry's own words, he has been 'breeding, growing, opening, selling and eating oysters for years . . . and years . . . and years . . . and years . . .' From here, we can look out on to the sea and Aughinish Bay, and the connection with the waters just beyond these walls is not lost as we sit at the wooden tables in the purification plant which doubles as a visitor centre.

Flaggy Shore Oysters was started by Ciara and Lorcan in 2016, under the tutelage of their father, as a way of celebrating the oysters from this wonderful location. Flaggy Shore take oysters from two local farmers a few miles away either side of Redbank; they are then purified with Grade A water in the original tanks from 1962, and then packed with local seaweed in beautifully branded wooden boxes. The Flaggy Shore Dainties from farmer Tommy at the mouth of Kinvara Bay are ever so slightly saltier than farmer Fergal's, who grows a larger-shelled oyster, which is slightly more on the mildly briny spectrum because of underground streams entering the bay from the Burren near his farm. Both farmers procure their seed from the same hatchery just 200 yards down the road, and all the oysters have a noticeably high level of salinity all year round. This is due to the particular conditions of the channel between Flaggy Shore and an island-type landform just 300m away called Aughinish, which was created by a tsunami after the Lisbon Earthquake of 1755. As a result, a powerful current of water enters the bay every day from Black Head, passes through Redbank along the southern shore of Galway Bay, and travels around the whole of Galway Bay anticlockwise and rushes back out on the north side. This means Flaggy Shore is regularly flushed with fresh oceanic water, producing the characteristic oyster tasting notes or merroir.

This area has long been recognised by locals and visitors alike for its first-class shellfish. Galway Bay stands deservedly alongside the big oyster names like Belon, Chesapeake, Coffin Bay, Bluepoint, Prince Edward Island and Colchester, but with Galway Bay just slightly north of Redbank, Gerry tells me that this has not always been the case. The Redbank bay has a private charter which dates back to King Charles I in the early 1600s. As a rule of thumb, charters were only given out to productive beds like Redbank, Connemara, St George's, Loch Ryan and so on. The other main native beds at the time were Tralee, Donegal (Foyle), Galway (Clarinbridge), Strangford Lough and smaller ones in Clew and Connemara. Around Redbank, each different bay had their own beds, and it was the Clarinbridge beds of Galway that eventually became the most famous; but, in earlier years, it was the Redbank and Pouldoody oysters that had the notoriety, with even King Henry VIII demanding that his oysters came from those two sources.

Gerry also points out proudly, like so many other producers have done in their own particular locations, that there is evidence of a long legacy of oyster activity here with records of ancient kitchen middens and banks of shells in Kinvara. It's also worth remembering, Gerry says, that oyster consumption in Ireland has not always been associated with delicious nutritious sustenance and enjoyment. The very fact that Ireland is an island would suggest that the population would be big fish eaters but, in recent history, that has not always been the case. Gerry believes that there is strong evidence to suggest that the Great Famine of the 1840s had a part to play; starving people would have survived by feeding off the naturally abundant food of the coast and the sea, and thus oysters and shellfish would have adopted the stigma of being a food eaten during periods of famine.

Another consideration is that Catholicism stipulated the avoidance of meat on a Friday, and so fish became associated with penance food. There must be some truth in this idea that negative connotations – relating to religion and famine – have surrounded the eating of seafood for many generations in Ireland. Perhaps the tide is literally turning now – we're living in an unsustainable way, and there's a growing distrust of highly destructive practices in many aspects of intensive meat-rearing, palm oil, soya bean production and so on. More and more consumers are becoming switched on to the sustainable benefits of our natural maritime and coastal resources, such as shellfish and seaweed. Alternative food sources that will protect the natural environment, rather than destroy it, are there for us on the foreshore and in our coastal waters, just as they have been for millennia.

Gerry, Ciara and Lorcan make a great team and their approach is clearly reaping dividends for Flaggy Shore. I'm shown around the visitor centre while Lorcan starts to shuck a Dainty; I assume it is for me to taste, so I'm surprised when he submerges it in one of the bubbling tanks of seawater. Peering over into the tank, it has a fine selection of live local marine animals – shore crabs, sea urchins, anemones and starfish. This is what they call the 'touch tank', which is used to educate visitors on the sea life that is just metres away on the seashore. They rotate the inhabitants of the touch tank regularly, it being a sort of temporary hostel for coastal fauna. An injured starfish checked into the tank the other week, and successfully grew back a missing limb. It has also been noted that the anemones will open and close with the tides, even when they are not in the sea.

This phenomenon of being subject to the lunar cycle has been well documented. Oysters also have a lunar rhythm, which is unsurprising, really, as the tides and the currents are all governed by the lunar cycle. When the moon is full or new, it is directly in line with the Earth and the sun, which exerts a strong pull on the ocean causing more pronounced tides. On the other hand, when the moon is half full, it is not aligned with the Earth and the sun and produces neap tides, the weakest of the tidal cycle. All of these astronomical forces have an effect on the oyster's food availability.

Studies have shown that oysters open wider during new moons and are more closed when the moon is full. Scientists are unclear as to why this happens, but it probably comes down to increasing food availability during a new moon. The moon's effect on the tides also impacts on the point in time at which different marine organisms choose to mate.

As soon as the small oyster has settled in the tank, the shore crabs are alert and scampering sideways to claim their prize. They guzzle the oyster meat as fast as they can in an impressive display of predator behaviour. Admittedly, they didn't have a moving target to contend with, but it's impressive, nevertheless.

I soon get my chance to sample my first Dainty. We move over to the tables again and Ciara pours a glass of dry white wine while Lorcan shucks some of their trademark smaller specimens. There is a little glass bottle of liquid of which two or three drops on the plump little oyster makes for a unique mignonette of wild samphire and dill; when chased down with the saltiness of the Flaggy Shore Dainty and a crisp white wine, this red building on the Redbank becomes a must-visit destination for anyone loving oysters, Ireland, dazzlingly beautiful scenery . . . or maybe all three.

21

Galway (*Gaillimh*)

Location: *Kilcolgan, County Galway, Ireland*
Natural habitat: *Inlet of Galway Bay*

Having waved farewell to the O'Hallorans at Flaggy Shore, I progress up the N67 with raindrops slowly becoming more regular and heavier. Fortunately, it is only a thirty-minute ride to Kelly Oysters in County Galway, just shy of Kilcolgan and Clarinbridge on the Clarin River. Halfway along Galway Bay, I turn off the road and I'm immediately in rural untamed countryside, arriving at Kelly's just before the downpour really gets going. Diarmuid Kelly is standing in the doorway of the main building and says, 'Not a good day to be on the bike then? Welcome to Galway Bay.' He puts the kettle on – there must be a rulebook somewhere for oyster folk that says: 'Thou shalt always brew tea and provide biscuits when greeting a fellow oysterman' – and he cracks open some ginger nuts over which we sit down and have a chat.

Diarmuid is an expert native oyster farmer, and he's keen to share his knowledge and experience of the area and its bounty. Behind him is a large map of Galway Bay; he points to the south-eastern corner and says his father, Michael Kelly, started working oysters in the early 1950s simply because he loved the area, having grown up here. He tried many things to make a living, including growing potatoes and corn, but found most satisfaction selling native oysters. His first oyster supply was from his own dredging boat, and his first customer for his produce was Paddy Burke, a restaurateur in Clarinbridge. Eventually, he used an old family holding ground in the bay and started his own oyster business.

In the early days, each oyster dredging family had its own storage area on the shore for storing their haul prior to sale. Michael Kelly supplied oysters to the second Clarinbridge Oyster Festival in 1955 and, ever since then, Kelly Oysters has supplied oysters to both Galway and Clarinbridge festivals. Diarmuid and his family now follow a similar model to that of the past, buying natives from around the coast and relaying them on Kelly beds. They mind, store and grade the oysters, which means they have them for the season which runs from 1 September to 30 April. They could technically sell them in August and May, but the family want to give them every chance for the natives to flourish, an excellent example of animal husbandry and conservation.

Native oysters are very fragile and the Kelly family are doing all they can to restore the once huge numbers of the bivalves in Galway Bay. There are currently 800 acres of wild oyster beds out there and they store several tons of oysters in a plot right next to the wild. The simple fact that all the oysters are contained together fosters a nursery environment that encourages reproduction. When the male releases sperm into the water, it is active for just ten minutes, leaving the female very little time to receive it and fertilise her eggs. A huge population of natives all amassed together is therefore needed to produce sufficient quantities of spat, or young oysters. Overfishing of native oysters in recent years has reduced these nursery areas, so the Kellys are redressing the balance by repopulating the beds through their approach. One oyster can produce up to one million new oysters, which represents mass production at its most extraordinary and natural. In reality, if you can get ten of those youngsters to survive, then you're doing well. Natives are highly sensitive to changes in the environment, especially salinity, so if you get a big flush of freshwater or agricultural fertiliser run-off, it will kill them – this has been seen particularly with the change of land use in the last fifty years. It's an important lesson in sustainable environmental stewardship from the Kellys, whose family have built up their extensive knowledge protecting and nurturing the shellfish on this stretch of coastline over the past seventy years.

Diarmuid is chairman of an oyster restoration project called 'Cuan Beo', a community-led collaboration that aims to reconnect the land to the sea through heritage, science and education events. Cuan Beo translates to 'living bay' and is funded by the EU and the Marine Institute. The catchment area of the project is the south-eastern corner of Galway Bay from Rinville Point in the north to Black Head in the south. There is a focus on native oyster restoration with an examination of the effects of different cultch substrates, and they also pay fishermen to observe the marine fauna during their working day and take pictures with smart phones, which are sent digitally to populate real-time maps and records. Recordings of substrates (sediments), flow-metre readings and salinity tests all assist in the understanding and restoration of the natural habitat.

Oyster reef restoration has been identified by Europe and North America as a conservation priority. In Britain and Ireland, the depletion of natural native oyster beds in the nineteenth and early twentieth centuries caused not only the industry to collapse but the destruction of the natural environment and food source. Oysters are an essential part of global ocean health; they provide food and employment for humans and a habitat for other organisms. Oyster reefs also provide vital barriers for coastal communities against storms and tides, preventing erosion through sediment stabilisation and protecting productive estuary waters with nutrient cycling, sequestration and water quality maintenance.

There were roughly 200 boats fishing from the huge oyster beds up until the 1950s and '60s in Galway Bay. It meant that money was still flowing into the local economy when others elsewhere were really struggling. There are lots of stories of fishermen at the time going to the pub after work, pulling £20 notes out of their pockets and offering to buy everyone a beer. The downside was that a lot of money went on drink because oysters were so plentiful, although fishermen were only allowed to fish for the month of December so, in the build up, they would be preparing their boats and hiring crew. It was common for Galway fishermen to hire Gaelic-speaking workers from Connemara because of their strong work ethic; many of these transient workers could not speak English and probably had not been on boats before. They were made to work hard and were given a menial wage, but it was employment at least. Most of the oysters were sold to buyers who would ship them out to England, the Netherlands and France to be re-laid. It became a truly international industry.

Although native oyster beds occur naturally in the counties of Galway, Mayo, Donegal, Kerry, Cork and Down, it was Galway that received all the publicity because of the annual oyster festivals of both Galway and Clarinbridge. And there's a story that testifies to the raw power of these little native bivalves; a Galwegian famously once said of the aphrodisiac properties of his local oysters that he ate a dozen on his wedding day and 'only six worked', which meant they couldn't have been true Galway oysters.

One particularly interesting midden in the Galway area suggests a practice that has rarely been seen elsewhere. Dating to about 4,000 years ago, many of the oyster shells from this particular midden show no signs of having been shucked or broken open, which suggests that the shells had been gathered into one big heap and smoked open over a fire.

Kelly oysters are sold all over the world today, but I also wonder where I could buy them locally. Within a stone's throw of the oyster farm is the world-famous Moran's Oyster Cottage, very much a traditional Irish oyster experience. They do a sample plate of three natives and three rocks with a side of soda bread and a pint of Guinness. There is Monks in Ballyvaughan on the pier, and in Galway City there are two options: the famous McDonagh's Fish and Chips Bar and Seafood Restaurant, or the Tartare Café for a more fine-dining experience.

Michael Kelly soon joins us, and I stand to greet this quietly spoken, thoughtful gentleman. He tells me that, over recent times, he has been worried that his customer base would soon dry up because it was 'only the older generation who were into oysters'. But he and his family are now much more optimistic about the future as they're seeing younger people now in restaurants 'ordering oysters over garlic mushrooms'.

Dunbulcaun Bay, on which Clarinbridge is situated, is the ideal environment for oysters, one which will have enabled them to thrive for thousands of years because of the clean, shallow blend of sea- and freshwater. I am standing in one of the few places in Europe that survived the overfishing of oyster beds that took place in the nineteenth century because of the regulatory environment and sound husbandry of the fishing grounds.

The Kelly Oysters of Galway have a distinct flavour profile taking influences from all points of the compass: underground water flowing through and around the karst limestone in the Burren; the Atlantic Ocean to the west rises and falls 16ft a day with the tides; there is sweet freshwater from the east via the Clarin and Dunkellin rivers; and there is the presence of sandstone-filtered water from the north. All the while, the oysters sit and feed and grow, filtering hundreds of litres of water a day.

The average salinity in seawater in winter is 24/25 ppt (parts per thousand), and in summer this rises to 32/33 ppt; but if the bay is subject to a north-west Atlantic breeze, combined with the Corrib

River coming in on a neap tide, salinity can drop to as low as 8/9 ppt and this effectively turns the bay into one big river. 'If this happens,' warns Michael ominously, 'it is curtains for the oysters.'

I wonder how the Galway oystermen eat their oysters, and the Kellys suggest breathing in the aromas first, then taking a sip of the juice to transport yourself to the coast and to prepare the palate. Then slide the meat into your mouth, take a bite or two and swallow. It is also important not to chill the oyster too much as the flavour begins to be lost.

Taking my leave of the Kelly family, there is only one place on my mind as my next port of call – Moran's Oyster Cottage is just a ten-minute ride round the Kilcogan River estuary to the mouth of the Dunkellin and Clarinbridge rivers. This renowned bar and restaurant stands by a weir in the village where, in the 1760s, Daniel Moran held a liquor licence which has been passed down seven generations to the present occupants. Over the centuries, Moran's has been serving Galway oystermen, turf-boat workers of Connemara, seaweed harvesters of Aran and everybody else who walks in through the door. They served bottled Guinness until the first barrel for draught pints arrived in 1966 during the oyster festival.

I step back in time as I cross the threshold into the eighteenth-century public house and sit at the wooden bar. I can almost hear the crackle and spit of a wood fire and the low chatter of ancient oystermen and labourers as a pint of Guinness settles to a creamy head on the table in front of me. This is followed by a mixed plate of the Kellys' natives and rocks with soda bread and butter. I am almost perfectly satisfied, but when there's a chowder on offer, it's rude not to order it. I've had a sensory overload today, earlier with the Kellys and now in this ancient seaside inn; the flavours, textures, sights, sounds and smells – they all are redolent of the very best that Ireland has to offer, along with the warmth and generosity of my hosts.

22

Achill Island (*Acaill*)

Location: *Achill Island, County Mayo, Ireland*
Natural habitat: *Ancient peat bogs on Atlantic island*

Crossing into County Mayo, the N84 takes me away from the coast and up past Loughs Corrib and Mask, a little further to the west of which is the holiest mountain in Ireland, Croagh Patrick. At 750m tall, legend has it that St Patrick fasted here for 44 days in AD 441; pilgrimages to this site stretch back 5,000 years, with today's pilgrims, hill climbers, historians, archaeologists and nature lovers all visiting the mountain for their own deeply personal reasons. The view from the foot of the mountain is fantastic, so I can imagine that the extraordinary vista at the summit is probably of biblical proportions.

My route takes me north beside the famous Clew Bay where there are 365 small islands, 'one for each day of the year' according to local folklore. Although it seems as if they have been snapped off the rugged coast of Mayo, they are in fact drumlins or small hills left over from the last glaciation.

In 1835, the Mayo oyster beds stretching from Clew Bay to Belmullet were some of the most developed in Ireland, so much so that when beds ran dry on the east coast, boats would come to Clew to fish to meet the demands of places like Dublin and Arklow in the 1860s. I swing due west on the N59 and climb until I gain quite some height at Mulranny and its beautiful sweeping Mulranny Beach below.

Winding through the woodlands and past villages I make my way over Achill Sound via a small bridge to a misty shrouded Achill, Ireland's largest island. Although there are five main settlements on the island, Achill and its misty mountains, crashing sea and the deserted stone village of Slievemore is every bit as wild and spectacular as any imagined, fairytale island. Nature is laid out here in all its splendour, and the regular visits of soaring sea eagles add to the spellbinding majesty of the place.

Before meeting Hugh O'Malley of Achill Oysters, I make a lap of the island on the Bonneville despite the deteriorating conditions with the wind whipping around the bike, bringing with it the threat of an unremitting downpour.

Riding south towards Keel Strand, I can hear the roar of the Atlantic crashing into the grey schist boulders below me. I am riding over the oldest rock formations in the whole of Ireland at 600 million years old, once home to the now extinct golden eagle. I continue to carve my way through the buffeting wind and look out to the churning ocean where, in 1588, the Spanish Armada lost 24 ships and around 7,000 men after the ferocious westerly gales dashed them against the rocky coastline.

The rain is bouncing off the tarmac a little harder now, so I descend carefully from the mountains through the lowland grassy plains to reach the sprawling, dense peat bogs with their pools of water stained the colour of black tea. These ancient bogs have formed over thousands of years because the area gets more than 125mm of rainfall each year, with plenty of it today, as I navigate a pot-holed track studded with puddles and mollusc shell . . . I'm definitely in the right place and, on the wettest day of my trip, I'm looking forward to getting out of my drenched gear. After half a mile of rutted track and heavy rain, I spy a huge pile of oyster shell on the horizon and a bright red wooden boat. Then a head pops above the parapet of heather and peat, and I see someone waving – it is Hugh. Grateful to be able to park the bike and stretch my legs, I wander down the remainder of the shell track and bear-hug Hugh as a long-lost friend and saviour.

Hugh's surname – O'Malley – is indicative of this part of Ireland, the most famous being the Pirate Queen of Mayo, Grace O'Malley, who lived between 1530 and 1603. The O'Malleys were a powerful seafaring family, who traded along the coast and controlled the waters of Ireland's western seaboard. Grace became a fearless leader and gained fame as a sea captain and pirate who stood up to the imposing English and famously stopped Henry VIII's ships sailing into Galway Bay. She is supposedly buried on Clare Island, the largest in Clew Bay. It's also very likely that she and her followers would have been sustained by the oyster beds of Mayo, particularly when travelling from coast to coast.

Leaning into the wind, Hugh and I march out on to the rocky beach covered in bright-yellow channel wrack seaweed towards the long lines of snaking trestles perfectly angled to maximise the water exposure for the oysters. Stopping at some bags, Hugh and I shuck some Achill oysters and devour them on the beach while co-worker Adrian checks other bags for storm damage. The peaty taste of the plump, meaty Achill rock is out of this world; the freshwater flowing down to the intertidal area gives the Achill oysters their unmistakable peat-based notes, which marry beautifully with the Atlantic salinity. It is everything that is great about Achill – wild, peaty, salty, sweet and charming, and it evokes a deep sense of connection with this historic, wildly rugged place.

We move on to a few more bags, as I learn more about the style of oyster farming that Achill Oysters undertakes here; Hugh favours an alternative to wild catch, with aquaculture allowing more produce to come from the sea, and thereby ensuring that there is increased employment in the area. By focusing now on

157

aquaculture, they are gradually moving towards their goal of allowing the sea to heal and let the wild catch return in sufficient quantities to sustain a commercial operation.

We take shelter in a wind-blasted shipping container at the top of the beach where Hugh points on a map of Achill to the house he grew up in, where the garden sloped to the Atlantic Ocean. A little further along is Keem Bay where, as a child, Hugh and his father used to fish salmon from a 16ft-long '*currach*', a traditional wooden-framed boat. There was a large basking shark fishing industry there, and they would return from fishing to see all the fishermen butchering the sharks. They used the oil for Swiss watches and rendered liver and the meat for dog food. Hugh remembers there were so many carcasses, people could walk over the entire catch from one side of Keel Harbour to the other.

Having worked away and lived in England, Hugh has returned to his home county of Mayo because of the love he has for this wild and beautiful place. Achill Oysters is living proof that it's possible to sustain a commercially successful year-round operation in a remote coastal area, and it's through businesses like this that rural communities are still thriving, despite the incessant march of the diaspora over the past 200 years to seek 'better lives' in the UK or America and beyond. Hugh works with a wonderful food source, bringing employment to the area by working with the water and the local natural environment in a harmonious relationship. Hugh is an intrinsic part of Achill and, when people eat his oysters, they can taste the beauty of this misty, peaty Atlantic island. Whether it is here on the island at his cousin's restaurant The Chalet, or moving further afield in Coragh Patrick Seafoods in Newport, Clarke's Salmon Smokery in Ballina, Butcher Grill in Dublin, or oyster bars in London or China, people know and love Achill. That is the power of the oyster, and a testament to the knowledge, skill and care of Hugh and his team.

It's a blessing that Hugh O'Malley has returned home.

23

Sligo (*Sligeach*)

Location: *Lissadell, Sligo Bay, County Sligo, Ireland*
Natural habitat: *Tidal bay*

I am brimful with respect and admiration for the oystermen in this part of the world after my whirlwind tour of Achill, and I head out on my journey to Sligo Bay in an optimistic, re-energised mood. As I enter County Sligo, the crest on the roadsign depicts a scallop shell, a book (for the rich literary history) and a steep hill (Benbulben is known as County Sligo's 'Table Mountain'). The shell is present because Sligo's name derives from the Gaelic word '*sligeach*', literally 'a place abundant with shells', which is attributed to the old name of the Garavogue River which flows from Lough Gill through Sligo town and into Sligo Bay. The people of Sligo are proud that their town was named before any other major town or city in Ireland in around AD 600, especially as it was a century-and-a-half before our earliest record of the two names of Dublin. That means that the name Sligo has been historically confirmed for around 1,500 years.

My two-hour ride concludes on the southern side of Sligo Bay, where I am met by Glenn Hunter at The Venue restaurant at the foot of Strandhill. I follow him to the water's edge where we cross a runway and arrive at the Wild Atlantic Oyster farm but, before exploring the operation here, I'm keen to find out whether it's possible to see another ancient midden, which I've heard exists in the area. Glenn is all too happy to let me crack on with the mission as he has quite a bit of oyster grading to do and needs to get his cart ready for a forthcoming event. So he slings me some waders and points out into the bay at Patrick's Fort (Dúnán Padraig) where I will find the midden.

Legend has it St Patrick took refuge on the islet from a storm and, since that day, the islet has never been covered at high tide. I walk down on to the beach past the Wild Atlantic Oyster nursery in pure Grade A waters where they start the oyster-growing process, as old shell crunches beneath my boots. Wild Atlantic's oysters stem from the original rock oyster brood stock that had been introduced to Ireland in the 1970s, and they carry on a tradition of oyster cultivation in Sligo Bay that goes back 150 years.

Venturing further out into the bay at low tide, the shells fringing the oyster farm and coastline give way to sand and various large and small channels of water. The most direct route to the midden is across a fairly fast-moving water course which is quite deep in parts and you need to watch your footing for soft sand. Glenn had explained to me the safest route, given all his knowledge of the local area, and I tried to take it all in; but he isn't by my side right now, so I'll have to rely on some scant knowledge of the coastal features and a lot of instinct . . . and luck. The water rises against my waders as I steadily move deeper into the channel, with the current pressing against my legs. Some small fish dart across my path as the water reaches my hips, nearly breaching the lip of the waders and ruining my day. Mildly alarmed and with my heart beating a little faster, I take careful steps forward, hoping that the ground will level out or rise again. After ten minutes of concentrated effort, the water level starts to recede and I make it on to the other side.

The islet is covered with tufts of long rough grass and flanked on top by limestone boulders. Walking round to the northern side, I instantly see the midden lying exposed to the elements as it must have been for centuries, existing as a thin 10cm–20cm deposit of oyster shells and scattered periwinkles about a metre above sea level. What a wonderful experience it is to stand next to an ancient midden about half a mile away from an active oyster farm in the middle of Sligo Bay. The powerful presence of oyster culture and the role the bivalve has played in our lives is stronger here than in almost any other place I have ever been. As a person who earns his living from shucking oysters, it's humbling to consider what those of us in the industry today, and all those who have cultivated oysters over the centuries, have managed to do to provide sustenance and livelihoods for people. And it has been done here in this very same spot and all around Sligo for millennia – a span of time that is simply too great to comprehend.

This midden has yet to be dated, as the site has not been excavated and no material has been recovered from it. As we have already seen, the most ancient of middens can date from the Mesolithic (approximately 8000 BC – 4500 BC) all the way through to the post-medieval period. The adjacent Coney Island was excavated by Dr James Bonsall to reveal a burnt mound which returned a date of the Late Bronze Age and, some time after the excavation, a midden was revealed by storm tides right next to it, proving that there had been activity in the area. Nearby at Strandhill, in an area known as the 'Shelly Valley', there is a large complex of middens, one of which was recently dated to the post-medieval period.

Just to the north of Patrick's Fort in Sligo Bay is the appropriately named Oyster Island. All around the bay and county there are recorded shell deposits. In 31 out of around 90 of the Sligo middens, they are all located less than 60ft from the coastline, meaning people would have consumed the majority of the shellfish by the seashore. One-and-a-half miles south of where I am standing in Culleenamore Strand, archaeologists discovered a large midden that could have been used for over 2,000 years between the Middle Neolithic, Bronze Age and possibly the Iron Age. Lastly, in Ballysadare Bay, the oyster remains range from 3660 BC – AD 1250, again proving that oysters have played a vital part in the lives of people here for over thousands of years.

I notice the tide starting to edge closer and, fearful of following St Patrick's lead and having to take shelter on the island, I wade very carefully back towards Glenn. I catch up with him on his tractor and he gives me directions to Sligo town, where I'll meet his wife, Aisling, who runs the Sligo Oyster Experience in the WB Coffee House in town; it was named after W. B. Yeats, the Dublin-born Irish poet, who spent most of his summers in Sligo and carried his fond memories of the region with him throughout his life.

The WB is like no other coffee shop I have ever been to – there is a shucking station for service and live demos, a wealth of books, and images and footage of the Wild Atlantic Oyster farmers working away on the trestles. Aisling shows me the range of various oysters sold by the farm – they have five main classes of rock oyster that customers can choose from, all named after various aspects of Sligo culture and heritage. Starting with the biggest, the Ben Bulben Oyster is 125g-plus and named after the iconic mountain that towers over the town; the next down is the Yeats Oyster at 110g–125g; the Lissadell Oyster is 90g–110g, named after Lissadell House which has been central to Sligo's rich shellfish farming history; the Coney Island Oyster at 70g–90g is a cocktail oyster from the original Coney Island, whose Gaelic name means 'island of rabbits', and which protects Sligo town from the ravages of the North Atlantic; and lastly, the smallest oyster is the Countess Markievicz at 50g–70g, a fantastic accompaniment to aperitifs, and named after the revolutionary Constance Gore-Booth of Lissadell House, Ireland's first female MP.

We're soon shucking at the station and Aisling dresses a few of the Coney Island oysters with some homemade Sligo seaweed pesto inspired by Prannie Rhatigan's recipe in her book *Irish Seaweed Kitchen*. Aisling also does a wonderfully flavourful, aromatic cucumber-and-gin dressing using Drumshanbo Gunpowder Irish Gin from neighbouring county Leitrim. I am experiencing maritime vegetal notes of the seaweed with umami from the oil sliced right through like a samurai sword by the cold gin.

Glenn had told me before I left him that he had proposed to Aisling not far from where I was in the middle of Sligo Bay today and I cannot resist asking Aisling for her take on this momentous event. She laughs, and blushingly agrees that I have her permission to retell the story. 'He woke me up saying he was going to show me a bit of romance and I got excited having been anticipating the proposal for the last six months. He took me to Coney Island, then we hopped on a boat and we went across the water to a lighthouse where he proposed. He said, "Anywhere you go in Sligo Bay, you will always see the lighthouse . . ."' As stories of proposals go, it's hard to beat Glenn's planning and execution – or the perfection of the wild surroundings that clearly still make it so magical for this charming couple.

After a good two hours sampling the Sligo oysters and talking with Aisling, I ride back to the hotel and freshen up before walking back into town to check out two highly recommended pubs – The Swagman and Shoot the Crows, which both offer live music. I have supper in The Swagman before venturing over to Castle Street and Shoot the Crows for an authentic Irish folk session. I walk in through the swinging wooden door to a rendition of 'Drowsy Maggie' which segues into the gloriously evocative 'Cooley's Reel', played by a talented group of musicians on the fiddle, melodeon, tin whistle, a couple of guitars, bodhran and a four-string banjo.

Looking around this traditional bar with its polished wood, shining brass and old-style lamps hanging from the ceiling, it's not hard to imagine what it must have felt like for those merchant seamen of the eighteenth century to have docked in Sligo Bay and rolled into bars like this to let off steam with a pint or two of the black stuff and sing along to some folk tunes. We've come a long way in 300 years – but in some ways, perhaps we haven't changed at all.

24

Donegal (*Dhún na nGall*)

Location: *Traigheanna Bay, County Donegal, Ireland*
Natural habitat: *Sweeping sandy bay*

Donegal can boast many famous sons and daughters, and today I'm on my way to meet another – Edward Gallagher, a legend of the Irish oyster game. His name has cropped up time and again on this trip, with many urging me to make sure his family-owned business, Irish Premium Oysters, is on my itinerary; he is purported to be one of the calmest, friendliest and most generous oystermen in the business.

Fourteen miles north of Sligo, the giant table-top mountain above Sligo, Benbulben, is on my right, catching the morning sun and elevating its status to something akin to epic. My journey from Sligo to Dungloe in Donegal will take around three hours, so there's little time to indulge in sedate sightseeing and admire the view. Leaving Sligo, I'll ride the N15 north for most of the journey. I pass into County Leitrim, one of the heartland counties of Ireland which also has a section of the Wild Atlantic Way, but it's only a three-mile stretch with the sea to my left and Lough Melvin to the right before I'm in Donegal and having to comply with the traditions of the Bundoran Fairy Bridges.

In *Scenes in Ireland* written by the author Rev G. N. Wright in 1834, he said of the coastal rock landforms, 'Although it is securely passable by simple mortals, visitors are recommended to avoid the [Fairy Bridges'] unhallowed surface, as troops of fairies are constantly heard, and sometimes seen, by those who possess the invaluable gift of second vision, flying hastily from end to end.' As time is of the essence, I just say hello to the fairies with a little wave to pay my respects, as all visitors are expected to do. I learnt in the Isle of Man that if you do not say hello to the fairies at Fairy Bridge between Ronaldsway Airport and Douglas, it will bring you very bad luck. They are sticklers for correct protocol and politeness, fairies, and I don't wish to upset them.

As well as the Fairy Bridges, the town of Bundoran gained popularity in the 1820s as a seaside town abundant in health benefits because of its position on the Atlantic Ocean and its wide, clean golden beaches offering the most bracing of promenade opportunities while filling the lungs with fresh, ozone-laden air. These natural conditions are not only enjoyed by humans, of course – the oysters in County Donegal also benefit from this idyllic setting, and are considered to be world class, too. Today, I am going to a wide sheltered bay just shy of Dungloe in Ireland's mountainous northern reaches.

Continuing north on the N15 to avoid roadworks, I climb into the hills around Ballybofey and then turn westwards, snaking out of the hills down towards sea level. As I look out over the Atlantic ahead of me, I am struck by the light shining off the surface of the sea in a huge bay on silvered, glasslike water. As I descend to sea level, the tide is working its way back in but, if I've timed it right, Ed and I should still be able to walk out to the trestles.

We meet at Ed's house and I'm immediately impressed with the towering presence of the man himself, exuding strength and resilience, all being softened by a wide grin. I hop into his red pickup truck and we trundle down to the water's edge. As we approach the beach, we are surrounded by grey, seaweed-shrouded boulders linking the grey-gold sand to the grass. Dungloe's Gaelic name – *An Clochán Liath* – means 'grey stones' and is a wonderfully appropriate name for the area.

The distinct plump white meat and sweet taste of the oyster is achieved by a combination of well-drilled husbandry and the perfect combination of naturally occurring conditions: there's the pure water from the Bluestack Mountains to the south; to the north, the Glenveagh National Park drains into the bay across nutrient-rich terrain which overlays granite and limestone geology. The sprawling bay is vast and the tidal forces at play ensure that pure oceanic Atlantic water rushes into and out of the area twice a day. These award-winning Donegal oysters also benefit from brackish river water that runs adjacent to the oyster farm, lending a distinctive peaty quality to the oysters.

At the trestles, Ed leans down to one of the bags and picks out a large-shelled specimen the size of his bear-paw hand. He digs out a knife from his windbreaker pocket and expertly shucks the oyster. I slurp the meat from the shell and it fills my entire mouth. It takes me a bit by surprise, and Ed laughs as I smile at my mistake while trying to savour the experience without choking. I have literally bitten off more than I can chew. As I gradually work through the flesh, the flavours start to release – I'm quickly overwhelmed by a brilliant sweetness and a hint of salty peat and lingering notes of iodine.

I can confirm that Donegal is perfectly situated for producing astonishingly flavoured oysters. Ed's oysters are mainly bought by consumers for the flavours – not too salty, not too sweet – their biggest selling point. Some oysters from other producers have 'big meat', Ed tells me, 'some oysters have beautiful shells . . . ours have a lingering taste of the mountains.'

Another contributory factor in the production of such wonderful oysters is the temperature of the waters in Donegal Bay – the relatively cold waters slow down growth and allow the flavours to mature. In Donegal, the water temperature is roughly 2°C colder than in the south of Ireland, which increases shelf life and the hardiness of the shell, and increases the meat content.

With the seawater now reaching the bottom of the metal trestles, we retreat back to the truck and make our way over to the other site where Ed and his family pack all of the oysters. Having their own transport company, they can ensure that the oysters are dispatched to the airport as carefully as possible before they embark on their trips around the world. When I initially contacted Ed when I was planning the Irish leg of my trip, he warned me that I would never find his oysters in Europe, which was unusual as the average oyster farm generally sells about 90 per cent of its output there. That may change in the future, but the majority of Irish Premium Oysters are currently exported further afield, principally to Asia and the Middle East, including Hong Kong, Taiwan, Malaysia, Japan, Singapore, Thailand, China and Dubai. It's the very definition of a world-class product, but there is still one way of enjoying the delights of Irish Premium Oysters without having to travel to Shanghai – Ed and his family welcome visitors to their farm in Dungloe with open arms, and guided tours, which include shucking and tasting the oysters, are well worth the modern-day pilgrimage.

Back on my bike and offering a final wave to Ed Gallagher and his hugely impressive rock oyster farm, I ride south on the N56 to Donegal. It is an hour-long ride which zigzags along the prehistoric coastline before cutting inland at Lettermacaward. I arrive in the historic town of Donegal just in time for dinner at The Olde Castle Bar pub in the centre of town. This stone-built pub is in clear view of Donegal Castle, home of the O'Connell clan chieftains who ruled this part of Ireland from the 1200s. The stables behind the pub are where they kept their horses and the restaurant section of the pub is named after Red Hugh O'Donnell, a famous chieftain. The town hunkers down beneath the towering Bluestack

Mountains where the Atlantic meets the River Eske, and has long served as a trading town – originally for the Irish to trade with Vikings and Gauls and, subsequently, the sea port was frequented by Spanish and Bristol traders. The importance of the fishing grounds here have long been one of the main reasons for Donegal's reputation as a trading hub, with the O'Connells becoming known throughout the European continent as the 'Lords of the Fish'.

Having been out in the elements all day and knowing I have only one day left in Ireland, I decide to follow tradition – I order the Oyster Isles classic of six Donegal Bay oysters, the Atlantic Seafood Chowder, a side of soda bread and a Guinness. Why change a winning formula? The menu offers a huge array of locally sourced, seasonal marine- and land-based dishes, and relies heavily on the quality and consistency of local producers.

Donegal's Gaelic name – *Dhún na nGall* – means 'fort of the foreigner', and the current inhabitants have really taken that idea of making strangers feel at home to their hearts – the friendliness of the inhabitants here is legendary, and their hospitality second to none. After a nice warm supper, it's a short jaunt back to the Castle Murray House hotel at St John's Point, a unique hideaway with stone floors and open fires which looks out on to the Atlantic.

25

Carlingford (*Cairlinn*)

Location: *Carlingford Lough, County Louth,
Ireland and County Down, Northern Ireland*
Natural habitat: *Tidal sea lough*

Pulling back the curtains of my cosy room at Castle Murray House near Donegal, I open the window to let some of the cool, crisp air into the room. The weather looks fairly bright today, which bodes well for my cross-country ride eastwards to Carlingford Lough. I gather my belongings and gear up the bike before settling myself in the breakfast room with panoramic views of green fields, Crownarad Mountain and the Atlantic. I order locally caught mackerel and scrambled eggs on toast with a wonderfully steamy cup of coffee.

After breakfast, I wander down Rohan Hill to the coast where, on a windswept promontory, I find McSwyne's Castle, named after the McSwyne clan of Banagh. There's a mussel farm bobbing up and down in the waves in the bay and, at the foot of the exposed cliff, are old oyster and winkle shells poking out of the dirt. With stone forts dating from 1000 BC – AD 1000 in the area, there is no doubt those who came here long ago were eating mackerel and shellfish just as we are today. I walk back up to the roadside to read a memorial to fishermen who lost their lives at nearby Bruckless Bay in 1813, when 200 sailing boats capsized in a sudden storm. I take a moment to remember them, and then set a course on the Triumph for the south-east.

The ride from County Donegal to County Louth will entail crossing into several counties and leapfrogging the political border between the Republic and Northern Ireland. As I embark on the two-and-a-half hour journey, I enter Northern Ireland at Petigo where I'm struck by the sheer scale of the lush green grazing pasture and the predominance of cattle and dairy farming in the area. Having been entirely focused on seafood for the past couple of weeks, it's really good to see another thriving industry and the sight of all the gorgeously healthy, doe-eyed dairy cows is very welcome. I pass through Armagh, where Viking-vanquishing Irish hero Brian Boru's bones are buried, before dropping further south of Belfast. I am now not far from Strangford Lough and, with Lough Foyle on the northern coast, both locations are synonymous with high standards of oysters over the last hundred years; native oysters were common to both loughs, particularly in the nineteenth century, until they were overfished in the early twentieth century.

After traversing the gently undulating northern counties of the Republic and Northern Ireland, I start to climb more steeply into wood-covered hills with the twisting, winding road weaving its way ever higher beneath lush green canopies. Circumnavigating Slieve Foye – or Carlingford Mountain and 'the mountain of the woods', as it's also known – I am now nearly half a mile above sea level, the county highpoint of Louth, which sits dramatically above the southern entrance to Carlingford Lough. I roll over the peak and begin my descent when suddenly my vision is filled with the dazzling electric blue of Carlingford Lough, quite a contrast with the relatively rural landscape of the past couple of hours. The sight of the lough with the backdrop of the Mourne Mountains is truly awe-inspiring and, as I pass through Omeath, the stunning beauty of Carlingford Lough opens up to my left, and I follow the shimmering waters along the coast road towards the old medieval town of Carlingford itself.

In the Dublin *Penny Journal* published on 21 July 1832, it was written: 'In all of Ireland ... there is not a bay so beautiful as Carlingford ... It would almost be well to be a Carlingford Fisherman or even a Carlingford Oyster, provided that an oyster could see through the sea and be susceptible of the picturesque, without the consciousness of being liable to be dredged for and gobbled by voracious Dublinians.' Indeed – if oysters could avoid being eaten ... and if they had eyes ... and if they were able to process the beauty of their surroundings ... then maybe they really do have the most wonderful life and idyllic view in this stunning part of the Irish Republic. There are a few big 'ifs' though!

I pull the bike over just shy of the town limits to look out on to the steep sides of the lough and the majestic peaks of the Mourne Mountains across the surface of water in Northern Ireland. C. S. Lewis grew up in the shadow of these mountains, and said of the natural beauty of the Mourne range, 'I have seen landscapes which, under a particular light, made me feel that at any moment a giant might raise his head over the next ridge.' He would draw on the power of this extraordinary landscape to create his mystical world of Narnia.

The Mourne area also lends its name to a traditional oyster bar in the Titanic Quarter of Belfast – the Mourne Seafood Bar – where you can enjoy locally sourced oysters at the right price. Only a century ago, hungry folk between here and Belfast would have scavenged the shores beneath me for oysters and shellfish as a last resort to overcome famine. Again, it's a reminder of the impact the oyster would have made in sustaining malnourished souls during times of hardship.

A few miles later, I arrive at Carlingford Oysters on the south-eastern side of this deep and expansive lough to meet the tall, bespectacled Kian Louët-Feisser, whose family own the farm. Kian exudes style with his close-cropped hair and sharp goatee and, like, Ed Gallagher, he's an expert oysterman with a huge presence and a warm smile. It's not surprising to hear that they collaborate a great deal and are wonderful ambassadors for Irish shellfish. Kian is the son of a Dutch father, Peter, and an English mother, Anna, who in the late 1960s sailed into Carlingford Lough with a crew of two chickens called Columbus and Mrs Gray. After a brief jaunt to Warrenpoint and back, the weather turned and foggy conditions forced Peter, Anna and their feathered friends to take shelter in Carlingford. They started an oyster farm, as you do, and have been here ever since.

Kian takes me into the plant where they are purifying thousands of oysters in the seawater under UV light. It is an impressively high-quality commercial set-up. There are umpteen boxes ready for local dispatch as well as to customers in Britain and Asia. It has not always been like this, though; when Peter and Anna started out forty years ago, they used to put a couple of boxes on a lorry with mushrooms bound for Manchester and other markets in the north of Britain. Then, when things expanded, they sent oysters through the regular mail service, before expanding further to become one of Ireland's best-known oyster farms.

Carlingford benefits hugely from a strategic position on the east coast of Ireland, facing the Irish Sea and equidistant between Belfast and Dublin. The Vikings are thought to have been exploiting the resources of the sheltered bay from the ninth century onwards, from which Carlingford gets its name – 'Fjord of Carlinn' – in Old Norse. It was deemed important enough in the 1200s for the Normans to build a castle here in 1261, now an imposing ruin named after King John. And the town eventually became known as an important trading port, enjoying significant prosperity from the fourteenth to sixteenth centuries.

With dusk fast approaching, Kian suggests we head out into the lough. We don some waders and gloves and make our way into the yard, where he starts the engine on a red-and-white tractor carrying a trailer-load of oyster mesh bags. I hop on to the back of the trailer while Kian starts driving down to the water. The tide is out, but it is starting to creep back in and the couple of inches of water we'll be wading through will soon rise up to submerge the trestles entirely. We don't have long.

Picking our way down between the imposing hillsides looking northwards to Northern Ireland and south out to sea, we're soon into the shallow water and chugging our way out to the trestles in the middle of the lough. There are rock oysters everywhere with the sound of bubbling water from the thousands of tiny little ecosystems in amongst the racks. Hooded crows flap lazily overhead and wading birds have a final forage before finding a roost for the night.

Back on the tractor, Kian points out various parts of the farm operation as we tour the site, explaining each feature and how everything works together; I take the opportunity to share some of my knowledge, too, having worked with Carlingford Oysters for a number of years now. It's risky, given that I'm currently in the company of the man who owns the business! For example, I've always found it easy to point out a Carlingford oyster on a display of rock oysters because of the little barnacles on the shell. Obviously, many oysters can have barnacles on them, but with Carlingford it is distinctive and almost a trademark. Second, the Carlingford oyster taste is usually quite salty, despite the freshwater flowing in from the mountainsides north and south of the lough. The actual position of the farm means that very little freshwater reaches it, being submerged twice a day by the full extent of the Irish Sea, which delivers all the nutrients the oysters need for healthy growth. It's true that once you taste a Carlingford oyster, you will most probably be able to identify it again in a blind tasting years later.

We hop off the tractor again, stopping by some baskets. Kian unhooks a black basket and pulls out a few oysters and says, 'This is the part of the farm that we have set up to get the most wave action.' One or two other producers have also taken this approach, letting nature do the work tumbling the oysters in the waves to create a desirable deep-cupped shell with an enlarged adductor muscle and high meat content. These are the premium oysters that they have called Louët-Feisser, after the family. It is a stunning mouthful of oyster – pearlescent meat, which is simultaneously sweet, ozone rich, tender and clean – leaving the palate with a perfect freshness as if paddling in the loch with the salty spray splashing your face! The lasting flavour is a delightfully salty sweetness on the palate. The scallop-like adductor muscle's sweetness comes from having been fully worked among the crashing waves like a bicep after a gym session, and the ozone characteristic contributes to a long shelf life and cleanliness as an end-product of purification.

In the past, the native oysters of Carlingford have been equally in demand, with the Marquis of Anglesey (who had local jurisdiction over the fishery) leveraging a tax on oysters – an annual 5 shillings per boat, not inconsiderable when you consider that there were up to 400 boats at the height of the industry here.

We continue with the tractor tour as Kian points to areas of the sea-bed which are covered in old native oyster shell. Native oysters were harvested here in the past as part of organised farming operations, having been brought here to be re-laid before being sent to Belfast, Liverpool and Dublin, and old stumps of posts and pebbles denote the systematic farming that must have gone on in the area over many hundreds of years.

The first records of natives are from 1622, which saw Carlingford grow to become a very popular fishery. In 1834, up to 2,000 people on hundreds of boats exploited the beds until they ran dry. Carlingford Lough was one of the places that brought over Virginica oysters from New York that had been landed in Liverpool and were re-laid here to prop up the dwindling oyster beds. Today, Carlingford is the last place between County Louth and Wexford where oysters are cultivated. This is largely due to the exposed sea, sandy beaches and a lack of sheltered inlets. Arklow in County Wicklow used to sell 3,000 tons of oysters a year, and Dublin Bay and the River Liffey used to provide ample flat oysters for the city and beyond. Now it is the rock oyster that is cultivated here.

The capital is just over 70 miles south and still traditionally strongly associated with oyster consumption. Even the Guinness advert proclaimed 'Guinness makes the oysters come out of their shells' and we were told 'Opening time is Guinness time', a 1932 poster depicting the black stout with five native oysters ready to be shucked. Benjamin Disraeli, the British Prime Minister from 1874 to 1880, described the experience of tasting Guinness and oysters on the night of 21 November 1837 as 'the most remarkable day hitherto of my life'. As well as the Guinness Store House, there are a host of fantastic oyster eateries in Dublin, including Klaw, Matt the Thresher, The Bank on College Green and, of course, many of the establishments in the Porterhouse and Temple Bar areas.

Kian's tractor wends its way inexorably back towards the shore as dusk gives way to a purpling darkness. There's an eeriness to the blue-black shapes and shadows around us, with the sound of the tractor engine grinding away as we forge a path along the muddy shallows. Just shy of the shore, Kian stops the tractor and jumps down from his perch, grabbing a 6ft length of steel bar lying nearby.

'Watch this!' he says, walking off the gravel pathway on to the mud, where he places one end of the pole in the water. 'How far do you think this will sink into the ground?'

'About two feet?' I offer.

He laughs and, with just his index finger, pushes the pole into the ground until the whole thing disappears. 'There are a few sink holes in the farm!' he shouts to me.

It's impressive – and another reminder, as if I need any more, that oyster farmers like Kian carry with them an intimate knowledge of their natural surroundings – essential if you've got unmarked hazardous geographical features waiting nearby to swallow you whole.

We head to the Anchor pub in the amber glow of the medieval high street. Known locally as PJ's after P. J. O'Hare, the pub ironically has the same name as the P & J Oyster Company, the famous oyster house on Toulouse Street, New Orleans, an establishment I've also had the chance to visit. Kian and I chat for most of the evening over some stout and seafood, enjoying the traditional feel of this old pub with its wooden panelling, brick hearth and warmly welcoming Irish charm.

As Kian and I part, I am sad to leave this wonderful country but I know I will return, especially for the chowder, soda bread, six oysters and a stout – the Oyster Isles special will always have a little place in my heart.

26

Porlock Bay

Location: *Somerset, England*
Natural habitat: *Bristol Channel*

Back on English soil, I am heading to the picturesque fishing town of Porlock on the south coast of the Bristol Channel, the last sheltered low ground before the county boundary with Devon. Upon entering Somerset, I whip past the Mendip Hills, Weston-super-Mare, Bridgwater and on to the A39 which runs along the southwest coast of Britain all the way down to Falmouth. Passing Minehead, I arrive in the beautifully rolling landscape of the Exmoor National Park, with its neat, well-tended fields that offer a direct link back in time to the agricultural revolution. The highest point of Exmoor, Dunkery Beacon, is just to my left and, to my right, are the crashing waves of the Bristol Channel.

Once in the small town of Porlock, I meander through the characterful ranks of seventeenth-century cottages to Porlock Weir, where I meet Mike Lynch; he is one of the leadership team of Porlock Bay Oysters, the community interest project that was set up by the local council to help revitalise the economy of the town.

Standing on the cobbles of the old Ship Inn, the freshening breeze sweeping across the vast expanse of beach before me, the gathering grey clouds and the churning, foam-topped sea are all signs of some heavy weather to come. Walking out on to the sand, I am struck by the purplish hues on the surface of the rocks, and notice that there are some giant 'pebbles' at the high-tide mark the size of basketballs; it serves to indicate the sheer power of the waves crashing on to the beach when 'perfect-storm' conditions occur. The cliff falls to the west and the high tides – rising and falling around 30ft – have helped to fashion the natural 6,000-year-old shingle ridge which geologists believe was formed with the rise in sea levels at the end of the last Ice Age. This is the main feature of Porlock Vale.

In the distance, further along the beach I can make out the black lines of trestles with their flattened oyster bags draped in seaweed lying neatly against the pale sandy-grey of the shingle. This is where Porlock finishes its oysters, having brought them up from their growing site in South Devon. Porlock oysters are known for their clear, almost sparkling mother-of-pearl appearance on the interior of the shell, which is thought to be due to the sheer force of the scouring action of the sea. They have the best of both worlds as the oysters are being grown in the nutrient-rich Bigbury Bay before they take on the high salinity of the Bristol estuary at around 34 ppt. Flanking the trestles in a section of the beach are the partial remains of rudimentary, 2ft-high manmade stone walls, the evidence of old holding pits for the oysters from times gone by.

Walking into an impressive stone-built shed at the end of the harbour that now acts as Porlock's purification facilities, an oilskin-clad lady called Emma is hard at work topping up the purification tanks ahead of the predicted bad weather so there will be sufficient oysters for next week's sales. Like all oyster producers, Porlock has to pay close attention to the climatic conditions and work closely with nature in order to meet sales demands. She fills up her last tank with pure seawater in order to support enough oysters to ride out the storm. Porlock intends to expand into the old stables next door as the business continues to grow. I pop a couple of beautifully clean oysters open and taste the unbridled high salinity of the Bristol Channel outside, perfect for pairing with a high-acidity white wine.

We walk along the harbour where, at low tide, the remnants of a prehistoric forest are visible, and we head over towards the white-walled and thatched Ship Inn, a celebrated local pub. Ducking my head under the lintel of the ancient doorway, I'm stepping back in time to around 1290 when this building was first established. Mike and I pick a quiet corner of the pub and we order a half of the local scrumpy. Over the past several hundred years, the timber walls and the wonky ceiling have been witness to many a smuggler, oysterman, coach postilion . . . and a fair amount of scrumpy-drinking. I am careful not to indulge in more than half a pint because the south-west is renowned for its strong cider; on top of that, I have Porlock Hill to tackle later, reputed to be the steepest road in England. Historically, the gradient of Porlock Hill – a 25 per cent incline – meant that two horses had to be permanently stabled at the inn to help the already exhausted stagecoach horses haul their loads to the summit.

Mike explains a little more of the unique nature of the Porlock Bay Oysters story; this oyster farm is one of the youngest of all those I have visited, and is definitely the youngest in England. Oysters were discovered by chance in the Bristol Channel by a man named Noel Pollard in the 1830s when returning from oyster fishing off The Mumbles in Swansea Bay. Pollard was from Porlock Weir and started dredging for oysters in this 'new site' in 1836. By the 1850s, the oyster industry had grown so much that thousands were being caught each day and were kept in an area of the beach called Oyster Perch, where we saw the crumbling low walls earlier. In the 1870s, the Minehead Railway opened, which took Porlock oysters into London where they became famed for their quality. As we have seen, the downside to this, of course, is that when Porlock oysters became more in demand, boats from Colchester and Whitstable would sail over here and dredge the lot to restock their own beds. This decimation of the native oyster population saw an end to the oyster industry in Porlock. I take a big gulp from my glass and apologise on behalf of everyone in Essex and Kent.

With the advent of the railways – in a theme repeated elsewhere – seaside towns were able quickly to increase the volume of oysters being dispatched to the big cities exponentially and this caused a boom in the oyster industry. The 1800s are widely credited with seeing the height of the oyster industry in Ireland and the British Isles, with the greatest volume of production and consumption occurring between 1860 and 1890. It is estimated that in England during the 1860s, 1.5 billion oysters were eaten a year. To meet this demand, oysters came from everywhere and anywhere and, although closed seasons had developed by then, a real focus was now placed on stopping fishing over the summer months to allow beds to stay stocked. This is the origin of the 'R'-in-the-month rule which we still apply to natives now. Oyster taverns in capital cities and oyster towns started to crop up, such as Moran's Oyster Cottage in Galway County, Wiltons in London, and Edinburgh was once famous for its oyster cellars. Oysters were pouring into the cities of Dublin, London, Liverpool, Edinburgh and Manchester and, when beds were depleted, oystermen just went further and further afield.

This plundering of other people's oyster beds became the norm around the turn of the century and the most aggressively entrepreneurial offenders were often those from Essex and Kent, primarily because they were so close to the biggest market in Britain – London. Another reason, of course, was that, by the 1890s, oyster beds were showing sure signs of depleted stocks from being overfished. Porlock is a prime example of why, perhaps, people do not think of England as having an oyster culture; people are not aware of – or have forgotten – the glory days of our proud industrial oyster heritage.

The current set-up at Porlock Bay Oysters is not only trying to reverse the demise of the oyster stocks – albeit with rocks rather than natives at the moment – they are also bringing in employment to the local area to offer local inhabitants a good reason to stay in this wonderful corner of Somerset. The main issues facing the area are the 'skewed' demographics as Porlock has one of the highest rates of over-65s in England, as well as lying in a fairly remote location.

In 2013, Porlock Futures group was set up by Porlock Parish Council which trialled oyster farming in the bay and now, a few years on, they are employing more local people, providing a new local attraction, and supplying local businesses, hotels and restaurants with a quality oyster. On top of employing local people, their oyster trestles were hand-built at the local Allerford Forge, a traditional seventeenth-century West Somerset blacksmith's business owned by the National Trust. The old forge is run by brothers Kyle and Kieran Roberts who make up West Country Blacksmiths.

The storm is blowing in and I reluctantly give up my cosy seat in the inn to brave the weather. I still have a lingering saltiness from the robust little Porlock oyster, and I'm sure many others will also be enjoying the bright shells and salty sweetness at the Harbour Gallery and Café by the weir – maybe not at their tables on the harbour front today, though. Mike Lynch assures me that visitors will be able to drop into their new premises and come away with a wooden box of oysters and a bottle of wine and, in fine weather, sit on the beach or by the weir and enjoy the most wonderful of impromptu picnics, dangling their feet over the water.

I gently coax the Bonneville away from the bay and tackle Porlock Hill – it's one thing to hear about the gradient in theory, but it's quite another to tackle the terrifying hairpin bends and wet tarmac on a bike. When I have a moment on the straights, I spare a passing thought for the poor horses who had to suffer in silence.

Once I reach the summit, I pull over and gaze out across the Bristol Channel with the south coast of Wales in the distance. It is a wonderful sight – whatever the weather.

27

Torridge to Porthilly (*Porthhyli*)

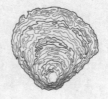

Locations: *Appledore, Devon; Rock, Camel
Estuary, Cornwall, England*
Natural habitats: *Brackish river; high salinity river*

My ride through Exmoor National Park is a memorable one for all the right reasons – I am surrounded by low-lying bracken and shrubs dusted with gorgeous late-summer/early-autumn hues of golds, deep greens and browns.

I occasionally catch a glimpse of a few fabled Exmoor ponies as I flash by, and startle the odd partridge and pheasant as they dash for cover from all manner of predator – blokes with guns and blokes on Bonnevilles to name a couple. The poet Samuel Taylor Coleridge also travelled this very route from Porlock Weir to Culborne, describing the journey as being full of 'wild deer, foxes, badgers and martin cats' in 1797.

Turning left at Blackmoor Gate on the western reaches of Exmoor, I join the A339 south to Barnstaple where I cross the River Taw. From here it is a short journey on to Instow which sits at the confluence of the rivers Taw and Torridge as they flow into the sea as one big estuary. I am now deep in the heart of *Tarka the Otter* country, and I can almost hear the strident notes of the bugle from my childhood over the roar of the bike. The Torridge catchment area supports one of the most thriving otter populations in England, one that is growing and is of international importance. The North Devon Tourist Board has recently developed the 180-mile Tarka Trail which is well worth a hike, taking intrepid explorers through sand dunes, salt marsh, woodland, grazing marsh and meadows. As well as otters, you might catch a glimpse of salmon, sea trout and brown trout, with the salmon now being protected as part of the Salmon Action Plan to increase their numbers.

The winds are freshening now so I waste no time in completing my journey by arriving at The Glorious Oyster Beach Café nestled behind the butter-coloured Sandhills at Instow Beach. The business name comes from the title of a book called *The Glorious Oyster* by Hector Bolitho who wrote travel and food books in the 1960s. The horizontal, weathered clapboard exterior of the café is painted a bright turquoise with wooden benches on sand and a serving hatch at the front with owner Lindsay hanging out of it to flag me down. I pull up next to a wooden sign encouraging a 'two-minute beach clean' with various paraphernalia available for enthusiastic litter-pickers. The Glorious Oyster is very much a part of the beach and its environment and it wears its heart on its sleeve in attempting to do all it can to sustain and improve the quality of the local natural environment. In addition to these efforts, south-west England is home to Surfers Against Sewerage, who have helped to make 96.9 per cent of the 636 designated bathing areas around the UK now classified as having excellent, good or acceptable water quality, compared to 27 per cent since the group's formation in 1990. It's an incredible achievement, and a lesson in the power of grassroots campaigning.

Lindsay and I have mutual friends, Lorna and Chunk, who have offered me a bed for the night, so I think it's perfectly acceptable to opt for a massive hug with Lindsay, bypassing the formal handshake. She leads the way up on to the sand dunes behind the Beach Café to get my bearings, pointing towards Appledore where Torridge Oysters are farmed at the meeting of the Torridge and Taw. The tide is out, exposing vast tracts of beach, with violent gusts of wind whipping up clouds of sand and bending the marram grass at right-angles to our boots. We hurry back down and take shelter in the café where Lindsay picks up where she left off before my arrival – peeling some quince.

As well as his cookery book being a great source of knowledge, Hector Bolitho wrote evocatively about oysters, saying: 'they are the loveliest of all foods, raw or cooked' . . . they are tender because of their 'talent for laziness' . . . and, best of all, that 'they are stupendous drinkers; they guzzle about a hundred and sixty quarts of seawater a day'. Lindsay was so inspired by the book she started selling local seafood from a converted horsebox on the beach at Westward Ho! in 2014, before opening this place up two years later.

Lindsay goes on to tell me of the rave reviews she has had and about her loyal customer base – some people have driven for two-and-a-half hours from as far as Salisbury to eat here, and she was a finalist on the BBC *One Show*'s Best Street Food award out of 600 nominations. The Horsebox and the Beach Café that make up The Glorious Oyster have become something of an institution across North Devon and beyond, with Lindsay admitting that the press and great reviews can sometimes be overwhelming. She says, 'Sometimes it isn't about the money, it's about the great feedback and having that connection with your guests. Just the other day the weather was awful and I was half thinking of not opening, but I did and I had a stream of guests saying, "Thank God you are open today," as they sat with their backs to the wind eating fresh fish with their hot cups of tea.'

Lindsay's aim is to promote the freshest of local seafood drawn from the Devon waters just outside her two sites, as well as renowned staples – it might be Clovelly herring, hand-dived scallops, Scottish creel-caught langoustines or locally farmed oysters. And with almost perfect timing, the door opens allowing a blast of wind to whip through the shack, and two figures are almost blown in along with it – they are Phoebe Chope and Martin Shute of Torridge Mussels & Oysters. The oyster farmers have just come in from their trestle farm over in Appledore, having made sure that their baskets were fastened securely ahead of this storm. The location of their farm in the Taw–Torridge Estuary is a Site of Special Scientific Interest with plenty of birds and wildlife, although I'm sure most creatures, like us, would have run for cover today at the earliest opportunity.

The wonderfully named Appledore and its attractive, multi-coloured terraced houses lining the curving, sloping cobbled streets are a clue to its seafaring past as these buildings were the dwellings of former fishermen, who would have caught salmon, bass and cod while everyday folk foraged for cockles and mussels at low tide in the Bideford Estuary. Appledore is also famed for its shipyard that built various boats, such as ketches, schooners and barks, that sailed out from the Bristol Estuary to North America. Martin tells me that although oysters were dredged at Clovelly and Porlock, and despite the rich maritime and fishing history of Bideford and the settlements of the Taw–Torridge Estuary, it seems that Phoebe and Martin have been the only people in recent times to farm oysters here. This makes them VIPs within the food scene of this local area in North Devon, despite mussels being more favoured by the local chefs.

I suggest we try some of the oysters and shuck for all of us in the sanctuary of the Beach Café. We compare shucking techniques and largely agree on the same hinge method, and enjoy the smooth taste of the Torridge. The oysters from the Torridge River make for a brackish taste with salinity averaging around the 21/22 ppt mark in an estuary with one of the largest tidal ranges in the world. The river is 48 miles long, rising in Baxworthy Cross and travelling in a loop before racing down to the estuary at Bideford to meet the Taw and flushing out into the Bristol Channel. The oysters are receiving nutrients from two of England's finest rivers as well as benefiting from the salinity of the sea. It is a remarkable location for an oyster farm, and to have The Glorious Oyster across the water is a true culinary treat.

With the weather worsening, I take my leave and ride carefully away, ending up in The Farmer's Arms pub in Woolsery, Bideford, for some hearty Devonshire ale by a log fire. It is a wonderfully designed, elegant establishment, with a perfect balance of comfort and style in a really characterful setting. It's one of the loveliest pubs I have been to all year and the food and beverage offerings match the quality of the surroundings – there's a well-considered menu which is a cut above the usual gastropub fare, and they have a great chef who really cares about the integrity of locally sourced, seasonal ingredients.

With the memory of that beautiful Torridge oyster still lingering the next morning, I am looking forward to sampling more treasures in the oyster-rich county of Cornwall down in the far southwestern reaches of Britain. Unfortunately, when I peer bleary-eyed out of the window, the rain is still lashing the panes and bushes and shrubs are being forced to bow their heads in the teeth of an almighty gale. On the upside, my Bonneville is still upright, standing proud in the vicious winds. So every cloud . . .

Part of me wants to sit out the storm, but I simply don't have the time to spare. Having steeled myself and muttering a silent prayer as I leave the warmth of Lorna and Chunk's cosy cottage, I ride into the wind, picking my way around scattered branches and boughs while the rain drives tiny bullets into my visor and the powerful gusts threaten to side-swipe me. It is not ideal, but I really have no choice – time, tide and an oysterman in the Camel Estuary wait for no man!

Once at Bude, the roadsign bearing the Cornish coat of arms reads in English and Cornish: 'Welcome to Cornwall . . . *Kernow a'gas dynergh'*. It's a timely reminder of this county's Celtic history and how strong the Cornish identity is today. The Cornish language dates back to pre-Roman times and the Celtic races that inhabited this part of Europe. Just as in Wales and Scotland, Cornwall's heritage lies with the Celtic people who were pushed to the western fringes by invading powers over the last 2,000 years. However, by 1500, only Tintagel and Looe were Cornish-speaking areas and, by the 1800s, Cornish was only spoken by fishermen. In 2014, the UK Government finally announced that the proud history, unique culture and distinctive language of Cornwall would be fully recognised under European rules for the protection of national minorities. Cornwall's St Piran's flag (black with a white cross) is also a powerful Cornish symbol, named after their patron saint of tin, one of the most precious natural resources to be mined in the area.

I continue south past King Arthur's Tintagel Castle on the Atlantic Highway and arrive in Rock, slowly winding my way down to Porthilly. Having battled wind and rain, I arrive bowed but unbeaten in the farmyard of Porthilly Oysters/Rock Shellfish, and dismount, leaving my bike beside some oyster-grading machines. I am greeted by owner Tim Marshall who kindly suggests that we take shelter. We step into a purification room, where mussels and oysters are filtering hundreds of litres of water in their respective tanks.

Having run a dairy farm originally, the Marshalls started oyster farming 35 years ago after seeing someone from Plymouth Polytechnic start an oyster farm in the estuary. Tim took inspiration from the French aquaculture systems and started out with 1,000 oyster seed and it literally grew from there. Now they have four sites in the Camel River where the whole farming process takes 16–24 months and involves continuous monitoring, sorting and separating of the oysters. Tim's son Luke started the mussels side of the business and now it is pretty much 50/50 when it comes to farming the oysters and mussels.

Tim shucks a Porthilly rock for me to try and with a 33ppt oceanic level of salinity, the crisp and clear salty flavour slaps me in the face with the essence of the sea. Not too long ago, based upon blind taste tests by a panel of expert judges, Porthilly won Gold in the Pacific Oyster Category at the British Oyster Championship, where the oysters were judged on appearance, meat-to-shell ratio and flavour. I can clearly see why.

Tim invites me to his house for some homemade lamb burgers, Cornish ice cream and a hot cup of tea. The risky journey has definitely been worth it.

Looking out on to the water, I can see where Tim and Luke Marshall farm their oysters and mussels. It is where the river opens to form a broad, flat estuary between the towns of Rock and Padstow on either side. The Camel Estuary itself is a drowned river valley that was formed by rising sea levels at the end of the last glaciation. It is a very unspoilt region, with winding creeks and tributary river banks that are home to all manner of wading birds and vegetation. The pace of life here is unhurriedly rural throughout the year, but there is inevitably a bit more hustle and bustle in the summer months from holiday makers. And just as we saw in the Taw–Torridge Estuary, the otter frequents this estuary, too, and one part of the river has been designated a seabass conservation area.

Porthilly Oysters are wonderfully located in the heart of an area geared towards not only seafood but fantastically high-quality gastronomy in all its forms. With fan favourite Prawn on the Lawn and Rick Stein's various seafood operations in Padstow, it is not hard to find Porthilly oysters on local menus. This part of Britain is a perfect model for a local economy which supports itself successfully. Oystermen and fishermen sell to local restaurants (literally off the boat in most cases), the restaurant procures the freshest local produce, the guests enjoy the best food and the word spreads as the whole cycle starts all over again.

Porthilly shows how the oyster is both local and global through physically being shipped and talked about. One customer in particular is Michelin Star chef and adopted Cornishman Nathan Outlaw. He proudly uses Porthilly oysters in his restaurants in Cornwall and beyond. The strong symbiotic relationship between chef and oyster farmer works its way along the chain of restaurant, hospitality staff and diners, and it all starts with Tim and Luke working the waters here. Tim says that the one thing he always tells people is, 'Make sure you chew your oyster and always store them at the bottom of your fridge – not in a bucket of water!'

Walking out on to the beach, the waves are choppy and the colour of the grey stone used to build the local church. With my stomach full and my body temperature almost stabilised after Tim's Cornish hospitality, I gaze beyond the coastline towards Padstow and wonder at the juxtaposition of the picture-book prettiness of the white-cottaged town nestling in the hills, and the sheer ferocity of the storm-lashed coast and rugged rocks surrounding it. I pull on my helmet and march back to the bike avoiding a thick fallen branch, feel the throb of the Bonneville as it reassuringly fires up, and wave goodbye to Tim.

28

River Fal (*Dowr Fala*)

Location: *Falmouth, Cornwall, England*
Natural habitat: *Drowned river valley*

Travelling south along the Atlantic Highway, venturing deeper into the wildly jagged landscape of Cornwall, my next destination is the famous Falmouth Oyster Festival which celebrates the start of native oyster season. It's held down on Falmouth harbour with cooking demos, shucking competitions, arts, crafts, local produce food stalls, beer and, of course, the highly prized Fal oyster. The festival is renowned for being proudly Cornish, offering an open door to anybody who wants to sample Cornish oyster culture on the boats, in the pubs or in the marquees. In addition to the allure of guzzling bucketloads of native oysters plucked directly from their natural habitat, it doesn't hurt that there's also a great variety of folk and rock music programmed to close each night. It's a little bit of heaven, as far as I'm concerned, and takes me back to my Essex childhood of raucous, joy-filled marquees in farmers' fields.

Following the A39 southwards towards the English Channel, if I continued on to the coast I'd end up at the historic Helford River oysterage owned by the Duchy of Cornwall. It has recently been taken on by oysterman extraordinaire Tristan Hugh-Jones of Rossmore, Cork, and Loch Ryan fame from London wholesalers and restaurateurs Wright Bros. Tristan is restoring the native oyster beds there to their former glory.

Having reached the UK's most southerly city, Truro, I turn into the onshore wind up to the aptly named Cliff Road above Gyllyngvase Beach towards the Lerryn Hotel. The storm is still whipping the sea into an absolute frenzy and it is quite tough to stay upright on the bike. I take refuge in the hotel and get chatting to the hotel owner, and I am devastated to learn that the festival has been cancelled due to the bad weather. However, all is not lost, as I have also arranged to meet a native oyster dredgerman called Ranger, who is hosting his very own unofficial oyster festival in the Front pub down on the quayside.

Falmouth is one of those fishing towns that has retained its smugglers' feel, and the buzz of youthful energy and illicit trades in dark corners is absolutely fantastic; the streets are thick with tanned surfer types and there are campervans pumping out music all over the town. Walking up Arwenack Street (named after the oldest building in Falmouth, originally built in 1385), there is bunting out for the oyster festival, so to raise my spirits, I dive into Harbour Lights fish and chip shop above the Front pub and order a pint of lager and some fish and chips with a seat facing out towards the harbour. It is a wonderfully immersive Cornish experience looking at the Fal Estuary. The Fal is the last wild native oyster fishery in Cornwall and considered home to the last commercially regulated oyster sailing fleet in the world – the other contender, Chesapeake, use motorised boats for a few days of the season. At one time, native oysters were found all over the Cornish shoreline in the rivers Fal, Percuil, Helford, Fowey and Camel, but now the Fal is the stronghold.

In 1602, a man called Richard Carew published his *Survey on Cornwall* which noted: 'They [fishermen] cull the oyster and cast away the residue . . . And serveth as a bed for the oysters to breed in'. His reporting of the fishing techniques of the Fal suggests that an oyster industry not only existed here over 400 years ago but an element of stewardship was conducted when pointing out that the extra shell (the cultch) caught in the dredge was thrown back to serve as an oyster bed for young oysters. Oysters here, as we've seen in many other locations around our islands, were bountiful in centuries past, and kept people sustained before the late eighteenth century's boom and bust which ultimately made the oyster a delicacy for the élite.

One of the key reasons for the survival of the Fal's native oyster beds is the set of by-laws introduced by the Truro Corporation in 1876 which dictated that harvesting the oyster should only be done 'under sail or oar' to propel fishermen's vessels. This meant working by hand with the wind and tide from traditional boats drifting along the oyster beds with no mechanical harvesting by any other means. This is the truest and most traditional form of oyster gathering in Britain today, and it's a wonderful thing to see the traditional Falmouth working boats all moored in front of me. The craftsmanship and heritage of the Cornish boat builders and fishermen is visible in each and every hand-hewn timber smack with their weathered red sails. I spot a local boat called *Willy Boy* that is over 150 years old, owned by local fisherman Tim Vinnicombe, who spends the winter oyster fishing and the summer catching mackerel. It must be quite a spectacle these days, all these historic boats sailing out to fish the oyster grounds, harnessing the power of the elements: surely a sight not too far removed from the times when the Romans fished here.

It's known that the Phoenicians traded along this coast, having been attracted here for the tin. And we know from the fifth-century Greek historian Herodotus that it was the Greeks who named the Phoenicians '*phoinikes*' meaning 'purple people', because of the dye used to make their exquisite purple clothes, which also stained the skin of the workers who applied it. In Drew Smith's book

Oyster: A Gastronomic History, he indicates that the oyster was a 'crucial contributor' to the Phoenicians' famed Tyrian dye used to colour imperial and royal robes. Drew points out that the purple dye is made from crushing the shells of sea snails which prey on oysters, and that collecting sea snails would have been an easy and lucrative cottage industry alongside harvesting oysters. So it follows that while the Phoenicians travelled to and from Cornwall for tin, it's likely that they discovered and exploited the rich oyster harvest in this part of the world as well. It would be wonderful to have definitive archaeological evidence for this but, unlike the Romans who came to Britain and settled, the Phoenicians would have sailed into harbours, traded and then moved on again, leaving very little evidence of their presence in our waters or on our land.

There is no doubt that Falmouth's deep and sheltered estuary would have been an ideal trading post for the Phoenician boats; the geology of the estuary was well explored by foreign traders. A nice deep channel with shallow banks either side would have been perfect for moving heavy cargo out of Cornwall. Up to about 200 years ago, you could sail a large boat all the way up to Truro but, sadly, since the china clay industry removed huge amounts of kaolin from their deposit sites, many of the natural river channels have silted up. If you go to St Austell today, you will see what Ranger calls the 'Cornish Alps', which were made from the five tons of waste for every ton of usable clay. In the nineteenth century, St Austell produced 65,000 tons of china clay, resulting in huge, white, slag-heap-style mountains of waste, with significant amounts also being flushed down the rivers.

The 'R'-in-the-month rule is also observed stringently here, as the native oysters are not allowed to be fished in the summer months to give them a chance to reproduce and allow spat to colonise and grow before the season starts. When the season finally opens from 1 October to 31 March, fishing is only allowed between 9.00 a.m. and 3.00 p.m. on weekdays and 9.00 a.m. and 12.00

p.m. on a Saturday; no fishing is allowed on a Sunday. It is largely accepted that the healthy stocks of natives in the estuary have been preserved over the last 150 years because of the 'natural inefficiency' of dredging using sail and oar. In addition, all Fal oystermen use a metal circular ring to measure the diameter of the oysters which need to be greater than 2in to be allowed to be taken from the water; anything smaller is thrown back. The metal ring was first introduced in 1926 stipulating that 'an oyster must not pass through a circular aperture to measure shell diameter'. This was updated in 2016 with a slightly new rule stipulating that an oyster must not pass through the ring when laying it flat across its longest length.

I finish my pint and fish supper and walk down the sloping street to the Custom House Quay pub. Walking into the cellar-style, vaulted-ceilinged bar, the festival atmosphere is still alive and well; Ranger greets me and presses an Atlantic Brewery Gold Ale in my hand and tells me I am entering a shucking competition which starts in ten minutes. I sink my pint and grab another. Moments later, a judge is announcing the contestants and throw myself into it: thirty Fal natives have to be shucked cleanly and not flipped, then presented on a platter and judged. Unluckily, I have mislaid my decent knife and have to borrow one of Ranger's. It's not the sharpest, but I'm not going to blame my tools – although when it comes to shucking, that rule really does not apply. A thick, stubby knife on delicate Fal natives will make shucking much harder.

Despite this, I shuck away and come second, losing out to Ranger. I will take that any day. Third place was a local fisherman from Venezuela called Adrian St Aubyn, whose ancestor was a Cornishman who left St Michael's Mount searching for a better life and ended up in Venezuela. Adrian has since returned and married a Cornish girl and works on the Fal. So, the first, second and third places of the competition were taken by a Kent-born Fal oysterman living in Cornwall, an Essex oysterman who shucks in London and a Venezuelan Fal oyster boat crewman with Cornish ancestry. We celebrate together with a bottle of Wolf in the Woods Cornish vodka, as if we didn't need any more reminders of just how global the world really has become.

The competition over, each contestant carries their platter around the pub with a collection box for the Fishermen's Mission for people to enjoy the Fal oysters and to make a donation. This charity was set up in 1881 and is dedicated to supporting fishermen and their families in times of need. It's a reminder to me that fishermen are 115 times more likely to suffer a fatal accident than the rest of the workforce, and that fishing is the UK's most dangerous peacetime occupation. I'm soon shucking more oysters behind Ranger's dedicated stall and he tells me about his boat *Alf Smythers*, named after its builder, and one of the last wooden boats built for the Fal oyster fishery. It was designed by Percy Dalton in 1966 specifically for use on the oyster beds. The boat gently works the 3ft frame dredge across the silty, muddy estuary bed that has been rotovated for hundreds of years. This method of oyster gathering is very low impact and any bycatch is returned to the water there and then, but the majority of crabs tend to move out of the way when they see the cloud of silt.

I shuck a few natives for me to go with my ale and it is a brilliant oyster. It has a very firm texture with a zinc flavour and faintly tangy notes, evoking images of earthy clay and it even has a vague tin colour in its hues as well, most probably due to all the minerals from the surrounding area.

While savouring the firm flesh of the oysters, I notice Ranger's wonderful Fal Oyster branding with the red sail, and there's also a stamp saying 'PDO'. This denotes that Fal Oyster has a protected designation of origin status, just like Stilton cheese. They qualified convincingly because the Fal oyster is produced, processed and prepared in a specific geographical area using recognised expertise – sail and oar.

I take a walk out to the edge of Custom House Quay away from the hubbub. I have fallen in love with Falmouth; it has such a wonderful charm that seems to be natural and timeless. The Fal oystermen are living and breathing history through their ancient practices and husbandry, protecting and nurturing the stocks of our native European flat oyster. I can feel the power and determination of the whole fishing community here to continue preserving the traditional fishing techniques that have played a critical role in making this fishery highly sustainable. The Fal Native Oyster Fishery wants to continue to protect their estuary with plans to create a Fal industry–community interest company led by the fishermen. They are the ones who work on the water, harnessing the wind and tides to sustain their livelihoods. They have unrivalled knowledge of this unique natural environment, and long may that be used for the benefit of the local community.

I pop back into the pub to say farewell, and take a midnight stroll through the narrow, dimly lit streets of Falmouth. I may not have won any competitions today, but at least I've played a tiny part in supporting the local fishing community while enjoying good beer, good company . . . and great oysters.

29

Yealm Estuary

Location: *Yealm Estuary, Devon, England*
Natural habitat: *Drowned river valley, high salinity*

Heading north out of Falmouth, I skirt round the northern flank of the Roseland Peninsula of wide open beaches, hidden coves and secluded farm shops to join the A39 and then the A30 towards Bodmin. I pass Castle-an-Dinas, one of the largest and most impressive hill forts in Cornwall, where King Arthur's mother supposedly met her maker, and I glide on to the A38 below Bodmin moor. I continue on through Cardinham Woodlands towards Liskeard and St Germans, pulling over at a yellow pub called the Rod and Line in Tideford on the River Tiddy; there, I tuck into some local crab and a half pint of Cornish Tribute bitter before pressing on to Saltash, eventually reaching the River Tamar, which marks the Cornwall–Devon border.

It is exhilarating riding over the Tamar Suspension Bridge which connects Saltash in Cornwall and Plymouth in Devon. The bridge is both a political and psychological border between the two counties – the proudly Celtic Cornwall and the staunchly English

Devon. I bypass historic Plymouth and continue down to the Yealm Estuary through the stunning Devon countryside. The River Yealm is everything you would imagine from an idyllic English river – it rises from the southern slopes of desolate Dartmoor, trickles through gorges and picturesque farmland and empties into the English Channel 12 miles later.

I decided to make this another destination on my oyster odyssey in order to meet Martyn Oates of Limosa Oysters. Instead of naming the oyster after the river, Martyn decided to use the scientific name for the black-tailed godwit, a rather majestic, long-legged, long-billed wading bird – *limosa limosa* – and it's no coincidence that the Latin word for mud has the same root. What makes the Yealm Estuary so special is its steep valleys and the rich agricultural landscape of South Devon. Over 80 per cent of the South Devon Area of Outstanding Natural Beauty is agricultural land.

I thoroughly enjoy being immersed in this quintessentially British of habitats, and soon arrive at Limosa Oysters. There are wild oysters here in the waters, but Limosa cultivate their specimens using the rack-and-bag method in a part of the estuary that is quite high in salinity because of the English Channel just over the sand bar.

Having been greeted by Martyn and swiftly shown to a comfortable chair for the obligatory welcome brew, I notice a rock oyster shell on the table that's doubling as a candle holder. Looking more closely at the cupped interior of the shell, the sun's rays catch the reflective milky hues generating tiny sparkles within the smooth surface. This iridescent white interior layer of an oyster shell is called mother-of-pearl or nacre, and is produced by many organisms belonging to the ancient order of bivalves, gastropods and cephalopods. A pearl is formed when a foreign body such as grit, stone or a grain of sand makes its way into the oyster and becomes enamelled by the mother-of-pearl. The oyster does this to protect itself from intruders, in a similar way to our own white blood cells being sent to engulf bacteria to prevent us from infection and disease. After layer upon layer of mother-of-pearl has built up around the intruder, a pearl is formed. Although you may find a pearl in your oyster one day – and I have found many – I believe the real prize is the oyster itself.

Oyster shells have long been used as ornaments the world over for as long as we have been exploiting the shellfish. Relatively recent examples are impromptu oyster grottos made by Victorian children at the feet of shucking costermongers, or the hugely ornate variety built as follies in the grounds of lavish country estates. One such example, discovered in Margate in 1835, uses 4.6 million shells, including oysters, and no one can really be sure whether it's a pagan place of worship or a Regency frivolity.

As well as objects, tools and vessels for liquids, oyster shells can be ground up to make medicine; Chinese culture uses the powder from shell to prevent or treat any conditions requiring calcium supplements, such as osteoporosis and rickets. In the British Isles and Ireland, other examples of the use of shells include mortar between stonework, lime-making, poultry grit and shell-tempered pottery.

The Yealm Estuary is also a drowned river valley just like much of the south-west coast of the UK and Bannow Bay in Wexford, Ireland. This means that the coastal inlets along this part of Devon are flooded unglaciated river valleys open to the sea. In the Yealm, as is common with many other rias, it was formed by the rising of the sea levels at the end of the last Ice Age.

Martyn is an expert who has been involved in the fishing and oyster industries for a number of years. He worked in East Mersea on the Pyefleet with Colchester Oysters, then moved to a wholesaler's, became a fisherman and finally settled on oyster farming with business partner Steve Allen in 1996. The Yealm Estuary is owned by the Bastard family who can trace their lineage back to the time of William the Conqueror, and Limosa Oysters lease the river from Rodney Bastard and have a fantastic relationship with the current progressive owner.

Martyn's inspiration for his move into oyster farming came from reading an article about Tony Maskell, who was breeding oysters in the 1960s as part of the original hatchery movement. The article was predicting doom and gloom for the oyster industry largely because of TBT (Tributyltin), an anti-fouling paint for boats to stop unwanted plant growth or organisms on the hull. This noxious chemical had polluted the water and catastrophically affected oyster stocks. Knowing that TBT had since been banned in the 1980s, Martyn believed that the waters must have recovered. So he went down to Steer Point and asked Rodney Bastard about taking on the oysters. It was all signed and sealed, and Martyn was soon selling oysters to Richard Haward in West Mersea, who was very encouraging in the early years and helped Limosa get off the ground.

The oysters here benefit from the plethora of organic matter making its way into the river via the lush wooded banks of the waterways that are packed full of all types of living and decomposing flora and fauna. The undersea world of the tidal estuary is equally teeming with nutrient-rich organisms, with ribbons of sea grass beds forming swathes of dancing yellow-green tufts. They enable marine animals to take refuge and grow in the safety of the dense foliage. Seahorses, pipefish, egg-laying fish, crabs and shellfish all use the underwater jungle to protect themselves and provide a stable environment for growth. The estuary is a nursery for seabass, too, and, when the tide is out, the Yealm reveals the mudflats which are bursting with life – diverse seaweed varieties, all sorts of shellfish and a number of birds are suddenly attracted to the area, particularly the kingfisher, little egret, oystercatcher and curlew.

The tidal part of the river extends four miles inland and the high sides of the valley keep the area relatively sheltered, while a sand bar at the mouth of the estuary inhibits the crashing waves from the open sea, all creating an idyllic environment for the oysters, who are constantly filtering a rich mix of nutrients from both the sea and freshwater sources. Sometimes, the seawater of South Devon can look cloudy and is often mistaken for being dirty when, in actual fact, the waters are full of tiny planktonic organisms which, in turn, support an immensely complex marine ecosystem.

I take my last slurp of tea, saddle up the Bonneville and ride down through Brixton and along the country roads until I reach Steer Point Road which runs along a prominent ridge separating the water channels of the Yealm River and Cofflete Creek until the road peters out. Switching off the engine and sitting among the trees high up on one side of the valley, I am suddenly enveloped by the sounds of the breeze in the leaves of the canopy above and around me, and the burbling of running water. I hop off the bike and clamber over a lichen-covered stone wall and see the Yealm at the bottom of a steep ridge, in all its glory, making its way out to sea. The oyster farm is just below me. My sense of connection with this special place has to be short-lived, though – I must press on, as there's always another oyster waiting to be shucked.

30

River Teign to Portland

Location: *Chudleigh, Devon; Chesil Beach,*
Portland, Dorset, England
Natural habitat: *Tidal estuary; tidal lagoon*

The pastoral idyll that I experienced gazing down over the Yealm is a distant memory as I splash through yet more torrential rain circumnavigating the southern edge of Dartmoor. It was here that the granite from the Haytor quarries was used, in part, to construct the former London Bridge when oyster sellers would line the Thames in the 1800s. As I ride, the River Teign skirts the northern side of the moor meandering on its 30-mile journey from the slopes of the moor to Teignmouth and the sea. The river is hugely diverse, with the tidal section extending from Teignmouth up to Newton Abbot where the mudflats host a rich and historic shellfish culture. Further up the river towards the heathland there are orchids, kingfishers, otters and salmon leaping at Drewes Weir. With England's highest waterfall near here – the 220ft Canonteign Falls – and the stunning hamlets of Trusham and Hennock, it's obvious why poet John Keats was so inspired by the natural beauty of this area, writing a beautiful poem entitled 'Teignmouth' celebrating Devonshire life. On the other hand, in letters to his friends while he was visiting the River Teign in 1818, it seems Keats was apt to complain, too, about that most British of gripes – the weather: 'There is a continual courtesy between the heavens and the earth. The heavens rain down their unwelcomeness, and the earth sends it up again, to be returned tomorrow.' And on the same theme, but with a passing reference to the shellfish that must have been readily available at the time, he wrote: 'The flowers here wait as naturally for the rain twice a day as the mussels do for the tide . . .'

After 40 minutes of the heaviest rainfall I have ever experienced on a motorbike, I'm hugely relieved to roll into River Teign Shellfish's yard in Chudleigh. Father and son Barry and Matt Sessions appear from a caravan and usher me in from the cold. On Matt's suggestion, we whip round the facilities at double speed, and retreat into one of their dry, warm outbuildings to recover. My eye is drawn to a tank of the largest oysters I have ever seen in my life. These huge rock oysters come from the River Teign and are reaching a kilogram in weight; they really are a sight to behold. They are beautiful green river creatures and their gnarly, rugged shells would need a monster of a knife to shuck them. They truly are exceptional.

We pile into a pickup truck and drive over to Matt's house with driving rain lashing the windscreen. It's quite a luxury for me to have a roof over my head and not mind the weather at all. Barry and Matt make their way into the house as I start the process of peeling off my drenched garments, and I'm soon down to my pants. Matt kindly lends me some jeans and a t-shirt and throws my sopping clothes into a tumble dryer. He then nips out to fetch some pasties, and serves them up with some tea and cake. I've now discovered that there's a foolproof way of breaking the ice with people you've never met – walk around their house wearing only your underwear and nibbling on a pasty. It'll work every time.

Barry advises me that it's probably not worth going out to the farm. Just around the corner from where we are sitting, the railway line along the stretch around Dawlish has been regularly in the news during stormy weather for having been completely impassable with sections being ripped up and having to be replaced. The force of mother nature down here can halt whole communities and threaten lives. I fear for my onward journey, but Barry reassures me that the worst of the weather will be behind me as I ride to Dorset later.

Historically, the River Teign was given to Exeter Cathedral and has been a managed fishery of one sort or another for 1,000 years. There are even tales of oysters from Devon being transported from Dartmouth to Rome in the first century supposedly via a three-day fast chariot, and Barry says it is rumoured that the Romans chemically produced ice using salt to facilitate the process. Ice was saved in the winter and moved into cave-like storehouses throughout the empire which allowed perishable stock to be chilled in transit.

The Sessions family are doing what they can to help regenerate the native oyster population by gathering any that they find and putting them all in one area to increase the chances of reproduction; they call these special sites 'oyster gardens'. After initially finding one or two natives in among the mussels, they now have a few thousand in different oyster gardens. They are doing the same for winkles, too, which like to graze on the oyster shells, cleaning them. And as if anyone needs more evidence that the native oyster once thrived here, the authorities were recently digging a trench 30ft deep in the River Teign to accommodate a pipeline, and all they managed to find among the waste material at that depth were oyster shells. So, for millennia before humans even appeared on the scene, oysters were happily populating this stretch of water.

Barry was born in Teignmouth just after the Second World War and used to have oysters for dinner back then because his family could not afford anything else. He remembers that, in the 1950s,

Baxters of Billingsgate would gather up all the unsold native oysters at the end of the day, load them into wicker baskets and pop them on a train down to Teignmouth. The train line runs right along the banks of the River Teign, so the locals stopped the train, unloaded the oysters and transferred them to the local fishing fleet, whose fishermen would spread them on the river bed until they were needed again.

A vibrant local economy exists here as a direct result of the oysters and mussels from the river. The team at River Teign Shellfish loves to work with smaller fish vans and restaurants, in addition to the larger and more powerful commercial operations, as they feel they are enabling the survival of small businesses in a tough industry, just like the fishermen.

I have had the pleasure of working with this remarkable oyster over the years and they are perfect for enjoying unadulterated, simply cooked and dressed. The River Teign's meat can be plump and juicy, truly world class, and when eating them raw they are best in the colder months; but if you want them in the summer when they are creamier, they can be incredibly sweet and very tasty when cooked. Barry tells me that he likes to make smoked oyster pâté with his large oysters, bringing all the ingredients together from within a five-mile radius of the farm.

Having made the most of Barry and Matt's hospitality, and with the amazing flavour of his stunning oyster still lingering on my palate, I take my leave and head back to the bike, easing it out on to the main road and continuing down the Jurassic coast. As Devon becomes Dorset near Lyme Regis, I feel the exalted presence of Mark Hix's celebrated Oyster and Fish House restaurant. The road gently rises and falls as I flash past emerald-green fields to my left and the churning sea to my right, carving an elegant sweep around Lyme Bay. The Isle of Portland gradually hoves into view rising out of the sea, standing 500ft high and proud of the sloping mainland. This huge mass of limestone rock juts out into the sea clinging on to the mainland at Chesil Beach, a pebbly sand bar extension of Lyme Bay. Portland is most famous for having produced Portland Stone, an immensely strong building material made from tightly packed limestone sediment that formed a million years ago, incorporating ancient fossils, including oysters.

Chesil Beach fills my vision and I can almost taste the fresh sea breeze as I leave the tarmac for the stony pathway that leads up to the award-winning Crab House Café, the home of Portland Pearl oysters. It comprises a single-storey, wooden-clad building bedecked with verandas, bright pink parasols protecting blue-painted picnic tables, and is surrounded by luscious palms and voluminous hanging baskets. Fortunately, too, it seems that the sun is finally making an appearance.

I park the bike next to the oyster bags and lobster pots in the car park right on the edge of the Fleet, the enclosed body of water on the western side of the causeway. Walking into the wooden-clad restaurant, I'm greeted by Nigel Bloxham, the oyster farmer and creator of this renowned establishment. We sit down at one of the wooden picnic-style bench tables in the shingle garden of the restaurant, and he shows me the menu – Nigel's a man who definitely has his priorities in the right place. The Crab House Café has one of the most delightful menus I have seen in England; it is joyously upbeat with a huge number of different fish and shellfish offerings. I opt for three different dishes: three Portland Pearl oysters au naturel; potted crab; and scallops with a bottle of Crab House Oyster Stout.

Waiting for my mains to arrive, I indulge in some bread dipped in yellow rapeseed oil, treacly balsamic vinegar and anchovy essence. It's a wonderfully piquant, aromatic blend, and makes a change from the standard bread and butter. When my main dishes arrive, I clean my palate with a sip of water and taste the first oyster – it is meaty, sweet, salty and full of umami. I take a bite of bread and oil again, and suddenly the liquor of the oyster and the unctuous oil mix in my mouth beautifully. Although I have ordered the oysters naked, I dribble a little of the sauce into the shell. The vinegar stays trapped in the oil, which in turn separates from the saline oyster liquor to create a pretty emulsion. I tip the rock oyster into my mouth and, oh my goodness, I am overwhelmed with a sense of extraordinary completeness and complexity. It reminds me a little of garum, the fermented fish sauce loved by classical civilisations of the Mediterranean. The culinary experience is so fitting, sitting as I am by the sea knowing that Romans and Phoenicians sailed these waters.

The potted local crab and scallop are also of exceptional quality, and I try to savour every mouthful as I enjoy the warmth of the sunshine. But however wonderful these two dishes are, I know that the star of the show – the Portland Pearl oyster – has already been logged in my taste memory for years to come.

Feeling wonderfully satisfied, I catch up with Nigel since we last met in 2017, and take a walk out to the Fleet to look at his farm, only a stone's throw from the restaurant. The native oyster has been harvested in the Fleet since Roman times; after the collapse of their empire, King Canute (AD 990–1035) gave the lagoon to a servant of his who is reported to have remarked, 'There is little in the Flete except for eels, flounders and grey mullet, but it is noted for its oyster beds . . .' The lagoon was then given to the local abbey and finally, after King Henry VIII dissolved the monastery, he sold this part of Dorset for £1,000 to one of his knights, Sir Giles Strangways, whose family still live here. But with overfishing and pollution the native stocks died out and now rock oysters are grown on the farm. Nigel buys part-grown stock from the Channel Islands and relays them in an innovative growing system of floating bags that he introduced in 2004.

Nigel explains that despite trestles being a hugely popular way of cultivating oysters in the UK, Ireland and France, he is convinced that the metal racks used to prop up the bags of oysters have an effect on the taste.

'How often have you heard people say an oyster has metallic notes?' he asks me.

Quite often, is the answer, particularly when you consider rock oysters produced on a large scale.

'Metal rusts and the salt in the seawater corrodes the rebars used in the trestles,' he says authoritatively. He has a point, but I do think this theory of oysters taking on metallic tasting notes from the racks must depend on the flow of water as well. In the case of the Portland Pearl oyster farm, it is protected by the huge and pebbly Chesil Beach which creates a much more tranquil aquatic environment, one that proves Nigel's theory after he changed his aquaculture techniques.

Nigel also allocates a zone within the site to trialling new methods of farming. Currently in the Fleet he has a floating bag system with a buoyant float attached to the bag which allows the oysters to move up and down with the tides. 'It creates a well-rounded, deep-cupped oyster shell which, in turn, creates a meaty oyster. The results of the test are proving really successful and I would like to devote more of the farm to it . . .' Nigel tells me. I can see these experimental bags bobbing with the undulations of the waves in total harmony with their surroundings.

We walk to the water's edge and watch the oyster workers tending to the oysters, wading in water up to their waist. The oysters stay in the farm for 7–12 months until they reach maturity and are then transported 60ft or so to the rear of the restaurant where the purification tanks are situated. After the oysters are purged, they are served in his restaurant and shipped far and wide. One very keen customer is well-known British chef Mark Hix, who gets through thousands of Portland Pearls at his Lyme Regis 'Food Rocks' festival every September, and who christened the oysters, apparently. Nigel says, 'Hixy jokingly said we should call them Portland Pearls . . . and the name was born.'

Standing on the coastal path at the high-water mark, down at our feet the sea herbs are growing in wild abundance, and are used as ingredients in the Crab House's dishes, especially sea beet – or 'caveman spinach' as Nigel calls it – the parent plant to all spinaches and beets.

The Crab House Café is a true gem in a world full of commercial, industrialised food chains and produce that is laden with air miles. I am standing in a thriving oyster fishery where diners can eat oysters right next to the farm that produced them, and from the very same waters that have nurtured and supported the natural production of oysters for over 2,000 years. And on the southern tip of Portland, one can see remnants of fossilised oyster shells millions of years old in the sedimentary rocks on the raised beaches and boulders surrounding the lighthouse.

Having popped briefly into Nigel's other place, Billy Winters, which looks on to Portland Harbour, I ride over Chesil Beach causeway past a family favourite, The Cove House Inn, through Underhill and climb the steep road to the top of Portland. I head into the gathering sea fret to go and visit Portland Bill lighthouse as it would be a shame not to see it in all its atmospheric splendour against a misty English Channel backdrop.

It is a short ride to the southern tip of Portland, where I park the bike and grab a takeaway cup of hot tea with some biscuits from The Lobster Pot. I head over to the large rocks by the sea and sit there looking at the hulking mass of Pulpit Rock. Flecks of Jurassic oyster remains catch my eye in the rock near me, and I zip up my jacket a little further as the murky sea mist does its best to bring a little more chill to the air. As I silently try to bridge the gap between the oyster I ate just an hour ago, and the visible shell remains embedded in the rocks around me that are millions of years old, I suddenly nearly jump out of my skin as the lighthouse sounds its foghorn at ear-splitting volume. My peace has been shattered, so there's nothing for it – I decide to dive into my packet of biscuits to calm myself down. Within a couple of nanoseconds, I am surrounded by squawking, flapping, biscuit-loving crows and gulls insisting that I share my bounty. I try to ignore them, but they won't give up, so half of my packet is donated to the hungry birds, all eyeing me up as though they're a gang of teenagers planning a mugging. With another blast of the foghorn, I nearly have another heart-attack, and Portland is subtly encouraging me to move on.

I get the message, tuck away my last remaining biscuits, and wander back to the bike.

31

Poole

Location: *Poole Harbour, Dorset, England*
Natural habitat: *Shallow natural harbour*

Taking the inland route along the A35 from Poole to Weymouth, I inadvertently find myself near Wareham, but there are plenty of worse places to lose yourself. Wareham was an important Roman port 2,000 years ago; the ships sailed down the River Frome, out of Poole Harbour and to the rest of the empire. The boats would have been laden with cargo of British commodities such as wool, tin and oysters, with the boat's crew guzzling Dorset oysters as they left Britannia.

For me, the towns of Wool and Wareham and their surrounding fields are at the very heart of really great beer-making in this country. In fact, all along the south coast you can find great beer with a healthy grain-to-glass ethos. The ales on tap in the pubs from Ringwood, Hampshire, to Swanage, Dorset, are second to none and I have fond memories of swigging refreshing citrusy pints of local bitter at the south coast's premier festival Camp Bestival at Lulworth Castle. If only I wasn't riding.

Forging a way through Caledonian pine on either side of the road, I am reminded of the Norfolk topography and this primordial pull that the forests seem to exert. The Bonneville is soon cruising along roads flanked by ferns, grassy soft verges and ancient bogs in the Holton Heath area, a mixture of ancient landscapes and purposefully planted woodlands, harking back to the original landscaping movements in the eighteenth and nineteenth centuries. Around 7,000 years ago, almost all of Britain was covered in forest. Now just 3 per cent is made up of ancient woodland, of which, according to archaeologist and woodsman Mike Skapa, only a small part of that 3 per cent is ancient forest. Given the way concrete, tarmac, brick and plastic have insinuated their way into our daily lives, it's no wonder we sometimes feel the tug of that primal urge for something altogether simpler, more natural. Fortunately, that urge is about to be satisfied as I near one of the largest natural harbours in the world – Poole.

It's around 8.00 a.m. as I make my way down the antiquated Poole High Street with sailing bunting fluttering above me in the breeze. It's a fine, bright day, and the distinctive, oak-beamed shops and houses stand proud in the sunlight. There are foundations of eleventh- and twelfth-century buildings in Poole made of thousands of crushed oyster shells, proving how long oysters have been eaten here and how thriving an industry there must have been 1,000 years ago.

I pull the bike up outside Storm restaurant where I wait for Pete Miles of Dorset Oysters, the marketing arm of Othniel Oyster Limited, whose restaurant this is and whose farm I am visiting today. Pete pulls up minutes after my arrival in a white pickup truck and unlocks the restaurant door. He is quite a character – he exudes the energy, strength and charisma of a man who spends much of his life outdoors crossed with rock-star looks, with the classic Poole bronze skin, a thick head of shoulder-length hair, and an amazing work ethic. He's a fisherman, restaurateur, the singer in a band . . . and, to cap it all off, he has a fantastic Dorset twang.

We get to know each other over a cup of tea and toast. He tells me that Storm restaurant started in 1999 with the sole aim to make use of the fresh fish that Dorset's coastline had to offer. His aim was to feed his guests in the same way that he fed his family – with good quality, natural, locally sourced ingredients prepared in interesting ways with care. The menu includes fish dishes such as oysters baked, au naturel and tempura; Poole cuttlefish and Poole gurnard. There are vegan choices, too, including the brilliant sweetcorn and foraged nettle fritters in a tomato salsa.

Storm also works closely with Lush Cosmetics, Mark Constantine's globally recognised ethical soap company which is native to Poole. Pete handles the staff meals for Lush and provides the company with fresh seaweed for their cosmetic ingredients. Mark Constantine is a well-respected local man, is a keen bird watcher and has a wealth of knowledge about Poole and its natural environment. Pete points out that the men on the ground – himself as a fisherman, bird-watching business owner Mark and local oyster farmer Gary Wordsworth – all share first-hand information with the authorities on bird numbers, shellfish levels and general environmental and commercial activities in the harbour. It is a great example of robust communication between different local interests for the greater good of the stewardship of a shared environment.

Pete and I jump into the pickup and make the short trip to Pete's boat moored in the harbour. The sun is sparkling off the water and illuminating a timeless scene as we breach the harbour wall and head towards Brownsea Island, the largest island in the harbour. The two headlands of Studland and Sandbanks converge north and south from the English Channel and Poole Bay, protecting the entrance of the 3,600 hectares that make up the surface area of the harbour, of which 200 hectares are leased for aquaculture. I am looking forward to meeting Gary, as his innovative work in oysters over the last thirty years has earned him a highly respected reputation in the industry.

As we approach Brownsea Island, a floating metal structure appears with Gary ready to greet us in his branded Othniel Oysters blue overalls and yellow wellington boots. We step aboard the huge, raft-like floating nursery and into a world of mechanised activity. We're now standing on what was once a car ferry which has been 'upcycled' into a nursery for growing oysters from 6mm until they are crab-proof at 35mm. The ones in my hands are growing a gram a day, which is very fast, Gary tells me.

The ingenious purpose-built and environmentally friendly oyster boats known as 'eco-harvesters' are a prime example of this industry's innovative skills, and Gary has built aquaculture infrastructure for fishing folk around the world. Gary takes Pete and me to a towering metal cage roughly 10ft in height and tips a variety of mesh bags into separate boxes to explain the various stages of growth. The cages hold different seed of different ages and hang off the floating structure, fully submerged, letting the oysters filter feed out of reach of predators. As we are looking at the bags, Gary is busy cleaning squirts off his young oyster bags. 'Everything grows like crazy here,' he laughs. 'Poole is a fantastic place for aquaculture, being warm and shallow, with fresh water inputs from four rivers, which encourages the growth of algae . . . lots of food for the oysters. In summertime during specific algal blooms, we can get a green-gilled oyster much like the French Fin de Claire. Sometimes the whole oyster turns green . . . it is truly special and highly sought after by the restaurants.' On top of soaring algae levels, the bay is teeming with wildlife and shellfish, with huge numbers of overwintering birds spending the colder months in the area.

I wonder at the name of the business, and Gary explains that 'Othniel' is an Old Testament name literally meaning 'lion of God' or 'strength of God'; it was the name of his original fishing boat thirty years earlier, when Gary was a fisherman originally, finally seeing the light and turning to oysters in the 1980s. Pete met Gary in Poole Harbour in 2009 after a day of prawn fishing, and the pair hit it off and decided to team up. Gary's Othniel Oysters is the

Judith Vajk of Caledonian Oysters at Loch Creran, Scotland. Photo by Richard Hunt-Smith.

Iberian tomato oyster (see recipes).
Photo by Ryan O'Toole Collett.

Oysters Rockefeller from Riley's Fish
Shack, Tynemouth (see recipes).

A Butley Creek oyster served au naturel on the half shell.

Carlingford Oysters facing the Mourne Mountains of Northern Ireland.

Tristan Hugh-Jones of Rossmore, Cork and Loch Ryan fame, holding a box of natives.

Masts of sailing barges not unlike those used in the eighteenth century to transport oysters.

The *Oyster Isles* Triumph Bonneville T120.

The terroir and merroir effect on an oyster's taste is illustrated perfectly by these two images. The image above shows the Isle of Skye's pure Highland water mixing with the high salinity marine environment, while the image below depicts Achill Island's peat bogs and the Atlantic.

Riding over the Lindisfarne Causeway at low tide.

Oilskins and gloves drying by a heater in Sligo.

Ed Gallagher.

Mark and his Faversham shucking bike.

Derek at Borough Market.

The legend John Bayes.
Image courtesy of Seasalter
Shellfish (Whitstable) Ltd.

Seventh generation West
Mersea oysterman,
Richard Haward.

Me and Bill Pinney of Butley Creek
Oysterage. Photo by Michael Leckie.

Pete Miles and Gary Wordsworth of Poole.

Stacey Belbin on her boat *Lady Grace*.

Hugh O'Malley of Achill (note the peaty water behind him).

The Triumph by the oyster bags.

Richard Loose showing Ben Sutherland some young Brancaster oysters (Scolt Head Island in the background).

Blue Walpole picks up his son who has returned from a long night of fishing.

Kian and I in Carlingford, Ireland.

Getting soaked on the Wild Atlantic Way.

5,000 miles along the oyster coasts of the British Isles and Ireland.

farm and Dorset Oysters would be the brand, under which a proportion of the produce would be marketed by Pete. Naming the oyster farm creatively rather than using the name of its location is akin to many North American oyster farms, where creatively named oyster appellations are equally as common as those of provenance.

Like a few of the oystermen and women I've met on my travels, Gary wears a number of hats. He is not only a fisherman-turned-oyster farmer – and farmer of clams – he is also Secretary of the Poole and District Fishermen's Association and sits on the Southern Inshore Fisheries and Conservation Authority, which is responsible for the management of local fisheries and whose Committee comprises representatives from local councils, the Environment Agency, English Nature, environmental NGOs and fishermen. His involvement with the bodies that surround the entire marine environmental infrastructure is paramount to increasing everybody's understanding of how different decisions affect the oyster and wider fishing industries.

The Marine and Countryside Act brought socio-economics more to the fore of decision-making within the various governing bodies, which encouraged people to listen to fishermen. It is important because, historically, those working the water were always perceived as being extremely low down the food chain in terms of influence or useful contribution, but now that the link has been made between the health of the environment and local economies, people like Gary and his crew at Othniel have a huge contribution to make, and can bring their experience and skills to bear on protecting livelihoods and natural ecosystems for years to come. They are the ones who work alongside the seahorses in the eel grass, the hundreds of curlews flying up the estuary, the cattle egrets perched vigilant on the shoreline . . . and they can gauge the health of the waters as the shellfish numbers fluctuate.

Gary, Pete and I walk around the nursery dodging the forklift moving bits of kit around while the crew are reseeding the cages.

Gary points towards Furzey Island across the bay and says we should go and look at the harvesting barges using a special low-impact mechanism for retrieving the oysters from the bed. Othniel farm 2.5 million oysters a year, depending on the availability of the seed, mortality rates and so on. Today, it is just rock oysters being farmed, but there is a natural settlement of native oysters here, too. Poole was always used as a fattening ground for native oysters from the Solent and, once the oysters had ingested the nutrient-rich waters of the natural harbour, they would be table ready and carry an increased value compared to where they would originally have been fished.

Cutting our way serenely through the water, Pete and I head over to the middle of Poole Harbour. In the distance is Cleavel Point at the tip of Studland, where there are Bronze Age remains of mass oyster consumption in the form of a shell midden. That means people were eating oysters here 4,000 years ago, and we're still farming them here today. The excellent preservation of coastal and marine structures and artefacts, submerged by rising sea levels, has led to Poole Harbour being heralded as one of the most important areas for coastal archaeology in the country. I am honoured to be here.

Pete eases back on the throttle and draws in close to one of Othniel's harvesting boats which is working the waters just north of Furzey Island. Again, it looks like a sci-fi designer's fantasy made from components found after an apocalypse – it's stunning engineering, and clearly does the job. The kit here is gently blowing the oysters off the beds and up on to the boat for grading, as the single crew member throws anything that is not an oyster back in to the water. While we watch, Pete tells me of an Iron Age wreck which was discovered in the depths below us in 1964. It was one of the largest surviving log boats from Prehistoric Britain and is thought to have been built by the Durotriges, a Celtic tribe, in about 300 BC, which means that Poole has been a working harbour for at least 2,300 years.

We sit there in the middle of one of the world's largest natural harbours watching an active oyster farm run by Gary Wordsworth and his well-drilled team of professionals, with a 4,000-year-old oyster midden to my left and 1,000-year-old Corfe Castle behind it.

I'm a lucky man.

32

Jersey (*Jèrri*)

Location: *Royal Bay of Grouville, Jersey*
Natural habitat: *High salinity large tidal bay*

High-level wisps of cloud over the sparkling, bright-blue sea surrounding Jersey suggest a wonderful day in store. I'm back on the road and zipping through verdant pasture dotted with the legendary golden-brown Jersey cows, the starting point for the highly prized rich milk and cream. When the grassy meadows thin out, they are replaced with acres of shimmering plastic-covered trenches sheltering the celebrated Jersey Royal potatoes. Jersey's other notable products are apples, cider, wool and, of course, seafood and today I am thrilled to be meeting Charlie Mourant of Jersey Oyster in the famous Royal Bay of Grouville.

Arriving in St Helier, I make my way on foot through La Route du Fort tunnel to my home for the night, the Hotel de Normandie. For a thousand years, Jersey spoke a Norman French language called 'Jèrriais', stemming from a time when the Duke of Normandy annexed the island in AD 933. Then when William the Conqueror (Duke of Normandy) invaded England in 1066, he brought the

Channel Islands and England under combined control. Although the King of England in 1204 lost control of Normandy, Jersey remained an isolated frontier outpost of the English Crown, despite being only 14 miles from the French coast and 85 miles south of that of England. It is only since the onset of train travel and boat connections from the British mainland to Jersey in the last 200 years that English superseded Jèrriais as the dominant language, although during the Second World War, the locals reverted to their original language wherever possible as the occupying German army couldn't understand them.

Sitting in the Bay of St Malo, the 9-mile-wide by 5-mile-long island of Jersey did indeed used to be part of what is now the French portion of the European continent before rising sea levels from the melting ice sheets created the Channel Islands 8,000 years ago. It is these shallow waters between Jersey and Normandy that are ideal conditions for oysters. And as with many of the locations I have visited, it was the native oyster which was fished here and would have provided sustenance to the inhabitants of Jersey for the last 6,500 years. Prior to that, there is evidence of Neanderthal presence on the island dating back 250,000 years at La Cotte de St Brélade ravine and La Cotte à la Chèvre cave. Archaeologists have found remains of butchered woolly rhino and mammoth, but shell remains have not been found, having been lost through rising sea levels in coastal areas. Aside from the *edulis* oyster being native here, the oyster heritage really took off from the Middle Ages onwards, although it's worth noting that the Romans settled here too, as well as the Vikings, who we've already seen have been prolific cultivators and consumers of shellfish.

After a quick turnaround at the hotel, I meet Charlie Mourant of Jersey Oyster in the car park and hop into his 4x4. He works closely with owner Chris Le Masurier, a third-generation Jersey oyster farmer, in whose absence Charlie has kindly agreed to show me around. We head east along the coast road in the direction of the Royal Bay of Gouville. As we skirt along the southern side of

Jersey, Charlie points to Le Hocq beach where the tide is out, exposing the expansive intertidal zone stretching as far as the eye can see. The thousands of scattered granite rocks pepper the sandy bed to give the landscape an almost Martian appearance. It is a stark reminder of how Jersey was connected to continental Europe in the past.

We pass the Le Hocq Inn – the most southerly pub in the British Isles – and take in the stunning vista out to sea. The Le Hocq beach on the south-eastern corner of Jersey is where the Jersey oysters are grown for the first year of their life in sheltered gullies between the granite outcrops which break up the wave action. The business procures roughly 40 million seed a year, which seems an extraordinarily large number, but Charlie says that through natural influences oyster farms can lose on average 30 per cent of seed a year, and sometimes it can even reach 80 per cent. Jersey Oyster imports its seed in springtime from France, and its proximity to both French and British nations means that it gets the best of both worlds in terms of trading opportunities.

Le Hocq beach is part of St Clement Bay which, in turn, is part of the Bay of Granville, which has a special treaty with France – The Granville Bay Treaty – negotiated in 1839. It is a trans-boundary management framework between the Jersey and French governments that allows shared fishing rights – Jersey boats can land fish in France and vice versa. Known to be the first international fisheries agreement ever negotiated, it came from years of conflict and violence between French and Jersey trawler boats targeting the same oyster beds in the 1800s, when an estimated two billion oysters were exported to English markets over sixty years. It is impressive how this relatively small, geographically isolated place retains its distinctive identity and punches well above its weight in the sphere of international treaties and global negotiations.

Charlie pulls the car over on to a slipway sloping down into the beach to point to the oyster racks, and explains how his father used this very slipway to escape the occupying Nazis. Turning north at La Rocque, we enter the Royal Bay of Grouville. The nearly five-mile long sandy beach was ennobled with the 'Royal' seal of approval after Queen Victoria saw the bay in 1859 and ordered her Home Secretary to commend the title to Jersey's authorities.

The States of Jersey developed oyster beds here between 1834 and 1837, opening them for fishing as a response to increasing disputes over oyster beds between Jersey, French and English boats. In 1797, abundant oyster beds were discovered in the sea just north of the Isle of Chausey between Jersey and France, which saw the small Jersey port of Gorey become a bustling boomtown. News of the oyster-rich beds reached England and, by the 1820s, dredge boats 2,000 men strong from Essex, Kent, West Sussex and Hampshire turned up to grab their share. The consequences for those involved in the 'skirmishes' were serious, as the *Sunday Times* of 23 March 1828 reported: 'An unpleasant affair has taken place between the English fishers off the coast of Jersey and two French vessels of war, which has led to serious consequences, many lives having been lost.'

Given that I am as close to France on this trip as I will ever be, I can't help considering the French approach to oyster fishing, and why they have become so famous for their oysters. Much of this reputation is due to their reaction to drastic oyster shortages in the mid-1800s. The nineteenth-century French Government and King conserved the supply of oysters by making the foreshore and sea-bed a public domain, which was the opposite situation in England, especially since the Magna Carta of 1215 saw the anti-authoritarian barons stop the King from having absolute authority and encouraged private fishing. The authorities had total control over the oyster beds to grant or cancel concessions for the greater good of the country's oyster supply. During the shortage, oystermen started to innovate with aquaculture techniques to get the best results for their oysters, but one man's work gained government approval over the rest. Monsieur Coste – a medical adviser to Empress Eugenie – conducted farming experiments in the Bay of St Brieuc just west of St Malo and 45 miles south of where I am in Jersey. He was inspired by Roman techniques he had seen in the Gulf of Napoli, Italy, in the 1850s. Napoleon III listened to Coste and oversaw the roll-out of a coastal restocking of France's oyster beds and the implementation of *parcs* and *claires*. It was in the salt ponds of Marennes d'Oleron that the famed Fine de Claire would be born. To show just how much the French cared about oysters, in 1868 the French Government paid for 300 *gardes-maritimes* (local oyster stewards) to watch over the stocks, while at the same time the English Government resisted paying for a single fisheries inspector for the entire country.

As well as strict government regulations over increasing oyster production nationwide, on the south-west coast of France a freak stroke of luck gave the oystermen a gift. In 1865, a storm forced a cargo ship carrying Portuguese oysters (*crassostrea angulata*) to jettison their entire shipment into the Gironde Estuary, where they began to grow in abundance. The people of the coastal area near Bordeaux cultivated their new oyster harvest as well as their European Flat variety, and the yield was increased considerably.

In the years from 1877 to 1887, the French produced 150 million oysters per year, compared with Britain's 40 million; and in the years 1910–14, France was able to deliver 500 million a year, while Britain mustered 25 million. The original vision and innovation of Coste and the French Government, and their ability to exploit excellent husbandry skills on a mass scale, meant that the reputation of the French oyster was secured.

Only a few miles off the French coast, I am standing overlooking the intertidal Royal Bay of Grouville, where Chris Le Masurier's grandfather started the Jersey Oyster farm in the 1970s, now the largest oyster farm in the British Isles. In 2017, Jersey produced a staggering 1,293 tonnes of oysters, showing that great husbandry and perfect conditions make for a very decent livelihood. Jersey sits in the Gulf of St Malo which has one of the largest tidal ranges in the world – a 40ft rise and fall between high and low tides. The clear, clean, nutrient-rich sea sweeps in and out of the bay, providing a huge exchange of seawater bringing abundant food to the rock oysters. Oyster fishing was Jersey's main industry until the bust years through overfishing, but it is the fine work and skill of three generations by the Jersey Oyster Company that is continuing the island's oyster and mussel tradition on their 36 hectares of beach. During peak periods of the year, Christmas and New Year, over one million oysters per week are dispatched from here.

Just at the top of the beach we pass the 'conditioning area' where the mature oysters are brought and acclimatise to being out of the water to develop strength between sea immersion and the restaurant table. The longer the oyster is out of the water – i.e. the higher up the beach it is, where it will spend more time exposed waiting for the tide to reach it – the stronger the adductor mussel becomes to hold the shell shut.

We turn inland from the beach to La Ferme, where Charlie and I walk into some large buildings where the grading and purification of the oysters occur. During the two years from seed to maturity, the oysters are graded here by a dedicated team at least three times. This allows Jersey not only to maintain an excellent level of husbandry, but helps Chris Le Masurier get to know his stock inside out and therefore gives him a clear idea of how to meet the specific needs of his customers. Charlie and I make our way up to a meeting room with a large wooden table overlooking the oyster plant floor, offering a bird's eye view of the seamless, efficient set-up. Charlie then presents me with some Jersey number 2 oysters (86g–120g), some Jersey butter, a fresh baguette and a glass of wine. Now that's the very definition of hospitality in my book! As well as number 2 oysters, Jersey also produce number 1s (121g–150g), number 3s (66g–85g), number 4s (46g–65g) and the little number 5s (30g–45g) – an oyster to suit every occasion. I regularly use the number 4s as cocktail oysters at events and for hungover folk on the Bloody Marys at the weekends.

With the baguette buttered, the glass full of dry white wine and the oysters shucked, Charlie and I tuck in while we discuss the farm and Jersey in general, to the soundtrack of the working oyster farm in the background. I am reminded of how intense the salinity of a Jersey oyster is. There is no freshwater coming into the Royal Bay of Grouville – in fact, there are no natural rivers on the island – and the salinity is in the high 30s ppt more or less constantly. But because of the crystal-clear waters, the taste of the oyster is supremely clean and fresh. It is beautiful on the palate and a gastronomic experience to be savoured. We cut through the salinity with some Sainte Marie medium-dry white wine from the local La Mare Estate, which gives a summer feel of mignonette and transports me to the beach. Visitors to the farm can enjoy a similar experience, being able to walk the island's Oyster Trail among the oyster and mussel beds, and then indulge in a memorable tasting at the Seymour Inn just around the corner from where I am sitting.

Pointing at old oyster shell being pulled out of a bag and graded, Charlie says that they do not use it as cultch; the Jersey Oyster Company crush it up for roads and for farmers for a valuable land conditioner; he adds that the company is the world's first accredited Aquaculture Stewardship Council (ASC) oyster farm for being sustainable and environmentally responsible while practising aquaculture. We raise our glasses, our baguettes and our oysters to that, and I head back to my hotel, grateful to Charlie for a wonderful visit.

Wandering down to the beach at dusk after being dropped back, I clamber on to a stone groyne jutting out into the sea, walk to the very end and watch the waves roll over the lip of the stone structure. Looking closely at the rocks around me, I hope to catch a glimpse of another elusive Jersey creature, the ormer (*haliosis tuberculate*). Also called the 'ormer abalone', the Channel Islands are the northern limit of the mollusc's geographical range. As well as being a delicacy, plenty of eighteenth- and nineteenth-century furniture was inlaid with mother-of-pearl ormer shell from the Channel Islands. Today, they are rare and highly sought after because of their low numbers and the restrictions over when they can be gathered – they may only be caught on the day of the new or full moon and the following three days. It's not surprising that they're shrouded in mystery and just a little bit of magic.

Sadly, I find no ormers and the sun has almost set, so I wander back, away from this other-worldly, rocky shoreline to the relative luxury of St Helier and its vast array of eateries. If it were summer, I would have tried my luck at Faulkner Fisheries at St Ouen; it's later in the season, though, so I pop into The Lamplighter pub for a quick pint of local cider, as it would be extremely rude of me not to try it when on Jersey soil. I then walk past the old fish market and into The Crab Shack for dinner. The restaurant is a relaxed affair, and entirely in keeping with its website claim that it's a reflection of modern Jersey – bright and breezy, funky furniture and bold interior design, and an extensive menu comprising locally sourced, fresh ingredients. It's exactly what I'd hoped it would be. I order six Jersey rocks, crab bisque and a schnitzel, all washed down with a pint of Liberation Ale in honour of the resilient people of the Channel Islands.

33

Guernsey and Herm (*Guernési et Haerme*)

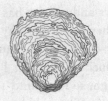

Location: *Bailiwick of Guernsey and Herm, Channel Islands*
Natural habitat: *Intertidal beaches*

It's an early start and I can feel the excitement building at the prospect of a fifteen-minute flight for me today as I pay a fleeting visit to Guernsey and the smaller island of Herm, where rock oysters hold sway. We hop over the deep-blue English Channel, the sea turning a rich Caribbean teal as we approach the shallows with rocky outcrops rising threateningly out of the water. As with its neighbour Jersey, Guernsey's location in the Bay of St Malo has the highest tides in Europe which can be seen from the iridescent turquoise shallows that fringe the island as we land at Guernsey Airport. The flightpath went over the eastern part of the island, where local knowledge has it that there were extensive native oyster beds in the 1800s near St Sampson's Harbour.

On the journey to St Peter Port, Guernsey's main town, I pass a number of 'hedge veg' sales boxes. They are miniature roadside stalls that sell local produce with an honesty box for payment; I grew up with a similar set-up in rural Essex. The taxi driver is a

Guernsey native with a Guernsey accent that sounds a bit like my mum's Dorset southern twang with occasional bouts of cockney. He tells me he is also among the 2 per cent of locals who speak Guernésiais, the local Norman French dialect which is known by some as 'patois'. His driving is 'leisurely', to say the least, because the maximum speed limit on the island is 35 mph with a recommended speed of 15 mph on *ruettes tranquilles* – the narrow, winding lanes where pedestrians, cyclists and horse-riders have priority.

I breakfast at the Coco Café in St Peter Port on the edge of the harbour, favouring a Latin American vibe of pork belly, fried eggs, tomatoes and salsa verde – it is as fantastic as it sounds. I also receive a phone call from Guernsey Oysters' Justin De Carteret who tells me that he has managed to get a boat to take us to Herm, and I'd better get ready – he'll pick me up in 45 minutes. This is great news, as it had been touch and go as to whether I'd be able to visit Guernsey Oysters' other farm on the tiny island, one of the Bailiwick of Guernsey's island cluster, in addition to Sark and Alderney.

Despite the Channel Islands being one of the sunniest places in the British Isles with more than 2,000 hours of sunshine each year, it's drizzly in St Peter Port today – a perfect day for a choppy jaunt across the channel to Herm with access only being possible by boat. The island's website makes this absolutely clear, along with the tagline: 'There's no place like Herm', which, when you say it out loud, makes you sound like you come from Hull. Try it.

Justin appears bang on time, and we walk along Fish Quay to a slipway where we board a boat run by Herm Island. The skipper, Tom Rawlings, and his Geordie first mate, Lee, have kindly offered to let us hitch a ride on Herm's official boat which is carrying provisions between the islands. The weather worsens as we leave Guernsey harbour and enter a body of water called Little Russell between Herm and Sark, which plummets to a depth of 120ft and is subject to large swells. The crossing is rough – constant rising, falling and rolling with the powerful waves, sometimes powering through the drops and occasionally surfing the crests, eventually completing the three-mile crossing and docking in Herm's tiny little harbour.

After unloading some of the cargo, and regaining my land legs, Justin and I thank the lads and head into the White House Hotel where we meet Craig Senior, who runs the hospitality side of things for Herm. He loves serving Herm Oysters to patrons of the hotel, telling them, 'The farm is a long drive and a pitching wedge and you are there!' Craig firmly believes his guests are 350 yards away from the best kept secret in the British Isles. Space is at a premium here – the island is one mile north to south by half a mile east to west, which makes for a hugely relaxing place to stay, while still offering some stunningly diverse natural environments to explore. In simple terms, the north coast is reminiscent of the Caribbean; it has its own mini 'Yorkshire Moors' in the centre of the island; and the rocky south coast is inhabited by pretty little puffins in amongst the cliffs. Visitors are warned to avoid 'Herm burn', as Herm tends to be roughly 10°C warmer because of the Gulf Stream than anywhere on mainland Britain.

The unique climatic and topographical conditions here create an extremely fast-growing environment for oysters, principally due to the huge tidal range and the prolonged submersion of the oyster trestles in the warm nutrient-rich waters of the Gulf Stream. The taste of the oysters here, though, in comparison to Jersey is quite different; the oysters are far less salty because of the sheltered nature of the farm, hemmed in between rocky outcrops that break up the waves. And although the oysters here grow very quickly, their shells are not as tough as those grown over on the five Guernsey oyster farm sites.

Justin and I leave Craig to his paperwork and stroll up a narrow road to a tiny settlement called Manor Village, which sits on the crest of a hill with panoramic views over towards Guernsey. It is a fascinating place to be and, despite the damp weather, it has the feel of an exotically foreign European country with all the luscious vegetation, beautiful beaches and clear waters. The oysters are worked and graded by boat, but this isn't any old boat; it is a landing craft called *The Crowe's Nest* which was used in Ridley Scott's 2010 Robin Hood film featuring Russell Crowe. *The Crowe's Nest* was given long oars as props for the actors when coming ashore with the boat's engine kept carefully out of shot. Strangely, it is one of a handful of films with an oyster-shucking scene: a character called Godfrey swears allegiance to the French king, while the king is eating raw oysters and has just cut himself opening one; he offers Godfrey the oyster laced with his blood, and Godfrey eats it. Now that's a mignonette I certainly wouldn't recommend.

By working this wonderful oyster farm the traditional way, Herm Oysters practise an environmentally low-impact approach in order to respect nature and minimise their footprint on the small island. Hugo Vajk of Caledonian Oysters started the farm on this site before moving to Scotland, and now Justin and Charlotte are intimately connected with the farm and the local environment, and the rhythms of nature itself. For example, they can recognise that the bass have been around the trestles from the circles in the sand where the fish have been rubbing their bellies on the ground; they also have a seal that comes to play among the trestles, who always moves the bags a little bit after scratching its back on the hard-edged structure.

We amble past the beautifully weathered eleventh-century St Tugual's Chapel, some French-influenced courtyards of grey stone and through the fields along Spine Road to the north end of the island where there is a concentration of prehistoric menhirs (standing stones) and dolmens (megalithic tombs) still remaining apparently frozen in time. We turn east to view the sweeping golden sands of Shell Beach, named because at low tide there are hosts of different species of shellfish from this corner of the world. It's a deeply peaceful place, with the deserted beach almost three-quarters-of-a-mile long from a rocky point all the way to the most northerly tip of the island at Alderney Point.

We cut back through the black-and-amber sloe bushes and brush to Fisherman's Beach where the oyster beds lie and on to the quay. Herm, its neighbouring island Jethou, and the rocky outcrops in the sea known as the Humps are a designated 'Ramsar' site, which recognises this ecosystem as a wetland area of significant importance. The intergovernmental treaty was named after the Iranian city of Ramsar where, in 1971, the Convention on Wetlands was adopted. Environmental sustainability is at the heart of Guernsey and Herm Oysters, and they are rightly recognised for operating in perfect harmony with the local wildlife.

Justin indicates the rocks out to sea where the kelp grows, and says, 'We have ormers here . . . not as many as we used to, but they are still present and found nowhere else in the British Isles.' The French call them 'oreille de la mer' or sea ear because of the shape of their beautiful shells. In the past, Justin used to gather and farm them in large numbers off the coast of Jersey, and then sell the ormers, whatever their size, as there was no limit; it all elevates him into virtual superstar status as far as I'm concerned. In Guernsey, people loved to cook them and make a stew or pan-fry their meat the same way you might cook sliced halloumi. British ormers are cousins to the abalone and love to feed on the kelp and take shelter under rocks huddled together. However, you might turn over a hundred rocks to find just one. Justin used to love watching them 'dance' during spawning season in the hatcheries; with the males and females in two separate buckets facing each other, when they are ready to spawn their little eyes come out from the top of their shell and they look at each other, just like two people flirting in a club. They climb to the top of the buckets and contort themselves, and then fire their eggs and sperm as far as they can – still not too dissimilar from most twenty-year-olds in any inner-city nightclub.

Justin tells me that it is possible to tell farmed ormers from the wild by checking the meat colour, explaining, 'Ormers love kelp, but they go crazy for palmaria, the red dulse seaweed that looks like a lettuce . . . it is like chocolate to them. So we used to feed them on that which would give the meat a red tinge as opposed to the pale white flesh of the wild.' These indigenous, rare creatures are a little to the Channel Islands as the Manx cat is to the Isle of Man and, for anyone wanting to see just how beautifully intricate they are, Sark Island's Sue Daly has documented them as part of her wonderful wildlife photography.

I can now blame the ormer for lowering the tone, and having highlighted a subject that needs to be discussed, as it is possibly one of the best-known 'facts' about oysters that almost everyone will have heard: are oysters really an aphrodisiac? In 1788, a priest in the Rosses, County Donegal, wrote: 'For scallops and oysters, when the tide was out, the younger women waded into the sea where they knew the beds of such fish lay; some of them naked while some of them went in with their gowns tucked up about their waist; and by armfuls, brought to shore whatever number of scallops and oysters they thought requisite.' There's no doubt that the link throughout literature between the erotic and oyster consumption is never very far away, and has been persistent ever since humans have enjoyed oysters. In Greek mythology, Aphrodite, the goddess of love, rose out of the sea on an oyster shell; the promiscuous Romans would eat British oysters at lavish banquets; and Casanova allegedly ate fifty oysters a day. I'm guessing he preferred them au naturel.

Nutritionally, the oyster is packed full of goodness and the vitality experienced when eating such an energising superfood will undoubtedly encourage and enable any 'pursuits' involving raised heart rates and sustained exercise. Even more significant might be the very high levels of zinc found in oysters, which enhance the immune system in both men and women but also, in men particularly, aids the production of testosterone. Recent studies have also shown that oysters contain dopamine, and they are rich in rare amino acids that result in increased levels of sex hormones D-aspartic acid as well as N-methyl-D-aspartic acid (NDMA) which are not the regular amino acids found elsewhere in mother nature. Between science, nutrition and mythology, I think it is fair to say that there is a very robust case to made for the aphrodisiac properties of oysters. Of course, the proof of the pudding . . .

Having calmed down, and once back in Guernsey after a smooth trip on the Trident Ferry, the heavens open as Justin and I dash to Le Petit Bistro on St Peter Port's seafront where we meet Charlotte Dickson, the owner of Guernsey Oysters, and Simon Granger, one of the farmers, for some evening food. The French influence on Guernsey is nowhere better felt than in a place like this. The interior is entirely French themed, with French waiters, low-lit Parisian décor and, of course, a French chef called Michael Pesrin, who starts by offering us some local Rocquette cider. Guernsey's rich history in producing cider goes back to the sixteenth century, and it's one that I'm very happy to extend by consuming it for as long as possible. I'm taking my first sip of this refreshing golden nectar when the first round of oysters hits the table. We have a mixture of Guernsey and Herm oysters, both tasting sweet and savoury at the same time with a refreshing and short finish. Next we try the cider-poached oysters with cucumber on a bed of apple sauce with a cider shot to go with it. It's quintessentially sweet Guernsey heaven in a mouthful. More dressed oysters follow, but the cider and apple sauce one is the winner for me, a cold dish with a cooked oyster and all ingredients sourced here on the island.

As well as *The Crowe's Nest*, Guernsey Oysters have an old blue boat for hire called *HMS Oyster* which travels to events on a trailer decked out like a beach with a model oyster trestle and bag set up for education while punters have the opportunity to taste the product. Justin sometimes brings a coffee cup along to show people just how tiny 500 baby oysters (seed) really are. The ethos behind the events is to encourage people to try oysters at £1 each; that way, if people do not like them, they have only spent a small amount on the experience, but if they do, then they're converts for life. Both Justin and Charlotte extend their outreach efforts further by leading beach walks, where people learn how the oysters are grown in this part of the world and understand how oyster farmers are working in a wholly organic way, living off the sea and not the land.

Although I have been here less than a day and I will leave tomorrow, the hospitality of Charlotte and Justin of Guernsey and Herm Oysters, the welcome I received on Herm and the beauty contained within these rocky outposts in the English Channel have all combined to give me a most wonderful oyster-fuelled experience. Victor Hugo described Guernsey as 'the noble little nation of the sea' and 'the rock of hospitality and freedom', which welcomed him when he was banished from Paris in 1856. His Guernsey home, Hauteville House, is just above the St Peter Port seafront, only a hop and a skip from where I will be sleeping tonight. I'll always think very fondly of this noble little nation . . . and tomorrow I'll be returning to my own rock of hospitality and freedom, the English mainland.

Au revoir . . . et merci.

34

Faversham

Location: *Swale Estuary, Faversham, Kent, England*
Natural habitat: *Estuary and marshland*

Arriving back on the south coast of England, I head north to enjoy some classic bike riding through the New Forest of Hampshire. It is an undulating landscape of sandy heathland, wild ponies, gorse bush and pockets of woodland. Deep in the forest are bogs and mires which, just as in times of old, can trap walkers and horse riders in the sphagnum moss with nothing but bog myrtle to grab on to to pull them out. William the Conqueror preserved this stretch of woodland for his hunting pleasures in the eleventh century; in the Domesday Book of 1086, it is referred to as 'Nova Foresta' and the constant land management on behalf of the élite classes has preserved an ancient feel within this part of England. The Normans also recorded British oysters in the Domesday Book while they were taking stock of their newly acquired lands, citing prolific fisheries in the Solent's Stanswood Bay just south of where I am now.

The charming Beaulieu River which runs through the little village of Beaulieu on the south-eastern edge of the forest drains into the Solent. The waterways are now part of the native oyster restoration project run by the charity Blue Marine Foundation, in conjunction with Portsmouth and Southampton Universities, as well as a host of funders. We have seen time and again that the oyster has survived umpteen setbacks over many centuries, usually because of man's ineptitude and greed, but it has persisted each time, and has even thrived. But we live in different times now – we have to accelerate our work in restoring oyster reefs to maintain the equilibrium we enjoyed only a few centuries ago. Reintroducing species to facilitate a balanced ecosystem is becoming more and more critical, just as it is with wolves in Scotland, saving Colonsay's bee colonies and re-wilding natural landscapes. Time is no longer on our side.

After the railways accelerated oyster production in Britain and Ireland, the industry boomed, creating employment and sustenance for an ever-hungrier population. The downside, though, was the inevitable loss of supply due to overfishing – something we've seen and heard countless times in many of the locations on this trip.

Oyster folk in Britain and Ireland would start to import oysters from other countries to keep up with the insatiable customer demand. On top of this, urban development and an increasing population brought a new scourge – sewage problems. High-profile food health cases started a wave of suspicion and distrust towards oysters, with such reported events as a typhoid outbreak at a mayoral banquet in Winchester in December 1902, where the Dean of Winchester and two other people died after eating contaminated oysters from Emsworth, Hampshire. In Cleethorpes, typhoid and cholera outbreaks between 1893 and 1905 were highly publicised and linked with oysters. The easiest thing for the authorities to do was to close the beds and effectively shut down the industry. The stigma attached to food poisoning from oysters all stems from this period in time, long before anyone fully understood the link between healthy food resources and pure, clean water. Soon afterwards, the oyster industry suffered yet another blow during the two world wars when many of the young men and adults from the British Isles and Ireland were killed in battle, wiping out a huge segment of the workforce. Oyster beds which lay depleted include the Mumbles, Firth of Forth, Solent, English West Country, East Anglia, Humber, Strangford Lough, Clew Bay, Liffey, Arklow . . . and so the list goes on.

Entering Kent, the Bonneville settles into a cruising speed of 70 mph as we blaze past the Bluewater Shopping Centre. Despite Kent being the 'Garden of England', much of the natural geography of this part of the Thames is unrecognisable, having been quarried extensively for chalk and gravel in the early twentieth century, but this area on the southern shores of the Thames can still offer a few surprises. Shell remains have been found, along with flint knapping deposits dating back to the Palaeolithic in Swanscombe. Bones from elephant, rhino and an extinct species of wild cattle, the auroch, have also been excavated, as well as hippo bones being discovered under London's Trafalgar Square. All this points to a time when the climate would have been swelteringly hot if we go back as far as 400,000 years.

Oysters in Kent were not only enjoyed as a food, they were used to make jewellery, too. In a village called Kingston between Dover and Canterbury, an early seventh-century Anglo-Saxon grave of a female skeleton was excavated in the late eighteenth century. The woman had been buried with a personal ornament that has come to be known as the 'Kingston Brooch' made from gold, glass, garnet and both pearl and shell. The 'step' pattern of the brooch recalls the centre of the St Mark carpet page in the Lindisfarne Gospels, and we've already seen how shells have been used in the creation of these important artworks.

I've soon reached the ancient town of Gravesend, famously the final resting place of Pocahontas (whose real name was Amonute) who died in 1617 from unknown causes at the age of 20–21 years. She was a Powhatan Native American whose tribe would have definitely eaten their fair share of oysters in the rivers surrounding the area of Jamestown, Virginia. It is said that, in the early stages of Captain John Smith's trip to the New World, he kept his men alive on a diet of sturgeon and oysters while privateering for the Virginia Company in 1607.

Pressing on eastwards, I'm suddenly sideswiped by a blast of wind as the road sweeps down towards the River Medway; I recover my composure, wrestle with the bike to maintain a straight path and cross the cantilever bridge with Cuxton on my right and Rochester on my left. Before too long, I'm off the motorway and into the leafy south bank of the Swale Estuary, cruising towards the medieval market town of Faversham. It has been a protected port since the Roman era, was famously the home of Viking-style 'peter boats' built in the shipyard and has King Stephen buried in Faversham Abbey, a king who granted a royal charter to the abbey which included oyster fishing in 1147. In 1824–26, the town was noted as a haven for smugglers, who took advantage of the trade in contraband on the black market facilitated by Dutch oyster boats.

Now on the edge of Faversham I look out for two pubs and a trackway that leads to Hollowshore Fisheries, the home of Lees Court Oysters. Leaving the road and continuing gingerly down the track, I can see masts of boats gently swaying in a creek up ahead and I'm soon turning into the yard of Hollowshore Fisheries, propping the bike up between a huge anchor and a propeller with a bullet hole through it. I'm greeted by Julian Walpole, who has just appeared from a wooden building at the other end of the yard and we make the usual introductions; Julian ushers me into a nearby shed where I find oysters in purification tanks just ahead of me.

As I'm having a look at the set-up, another chap appears from behind me wearing tinted glasses, a black cap and red smock. He introduces himself as Mark, and gives me a solid handshake and a warm smile. He tells me that he does a bit of work around the yard and owns the vintage Pashley bicycle in the yard I'd admired on the way in; he uses it to shuck fresh Lees Court Oysters in Faversham for £1 each or 60p for a small oyster and says he is the last person in England shucking from a bike. Mark has designed a neat shucking block which is attached to the front basket of his bike, comprising a foot-long wedge of scaffolding board with a rubber buoy ring screwed into the top of it to hold the oyster in place. I've never seen one like it and I love it.

Mark reaches into the tank and picks out a craggy shelled Lees Court oyster for me. The plump, meaty muscle is packed full of flavour, stimulating my tastebuds with the tang of wild, herbaceous marine umami. The quality of these hand-picked oysters and their uncompromising jagged shells is astounding, and I can only assume that they must fly off Mark's bike quicker than he can shuck them. The estuary is highly productive, proof of which is provided by Mark when he shows me a fossilised native oyster the size of a football.

Julian sets a mug of tea down for me next to a box of skate wings and he tells me about the Lees Court oyster farm; it is located in the middle of the water course between the Isle of Sheppey and the Oare Marshes Nature Reserve on estuary and creek bed, which makes up part of the 6,900-acre Lees Court Estate. The stately home itself is further up the road in an idyllic village called Sheldwich, where the Sondes Family have lived for the past 700 years. The Swale Estuary, Oare Creek and Faversham Creek have been part of the Sondes Estate for nearly 400 years, which is quite rare in the British Isles as the vast majority of the remaining land below the mean high-water mark is usually owned by the Crown Estate. Countess Sondes is extremely keen on traditional activities on her land and encourages wild fowling, moorings, fishing and, of course, oyster farming.

Although the area has a long tradition of native oysters, Julian's dad Barry 'Blue' Walpole has predominantly worked with rock oysters since the early 1980s. Blue and his family – Julian, his other son, Wink, and his daughter, Fiona – all work in the business, sending oysters to Billingsgate Market and supplying the Kent area, but they recommend that the best oyster experience is had by making a trip down to Faversham on a Saturday to eat the oysters first-hand in their shop.

Julian and Mark lead me into another part of the building to a small room filled with photographs, fishing paraphernalia and an empty seafood counter. This is where they sell their fresh fish every Saturday to the local community as well as those who travel far and wide to buy good-quality local produce direct from the specialist producers themselves.

My eye is drawn to a framed newspaper clipping from 1989 with graphic pictures of sewage spills and dead fish. 'What the hell happened there?' I ask.

Julian explains that disposal pumps from a paper reclamation plant had been switched on during an ebb tide, resulting in purple-coloured waste containing mercury being disgorged into the waters. The chemical-laden paper fibres sank to the bed and choked everything, and kept the fish away. 'The Swale became barren and we lost a good percentage of our business,' Julian adds. It's a universal truth that the good stewardship of our inland and coastal waters relies upon legislation that works, transparency and an awareness among all stakeholders – from environment agencies, water companies, government, to those working the water and even us at home choosing what to pour down the sink – to do everything we can to care for our precious ecosystems. We're all linked, and we all have a part to play to maintain the precious biodiversity of our planet. Thankfully, wrongs were righted and the water environment recovered to allow beautifully fat oysters with strong gnarly shells to thrive once again. As proof, I can see them all slurping away in front of me.

We hear the crunch of approaching footsteps on the gravel outside, and in bounds a soggy, excited dog followed by Blue Walpole himself. He introduces himself and joins the conversation about the environment, observing, 'In the next 50 to 100 years, the effects of population growth and industry from London that makes its way into the Thames will be devastating on the marine environment if people don't start to understand nature and our interactions with it.' He adds that it's already being seen with decreasing shrimp and flounder numbers and, if we end up destroying the lower forms of life, it will cause major problems higher up the chain. His view is that this is not rocket science – if developers carry on building up the riverside areas as intensively as they are doing at the moment, then there can only be more problems with discharge. 'We've lost so much of our intertidal regions, particularly in Kent and up the Thames corridor, you cannot but wonder if the higher-ups will ever wake up to the problem.'

While we absorb the stark reality of the newspaper clipping, the mood in the room becomes downbeat, and for very good reason. They are witnessing the effects of mass development, population surge and wilful malpractice on our natural environment at first hand, and are very concerned about the future health of their fishing grounds, and the authorities' willingness to protect them. And if *they* are, then we should all be as well.

To improve the mood, Blue invites me to hop in the pickup truck to help his son Wink bring in the catch from the night's fishing. I'm happy to oblige, and the truck is soon trundling along the country roads towards the Oare Marshes. Blue tells me how he used to work with the local oyster hatchery legend John Bayes, who seeded millions of native oysters on the Kent Flats in the 1950s. Today, the resurgence of the native oyster population in this area is down to John Bayes and, apparently, a map exists somewhere showing all the native oyster spots, a virtual Holy Grail to anyone with an interest in oysters.

We meander through the *Great Expectations* landscape that is the North Kent marshes; Blue points to the old boathouse they used to use which now sits in a conservation area belonging to a nature charity. He is concerned over the draining of the marshes in order for them to be designated nature reserves which, in turn, has destroyed the native oyster's natural habitat. Blue recounts the time he laid oysters all around the Oare Marshes as it made for a perfect sheltered environment where our indigenous natives could fatten. Looking at the fast-flowing river, it is clear that natives would not stand a chance out in the Swale as the spat would not have time to settle before being swept away, whereas the marshes were a perfect environment. The rock oysters, however, do not seem to mind the Swale conditions; they are hardier by nature. It is the first time I have really encountered the other side of the conservation argument – not all conservation is necessarily a good thing. It depends on the type of conservation, and what will be adversely impacted as a result. Some have said that it seems to defy logic to alter a natural salt marsh from brackish water to freshwater to enable the public to photograph birds which would probably already be there, and possibly make some commercial gain as a result, while losing the natural habitat of our prized native oyster species.

We arrive at the shoreline and I greet Wink as he heaves his catch of sole into the back of the truck. Blue points to the submerged oyster beds where the little creatures are enjoying a good feed. The wind picks up and the tide has turned, so we head straight back and a few beers are opened to bring a relaxed end to Wink's nightshift. While the family chat a little about business, Mark reappears, whizzing into the yard on his bike. He trots over to me and, grinning, produces a freshly made shucking block and hands it over as a gift for me. I am a little embarrassed and genuinely delighted at my new toy, and ask Mark what it is called.

He chuckles proudly. 'My friends call it my tombstone!'

And that is what I have christened it.

After a bit more chat, it's time to let the Hollowshore team get on with their work and I depart, shaking with all the lads and thanking them for their time and their stories. But the one person I did not get to say goodbye to was Mark. He'd disappeared just before I left, having crossed the track and vanished over the grassy banks of the creek towards the clinking boats I had seen earlier. Perhaps it's a fitting and poetic departure for such a generous soul. Thanks for my Tombstone, Mark.

Leaving Hollowshore, I know I will be back for a plump, herbaceous Lees Court oyster. I'm heartened by the kindness and expertise that is intrinsic to this small team, and their willingness to fight for the protection of our precious marine environment; their livelihoods depend on the water. But Blue's ominous warnings still ring in my ears – it's not just *their* livelihoods that depend on clean water, it's all of ours. We're all connected and, if we don't protect our natural ecosystems now, then the time will come soon when it will be too late to do so.

35

Whitstable

Location: *Horsebridge, Whitstable, Kent, England*
Natural habitat: *Shallow sandy muddy tidal estuary*

I'm nearing the end my journey, so it seems fitting to be completing it in Whitstable in the south-east of England. A place, like my beloved River Blackwater, that was equally loved by the Romans who made these oysters famous. This feeling of coming full circle is also apparent as I stare over towards my native Essex where, not only did I start my Oyster Isles journey, but it was on the Thames Estuary coastline that I went to school in Westcliff and started out in oysters. I used to deliver to all sorts of establishments in and around the area and, after having discovered so many new landscapes on this trip, it feels good to be within touching distance of the coastline I know so well.

The sky is clear and the air is crisp as I sit at a wooden picnic table on the pebbles of Whitstable beach gazing out on to the grey-blue waters of the Thames Estuary. At the end of July every year, the Whitstable Oyster Festival sees thousands of ostrophiles line this beach as children build fantastical grottos out of the empty shells – an age-old tradition.

I'm waiting for James Green of Whitstable Oyster Company, having only made a short journey from Faversham. On my way, I took a little detour to the Goods Shed, a farmers' market set-up in historic Canterbury, where I took advantage of a few little plates of deliciousness at the Wild Goose. I then had a chance to ride the bike through Canterbury along Watling Street beside the River Stour and enjoy the wonderfully evocative historic architecture, with the crowning glory being the cathedral, still awe-inspiring, despite the number of rebuilds it's endured over the centuries.

I'm still thinking about the ride up here when James pops his head around the corner and invites me to join him at his Lobster Shack restaurant a few yards along the beach. We sit down with a couple of drinks and he proudly places a stunning plate of twelve rock and native oysters in the centre of the table, perfectly shucked and on a bed of crushed ice. Despite the Kent–Essex rivalry, I am struck by the quality of the produce in front of me, and I'm keen to find out as much as possible about one of the most famous oyster fisheries in the world. I'm looking right now at the famous Whitstable natives and Whitstable Pearl oysters; the pearls are scattered on the sea-bed much like the wild oysters of the Blackwater and typically have a hardened, deep-cupped shell with great meat content. I can't wait any longer, so I dive in and the meat is so plump it sits proudly in the shell like a boiled egg crammed full of sweetness. The natives lie lower in the shell as they always do, but are just as firm in texture on the more tannic side.

These oysters show that Whitstable Bay has always been a good area for growing and fattening oysters, because of the huge variety of nutrients running down the Swale and Medway rivers, which hits the vast expanse of seawater in the Thames Estuary and encourages algal growth. In addition to that is the very considerable tidal flow.

Whitstable's geographical position provides significant benefits when it comes to oysters. As well as having a strong market in the town itself throughout the year, it's also in the perfect location between London and France, the biggest UK market and Europe's biggest producer. And historically, the English monarchy would always safeguard Kent's trade because of the business it could conduct with Europe. Undoubtedly, oyster folk would have been involved because of their seafaring skills and influence. Something else that really helps with recognition of oysters in this area is the name – Whitstable. It's synonymous with the top-quality British oysters, just like Fal, Colchester and Galway in Ireland.

Royal patronage will have helped the oyster trade in this area as well. The oysters here go way back to the Roman times and beyond, but most of the Whitstable history starts in 1793 when the first company, called the 'Free Fishers and Dredgers of Whitstable', was formed by an Act of Parliament and then, a hundred years later, it became 'Whitstable Oyster Fishery Company' in 1896, a name that still persists today. In the 1850s, 80 million oysters were being sent to Billingsgate Fish Market a year, which meant that the company had increased considerably in size and soon caught the attention of the royal family, who lent it official recognition. Royal association must have imbued Whitstable with an element of sophistication and, by default, the product would have been promoted far and wide as part of an early popular marketing strategy.

This part of Kent is a particularly oyster-rich area – as I made my way down here I passed Claxfield Farm where a number of refuse pits were excavated, all containing medieval pottery and large quantities of oyster shell. On the east coast in Ramsgate, a relatively uncommon Neolithic shell-rich deposit was found. In Goodnestone, just the other side of Canterbury, archaeologists have found oyster shell deposits from the post-medieval period; and on the Isle of Thanet, Roman and Anglo-Saxon digs have uncovered remains of oyster, mussel and whelk. What is particularly interesting here is that some of the medieval oyster shells have had large holes bored into them, which still remains unexplained.

They are similar holes to those found on the Thames foreshore in London at low tide. The archaeologists of Thanet Earth tend to think that they are from the use of rakes which would have been deployed to gather the natives all at once. They seem to think that rakes were preferred rather than axes, which would have caused a greater number of damaged shells.

The Romans in this area dominated not just the land but the waters, too. A Roman shipwreck and its cargo of Samian pottery was discovered on the sea-bed of Pudding Pan just off the coast of Whitstable to the north of Herne Bay. It is thought the boat with the rare earthenware got into trouble and became lost en route to Roman London. The pottery which has been dredged up by oyster-men over the centuries is typical of the ceramic tableware used throughout the early part of the Roman Empire and, because the Pudding Pan artefacts are stamped with the ceramicists' names, they have been dated to the late second century. And not far from where we are standing, Roman coins have been discovered in and around the Horsebridge, too, a cobbled ramp that slopes into the water just in front of the Royal Native Oyster Stores restaurant. It has recently been restored to its former glory, when horses would reverse carts down the jetty to the boats to unload the oysters and fish from the day's catch. This example of ancient engineering has played a key role in the town's maritime history and that is where we are heading now.

We take a short walk along the beach to the Horsebridge, where James and I grab our wellington boots and hop over a sea wall that was built after the flood of 1953, landing on a heap of oyster shell sloping down to the boardwalk. We march down the cobbled jetty and on to the exposed beach where we make our way out to the trestles of oysters being attended to by the oyster boys. James's father, Barry Green, grew up in Weymouth near Portland Pearls and moved his family to the now well-to-do seaside town of Whitstable when James was eight years old. They were inspired by Suffolk oystermen Bill and Richard Pinney when they took over the business and have since built it up into a force to be reckoned with both locally and on the national stage. The Lobster Shack in winter has a cosy log burner but is equally a perfect summer destination with its outdoor Oyster Shed serving day-trippers by the harbour. The Lobster Shack was originally the headquarters of the famous Seasalter Shellfish Company, having been built in 1860 during the boom years of the UK oyster industry. The Whitstable Oyster Company's empire continues, just a little further along the beach, with the Whitstable Oyster Company Restaurant, which gives you some idea of the wealth that was in Whitstable at the time when there were about 100 million oysters a year coming out of these Kentish waters.

The oysters sold by the Whitstable Oyster Company range from the famed, seasonal, native, trestle rock oyster numbered 1–5 (which represent 80 per cent of the farm), Wild Seasalter jumbos (over 150g), sub-tidal reef oysters dredged with a fishing boat (naturally spawned), and the ranched pearls from the sea-bed in and around the trestles. All the oysters are run through a seawater purifier and are available to order on the seafront.

James and his team run a fantastic business and it is truly inspirational to see how they celebrate the oysters here, just as in many of the other locations I've visited on my travels. One of the key dates of the year in this area is the Whitstable Oyster Festival, when hordes of people spill out on to the pebble beach to celebrate Kentish oysters, seafood and their paired drinks. There's no doubt visitors always have a wonderful time in this part of the world, whatever the season, but it's particularly special if you happen to make it here for the festival.

Despite the royal seal of approval, James is adamant that it is not just royal patronage that has helped to make the Whitstable name internationally renowned. 'When we first opened our restaurant in 1988, it was generally the well-to-do aristocrats who came down for their native oysters during the season and, although that high-end clientele has diminished a lot in the last five years, I have seen a growth in younger people eating oysters who are more interested in provenance and nutrition.' James has also literally kept the door open during the quiet times, and has put in the hard graft in expert husbandry and at getting the Whitstable name out there throughout the last thirty years – it hasn't just happened by luck and he hasn't relied on past glories. 'We turn up each day really ... it is where most people fail, with whatever you do. As the fishermen say, "If the prop ain't turning, you're not earning!"'

Taking my leave of the fishery, I walk back up the beach and through Whitstable High Street, which is steeped in maritime history, to the oldest restaurant in town called Wheelers Oyster Bar which has been going for over 150 years. It is a famous pink-and-blue-clad oyster and seafood parlour run by Delia Fitt, who keeps things brilliantly simple on the à la carte menu with six starters, six mains and six desserts, all cooked by chef Mark Stubbs and his team in the kitchen. I sit with Delia in the back room where we could easily have slipped through a time-warp to 100 years ago; the sound of other diners clinking cutlery and crockery, and the murmur of quiet conversation is extraordinarily familiar and hugely uplifting – seeing people enjoying the very best of the local seafood always fills me with joy and optimism. Wheelers was started by a local oysterman and master mariner called Richard Leggy Wheeler, and the building has survived two world wars, a great flood of 1953 and several different owners. It's a much loved Whitstable institution, and given the quality of the produce I've just seen with James and his team at the fishery, I thank the Lord for Whitstable, and all it has done for our love of British oysters.

Final Pearls

Riding back into London as night draws in, a few hot-dog vendors have rolled their carts out of the darkness into strategic spots to catch some passing trade. A hundred years ago, they would have been oyster stalls feeding the capital's rich and poor. Rolling over Tower Bridge above the swirling black waters of the Thames, the smell of fried onions would have been replaced by the unmistakable aroma of fish and the sea, and across the shiny cobbles, between brick alleyways, Victorian costermongers would have slung shells from their carts. The oyster is loved by all, and can be enjoyed everywhere – you can guzzle them in markets, slurp them in airports or savour the firm, sweetly salty flesh and liquor in a luxurious restaurant.

We can learn a lot from a creature that has survived the separation of the world's super-continents over millions of years. They were present when the dinosaurs roamed the earth, when megafauna evolved to extinction and silently persisted when the world's greatest civilisations rose, conquered, ruled and then died. Vast aeons of time have passed while the oyster has simply filtered pure, clean water and thrived. Our history books tell us that the oyster was once referred to as a prize stolen from Neptune's larder that should be cherished, but we've seen what the 'stealing' of this prize can do to the oyster, and all the livelihoods that rely upon it. That lesson is worth repeating – we now have a responsibility to nurture and protect our intertidal friend, and the waters that support it, working together for the benefit of both of us and our ecosystem's future.

The hundreds of people I have met on my journey around the British Isles and Ireland have proven time and again that the oyster industry is both progressive and traditional. We have seen innovative technologies in the Morecambe, Guernsey and Tralee hatcheries that ensure people will have a reliable food source for the future; at the same time, trestle culture and sail boats without motors are still gathering oysters sustainably in the Fal Estuary as they have done for centuries. A high-tech, state-of-the-art nursery is in use in Poole Harbour, while in Suffolk the same principles for growing baby oysters make use of disused scaffold boards and old mushroom boxes. Whatever the aquaculture or fishing technique, successful, efficient and sustainable oyster-gathering produces a highly nutritious, protein-rich food source while remaining supremely environmentally low impact. This is surely something to celebrate.

Oyster folk are a vibrant and constantly changing community of farmers, aquaculturalists, fishermen and women, shuckers, restaurants, bars, market stalls, universities, governments, naturalists and scientists who all talk and work together. The knowledge gained from working with this extraordinary little creature proves how beneficial it is to share best practice and insight for the greater good – as well as to recognise and then act on the warning signs.

The coast has taught us that there are no absolutes when it comes to such a diverse region as the intertidal zone; there is simply too much variety to apply a one-size-fits-all approach to legislation or governance. Oyster folk themselves, working in and around the waters every day, are the most reliable source for understanding this complex environment.

Oysters can also spark collaborative communication between nations, with Irish producers trading with China and the UK,

Scotland buying seed from England, the Channel Islands developing treaties with France and Northern Ireland exporting to Wales. Oysters are both local and global – no fuss, no fanfare, just an authentic, honest product that has consistently provided value to so many around the world.

Our native oyster has come a long way from its ancient beginnings, through Stone Age middens, right the way through to the Victorian commercial boom and bust, and it is only now, in the twenty-first century, that the respect for *ostrea edulis* and the recognition of its worth are the drivers for a new era of renewed commercial success for the industry. This rediscovered interest in our native oyster falls in line with a growing awareness of environmental concerns, which seemed to have been lost in the latter half of the twentieth century.

Throughout modern times, oysters have acted as a sort of biological water meter, accurately gauging water quality, and sounding the alarm when the harmful effects of human activities threaten to destroy the natural environment. They are an intrinsic part of the food chain and, as such, are inextricably linked to our own health and that of the world around us. All the while, the oyster is a sessile creature, offering 'superfood' benefits to all humanity through the simple action of ingesting sun-fuelled phytoplankton. And over and above their nutritional benefits, the oyster has helped us to construct roads, neutralise acidic soils, build homes and public structures, inspire and lend materials to our artistic and cultural endeavours, and heal our bodies of ailments.

After 5,000 miles, my motorcycle odyssey has taken me from the most dazzling of sunlit landscapes to the darkest, wildest and most ferocious of storm-lashed coasts – with everything in between. At journey's end, I'm satisfied that I've managed to explore as much of the current state of the oyster industry as possible – some sights and practices have been familiar, and some have been extraordinarily unexpected. I'll carry with me for ever the sound and sensation of the Bonneville thundering along the tarmac through the most wonderful landscapes, with the mouth-watering prospect of the humble bivalve waiting for me at the end of rutted tracks, on sloping, seaweed-laden trestles, along rock-strewn beaches or bobbing in mesh bags from floating rafts. I've heard the song of the curlew, the turnstone's chirp, the crashing of the waves and I've seen the steady ooze of the salt marsh water. And I've done it all on the back of a Triumph Bonneville – life doesn't get much better than that.

In 2019, oysters have been earmarked to play a key role in the UK's 2040 Seafood Strategy; they have been recognised as an important food source for a global human population. It is estimated that, by 2050, the global population will be 10 billion with researchers suggesting that food from animal production will have to increase by 50 per cent. Not only can oysters help to feed this growing population, they can ease the pressure from intensive land use and meat production.

The oyster has given us so much – and if we've learnt anything along the way, it's that it's time to make sure we protect the future of this extraordinary little creature. This journey has reinforced the importance of sound stewardship and what we have to do to ensure the cleanliness of our coastal waters and the wider natural environment. This is no longer a choice – we simply have to act positively, encourage sustainable farming and cherish the treasures that have become *our* responsibility on *our* watch. It's the least we can do for one of our most important and ancient of species.

I started this book with a bustling Victorian street scene – and at the heart of that scene was the oyster, enjoyed by, and sustaining, the whole of society. It has been a great leveller, simply giving people of all ages, races, creeds, colours and classes a lot of pleasure. Maybe . . . just maybe . . . we're seeing the beginning of such an appreciation of the oyster once again.

I'll raise my glass, clink my shell and slurp . . . to the glorious oyster.

Appendix

Glossary

Aquaculture – the breeding, rearing and harvesting of fish, shell-fish, plants, algae and other organisms in all types of water environments.

Bivalve – an aquatic mollusc enclosed within a double-hinged shell, such as oysters, mussels and scallops.

Brackish – the mixture of freshwater and seawater in an estuary.

Cultch – a substrate which oysters attach themselves to on the sea-bed, usually remnants of other shell.

Estuary – bodies of water usually found where rivers meet the sea.

Filter feeder – an aquatic animal that feeds on particles or small organisms strained out of water by circulating them through its system.

Halophyte – 'salt-loving' or salt-tolerant plants, e.g. samphire.

Hatchery – an aquaculture (or mariculture) practice in which oysters are raised for human consumption. They mimic the natural conditions of the oyster's habitat and use various types of phytoplankton to feed the shellfish.

Intertidal – a flat, muddy coastal wetland, with a cover of salt-tolerant grasses that is inundated periodically by the tide.

Merroir – the distinctive taste of a particular oyster depending on its place of origin, as well as the effect of seasonal environmental and climatic conditions.

Mollusc – an invertebrate of a large phylum which includes oysters, snails, slugs, mussels and octopuses. They have a soft unsegmented body and live in aquatic or damp habitats, and most have an external calcareous shell. They are the second-largest phylum of invertebrate animals.

Native oyster – (*ostrea edulis*) the indigenous oyster to Europe. It is also known as the flat oyster and is disc-like in appearance with a shallow cup. The meat is beige and the oyster famously produces a nutty, gamey and mineral taste. They are seasonal and can only be eaten during the colder months of the year when there is an 'R' in the month. They spawn roughly 1 million eggs per season, take longer to grow than rocks and are highly prized.

Neap tide – when the sun and the moon are at right angles to each other, they pull in opposite directions. This causes lower high tides and higher low tides than usual.

Ostrovegan – a vegan diet that accepts oysters because of the oyster's lack of central nervous system.

Oyster – a sea creature that lives in a shell. A member of marine bivalve molluscs (family *ostreidae*) that have a rough irregular shell closed by a single adductor muscle and include commercially important shellfish.

Oyster reef – a collection of oysters that form a reef which, in turn, creates an important habitat for other marine flora and fauna as well as doubling up as an important coastal defence against the sea.

Phytoplankton – very small plants and animals that float in the sea and on which other sea animals feed.

Psammosere – is an ecological succession that started life on newly exposed coastal sand. In addition, sand dune systems are the dynamic elements of the landscape and they're the most common psammoseres.

'R' *in the month* – is the traditional rule for eating oysters in the colder months of the year (September to April) when the mollusc is not spawning (creamy-tasting) to allow the oysters to reproduce. This rule still applies to native oysters but not the rock, which can be eaten all year round.

Rock oyster – (*crassostrea gigas*) a Pacific species of oyster most common throughout the world, particularly in aquaculture for its hardy nature. It has a deep-cupped shell, is arrow-like in appearance and contains a cream-coloured meat. It spawns up to 50 million eggs external to its shell.

Sail and oar – fishing without a motor using only a sail and oar (wind and hand power) to manoeuvre the boat.

Salinity – the amount of salt in the water measured in parts per thousand (ppt). Full oceanic salinity is 35 ppt or 3.5 per cent (for every 1 litre of seawater there are 35g of dissolved salts). River water is usually around 0–0.5 per cent salinity and is called sweetwater.

Saltmarsh (saltings) – an area of coastal grassland that is regularly flooded by seawater.

Shellfish – an aquatic animal having a shell, e.g. the oyster and other molluscs and the lobster and other crustaceans.

Shuck – the verb to open an oyster.

Shucker – the person who opens the oyster.

Smack – a traditional fishing boat used to gather oysters.

Spawning – to release eggs. The native does this within its shell and the rock pumps out eggs into the sea, turning the water around it white in colour during the summer.

Spring tide – when the sun and the moon are in line with each other, they pull the ocean's surface in the same direction. This causes higher high tides and lower low tides (nothing to do with the spring season). The word 'spring' comes from the idea of the tide springing forward.

Tide – the regular rise and fall of the ocean's waters are known as tides.

Trestle – a table frame used to secure oyster bags to keep them off the sea-bed away from predators such as starfish and crabs. A very common French aquaculture technique.

Nutrition

Oysters are a commonly accepted 'superfood'. They are a significant source of zinc (50 times that of chicken), vitamin B12, copper, iron (8 times more than chicken), vitamin D, iodine, protein and omega-3. In the past, they were even prescribed by doctors for the infirm, because of being so packed with beneficial nutrients, and the Roman writer Pliny believed they were good for the complexion.

Twelve oysters offer as much protein as a 100g steak, contain as much calcium as milk and are less than 100 calories. The oyster imparts the umami taste triggered by glutamate which has been used to enhance flavour in cooking for thousands of years, triggering those special receptors in the mouth that give you that savoury 'wow' flavour.

Lastly, farmed oysters feeding on phytoplankton are one of the most efficient and sustainable methods of protein production for the human food chain.

It's also worth noting that oysters are one of the few items of animal product that vegans are sometimes willing to make an exception of – and so becoming 'ostrovegan'. It is a highly debated and contentious issue, provoking a great deal of website traffic. Yes, it's undeniable – oysters are animals, contain animal protein and are definitely not a plant and so, by definition and adhering to strict vegan principles, they are not suitable for vegans. The source of confusion is the fact that they do not have a brain or a central nervous system, with many believing that they therefore cannot feel pain. Sponges – which have no central nervous system – are considered by most vegans to be acceptable as a viable foodstuff, but vegans and scientists cannot seem to make their minds up over bivalves. Oysters do have clusters of nerves that act as mini-processing stations and a kind of pre-brain that can order the shell to snap shut when threatened. This means that oysters may not be the ideal dinner-party guests as their conversation will probably be quite limited, but they do exhibit a basic level of sentience in order to survive.

In the spirit of health and wellbeing, it is essential to mention that people can be allergic to molluscs (oysters). It is best to avoid raw oysters during pregnancy to reduce the risk of food poisoning; however, the NHS says it's safe to eat shellfish during pregnancy if they have been thoroughly cooked.

And continuing the theme of general fitness, the cholesterol issue must also be discussed. According to the Shellfish Association of Great Britain (SAGB), confusion can arise when people with a high cholesterol level are wrongly advised to avoid certain foods because they are 'high in cholesterol'. Only a small amount of cholesterol in the blood comes directly from our food; cholesterol in the blood is produced in the body by the liver. Generally, cholesterol from food has very little effect on blood cholesterol level; the amount of saturated fat you eat is far more significant. Shellfish, which are molluscs (such as cockles, mussels, oysters, scallops and clams), are very low in cholesterol; they have about half as much as chicken and contain much less cholesterol than red meats – so shellfish is ideally suited for those seeking out low-cholesterol options.

For the small group of people with familial hypercholesterolaemia (FH) or familial combined hyperlipidaemia (FCH), dietary cholesterol may need to be more carefully managed in line with the advice of their doctor or dietician. In short, shellfish can count towards the recommended two portions of seafood a week.

For further evidence of the nutrient composition of the oyster, see the following table produced by the SAGB:

Per 100g oyster meat (roughly 8 oysters 80g–100g)	RDA for adult men %	RDA for adult women %	Health benefits
Zinc	623	845	Zinc helps process the carbohydrate, fat and protein in the food we eat and supports the immune system; aids production of testosterone
Omega-3	6 rock oysters = 43% weekly recommended intake 6 native oysters = 40% weekly recommended intake *(based on a recommended 3,000mg weekly intake)*		Protects the heart and can help to prevent development of certain forms of cancer
Protein	20	24	Building, maintaining and repairing body tissues; supports the body's structural components, such as blood, cartilage, skin, muscles, bones, and organs; intrinsic to the production of enzymes, hormones and other chemicals in the body
Copper	625	625	Helps produce red and white blood cells and triggers the release of iron to form haemoglobin. It is also important for infant growth, brain development, the immune system and for strong bones

Vitamin B12	1133	1133	Important for the normal functioning of the brain and nervous system and plays a key role in the formation of red blood cells; lightens our moods
Iron	67	39	Iron is key in the making of red blood cells that carry oxygen around the body; helps to prevent anaemia
Vitamin D	20	20	Regulates the amount of calcium and phosphate in the body, to help keep bones and teeth healthy
Iodine	43	43	Naturally present in seawater, is a key constituent of the thyroid hormones, essential for the good functioning of the metabolic rate and to keep cells healthy
Other vitamins and minerals	Vitamins A, E, B1, B2, B6, Niacin, Sodium, Potassium, Calcium, Magnesium, Phosphorus, Chloride		
Calories	65 (3.3% RDA)		
Fats, sugar salts	Fat 1.3g (1.9% RDA); saturated fat 0.2g (1.0% RDA); sugars trace (0% RDA); salt 1.3g (21.3% RDA)		

On the subject of omega-3, it is crucial to note that our bodies do not produce this naturally, meaning a dietary supplement is essential (other main shellfish sources of long-chain omega-3 are mussels, crab and squid). For more on this, I can highly recommend Paul Greenberg's *The Omega Principle,* and his *Four Fish* book is essential reading, too.

Drinks Pairings

I am a great believer in drinking whatever you want with oysters, particularly when both oysters and drink are from the same area. For example, you'd do well to pair a Murphy's stout with a Dungarvan; an Adnams Golden Ale with a Butley Creek rock; a peaty Bruichladdich single malt whisky with an Islay oyster; a dram of Talisker with an Ockran rock oyster, a Guinness with a Carlingford; a Rocquette cider with a Guernsey; or an English sparkling wine with a Whitstable. Whichever of our islands' drinks you choose, I'd recommend tasting the oyster first before deciding what to pair it with and, once you're all set, alternate eating a couple of oysters with sipping the drink.

Beyond our shores, the global options for great drink pairings are almost infinite. Why not try vodka in a Bloody Mary to combat a hangover? And thinking about the perfect marriage of oysters with white wine or champagne, Chablis and Sancerre are great with flat oysters and Muscadet with rocks. Often paired with a dry white wine, the oyster's salty, briny and brackish notes are 'cut through' by the acidity of the wine. The champagne house Lallier's Blanc de Blanc or Loridon will certainly provide a very satisfying experience as would champagne Agraparts & Fils

Minéral Extra Brut. Or if you like vermouth, why not try a Noilly Prat Extra Dry with lime zest or a London Dry gin and tonic on a summer's day?

For those preferring non-alcoholic beverages, chose a virgin cocktail based around the Bloody Mary or go down the acidic citrus route – Seedlip offer a non-alcoholic range of 'gin' drinks and they'd work beautifully with oysters, as do some of the Rare Tea Company's blends. Whatever you choose, the drink should complement the oyster and elevate the gastronomic experience.

Eating Oysters

Oysters are extremely versatile when it comes to gastronomy. When eating raw (on the half shell, naked and au naturel) always chew and do not swallow whole. Wherever the myth of swallowing oysters whole came from, I can confirm that it is a colossal waste of time ordering oysters if that's how you are going to eat them. Chew oysters like you would chew any other food. They are one of the world's best foods, so take the time to extract the maximum pleasure from them.

Regarding an eating technique, drink a little of the liquor first before eating. If the oyster's adductor muscle has been cut (as is customary in the UK and Ireland), then just tip the oyster into your mouth, chew and enjoy. If the adductor muscle is still attached, often in the belief that a 'second' water is released after being cut (as is customary in France), just cut the muscle loose, drink the liquor and tip the oyster into your mouth and let all the flavours dance on your palate.

Natives should be enjoyed on the half shell au naturel with a small squeeze of lemon if you want. Rock oysters can be eaten raw, cooked, smoked, made into sauce, deep-fried, pan-fried . . . the list is endless.

Lastly, it is *your* oyster and you can do whatever you like with it – just make sure the first one you try is naked so you can taste the natural flavours and notes of the merroir.

Condiments often used and readily available are Tabasco, lemons, cracked black pepper and mignonette. Mignonette is easily made by finely dicing shallots and adding them to red wine vinegar with some black pepper and brown sugar. Make sure the mixture is thick with shallots. You can have a lot of fun mixing the ingredients or swapping the vinegar for apple cider and other acidic or tart flavourings.

How to Open Oysters

The verb to open oysters is to 'shuck'. It is a word specifically used for the action of removing an outer layer of husk around maize, a pod enclosing peas or the shell protecting oysters.

There are many ways to shuck an oyster and neither one is more correct than the other; my preference is the hinge technique that I learnt when I started shucking. The main aim is to separate the two shells and extract the muscle without damaging the food or yourself.

You will need an oyster knife (a short stubby knife no longer than the handle with a sturdy sharp blade). Hold the oyster cup side down using a tea towel on a sturdy surface such as a wooden block. With your non-writing hand, apply sufficient pressure to the shell so it cannot move. Take the oyster knife in your other hand and insert the tip of the blade into the hinge of the bivalve at a downward 45° angle (so that if you slip, the knife goes down and away from you, and not into your own arm or hand).

Once the knife is in position, confidently grip the handle of the knife and make little wriggling movements with the blade into the oyster in a chisel-like motion, while keeping the pressure on the shell with your other hand. The more you hold the oyster in place and the stronger your grip on the knife, the more control you have and the less likely you are to have an accident. Only the tip of the blade should enter the oyster so as not to butcher the meat. You'll know when you are 'in' if you can take your hand off the handle leaving the knife in position.

Now with a gentle slicing action, work the blade sideways towards you in a gentle scooping motion until the oyster pops open.

Lastly, run the knife along the inside of the top shell and cut the adductor muscle which the oyster uses to open and close its shell. Once the muscle has been detached, lift the top shell off, cut the bottom of the adductor muscle in the cupped shell and enjoy your oyster in whatever way works for you. Be careful not to spill any of the oyster liquor as it is incredibly tasty.

If you have shucked a 'bad oyster' that is not fit to eat, you will know it from the smell that hits you as soon as the shell opens. Other tell-tale signs are if there is no liquor present and the oyster is dry; if mud has got inside the shell; if it smells fishy and not like the sea; or if the meat is black or greyish in colour. Trust your natural instincts.

Bobby's Good Oyster Guide

From beach shacks to fine dining, this is an extensive list of recommended places to eat oysters on the coasts and cities of the British Isles and Ireland.

East Coast of England

Blackwater Seafood, Maldon, Essex
Dante's Brasserie, Maldon, Essex
Company Shed, West Mersea, Essex
Mahalah's, Mersea, Essex
Burnham Seafood and Oyster Bar, Burnham-on-Crouch, Essex
Oyster Smack Inn, Burnham-on-Crouch, Essex
Osborne Bros, Leigh-on-Sea, Essex
Simply Seafood, Leigh-on-Sea, Essex
Toulouse, Chalkwell, Essex
Butley Creek Oysterage, Orford, Suffolk
Pinney's of Orford, Orford, Suffolk
Regatta, Aldeburgh, Suffolk
Solebay Fish Company, Southwold, Suffolk
The Lighthouse Restaurant, Aldeburgh, Suffolk

The Riverside Restaurant, Woodbridge, Suffolk
The Station Hotel, Framlingham, Suffolk
Brummells Seafood Restaurant, Norwich, Norfolk
Rocky Bottoms, West Runton, Norfolk
The Old Forge, Thursford, Norfolk
Wells Crab House Seafood Restaurant, Wells, Norfolk
The Hoste, Burnham Market, Norfolk
The White Horse, Brancaster Staithe, Norfolk
Titchwell Manor, Brancaster, Norfolk
Charlie's Shellfish and Oyster Bar, Skegness, Lincolnshire
Café Fish, Scarborough, Yorkshire
The Marine Hotel, Whitby, Yorkshire
The Moon and Sixpence, Whitby, Yorkshire
Star Inn on the Harbour, Whitby, Yorkshire
Latimer's Seafood, Whitburn, Sunderland
The Grotto, South Shields, Tyne and Wear
Coleman's Seafood Temple, South Shields, Tyne and Wear
Riley's Fish Shack, Tynemouth, Tyne and Wear
Longsands Fish Kitchen, Tynemouth
Saltwater Fish Company, Fenwick, Newcastle
The Broad Chare, Quayside, Newcastle
House of Tides, Newcastle
The Patricia, Newcastle
Staith House, North Shields, Tyne and Wear
Roxburgh, Whitley Bay

Scotland

Henry's Bay House, Stranraer
MacCallums Oyster Bar, Troon
The Oyster Catcher, Tighnabruaich
Ondine, Edinburgh
Fishers Leith/Fishers in the City, Edinburgh
Aurora, Edinburgh

Chophouse Bar & Butchery, Edinburgh
White Horse Oyster Bar, Edinburgh
Loch Fyne Restaurant, Edinburgh
Mussel Inn, Edinburgh
The Ship on the Shore, Edinburgh
Champany Inn, Linlithgow, West Lothian
The Seafood Ristorante, St Andrews, Fife
The Tailend Restaurant, St Andrews, Fife
Tolbooth Seafood Restaurant, Stonehaven
Bistro Verde, Aberdeen
The Silver Darling, Aberdeen
Atlantis (The Mariner Hotel), Aberdeen
River House, Inverness
The Oystercatcher, Portmahomack, Tain
Rogano, Glasgow
Loch Fyne Restaurant, Glasgow
29 Glasgow, Glasgow
Mussel Inn, Glasgow
Inver Restaurant, Strachur, Loch Fyne
Loch Fyne Oysters, Clachan, Cairndow
The George Hotel, Inveraray
The Oystercatcher, Easdale
The Puffer Bar & Restaurant, Easdale Island
Waterfront Fishouse, Railway Pier 1, Oban
Oban Seafood Hut, Oban
Ee-usk, North Pier, Oban
Oyster Croft, Isle of Lismore
Mishdish, Isle of Mull, Inner Hebrides
The Boathouse, Isle of Mull, Inner Hebrides
The Creel Seafood Bar, Isle of Mull, Inner Hebrides
Fish Café, Isle of Mull, Inner Hebrides
Colonsay Hotel, Colonsay, Inner Hebrides
Colonsay Pantry, Colonsay, Inner Hebrides
Lochleven Seafood Café, Fort William, Inverness-shire

Waterside Seafood Restaurant, Kyle of Lochalsh, Kyle
Plockton Shores and Coffee Shop, Plockton
Kishorn Seafood Bar, Strathcarron, Wester Ross
Oyster Shed, Carbost, Isle of Skye, Highlands
Sea Breezes, Isle of Skye, Highlands
Kylesku Hotel, Sutherland, Lairg, Northern Highlands
Captain's Galley, Scrabster, Caithness, Northern Highlands

North-West England

L'Enclume, Cartmel, Cumbria
Hipping Hall, Kirby Lonsdale, Lancashire
Robert's Oyster Bar, Blackpool, Lancashire
The Con Club, Altrincham, Trafford, Greater Manchester
George's Dining Room and Bar, Worsley, Manchester
Sinclair's Oyster Bar, Manchester
Randall & Aubin, Manchester
Restaurant Bar & Grill, Manchester
Restaurant Bar and Grill, Liverpool
Wheelers of St James Oyster Bar, Kings Dock, Liverpool

Wales

Marram Grass, Anglesey
The Lobster Pot, Holyhead, Anglesey
Sosban & The Old Butchers, Menai Bridge
Dylan's, Menai Bridge
Mr Villa's Fish & Chip Restaurant & Oyster Bar, Barry, Cardiff
Le Monde, Cardiff

South Coast of England

Loch Fyne Seafood & Grill, Bristol, Somerset
Harbour Gallery & Café, Porlock, Somerset

Glorious Oyster, Instow, Devon
Glorious Oyster (Horsebox), Westward Ho!, Devon
Nathan Outlaw Restaurant, Port Isaac, Cornwall
The Boathouse, Newquay, Cornwall
Catch Seafood, Newquay, Cornwall
Rick Stein's Seafood Restaurant, Padstow, Cornwall
Stein's Fishmonger's Seafood Bar, Padstow, Cornwall
Prawn on the Lawn, Padstow, Cornwall
The Cally Oyster Bar and Grill, Padstow, Cornwall
The Cracking Crab, Polzeath, Cornwall
The Wheelhouse, Falmouth, Cornwall
Hooked on Rocks, Falmouth, Cornwall
The Shack, Falmouth, Cornwall
Flying Fish Restaurant, Falmouth, Cornwall
Ferryboat Inn, Helford Passage, Cornwall
The Watch House, St Mawes, Cornwall
Oyster Shack, Bigbury, Devon
The Salty, Teignmouth, Devon
The Crab Shack on the Beach, Teignmouth, Devon
Seahorse Restaurant, Dartmouth, Devon
River Exe Café, River Exe, Devon
Circa1924, Exeter, Devon
Rockfish (Exeter, Brixham, Exmouth, Plymouth, Torquay,
    Darmouth), Devon
Hix Oyster and Fish House, Lyme Regis, Dorset
Crab House Café, Chesil Beach, Dorset
Billy Winters, Chesil Beach, Dorset
Lobster Pot, Portland Bill, Dorset
Gee Whites Seafood Restaurant, Swanage, Dorset
Storm, Poole, Dorset
English's of Brighton, Brighton, West Sussex
The Salt Room, Brighton, East Sussex
Riddle and Finns, Brighton, East Sussex
Brighton Shellfish & Oyster Bar, Brighton, East Sussex

The Belgian Café, Eastbourne, East Sussex
Taylor's Seafood Restaurant, Hastings, East Sussex
Whites Seafood & Steak Bar, Hastings, East Sussex
Webbe's Rock-a-Nore, Hastings, East Sussex
Tunbridge Wells Bar & Grill, Tunbridge Wells, Kent
The Court Yard Oyster Bar and Restaurant, Deal, Kent
Buoy and Oyster, Margate, Kent
Hantverk and Found, Margate, Kent
Whitstable Oyster Company Restaurant, Whitstable, Kent
The Lobster Shack, Whitstable, Kent
Wheelers Oyster Bar, Whitstable, Kent
Wild Goose, Canterbury, Kent
Hollowshore Fisheries (fish counter on Saturdays), Faversham, Kent

The Channel Islands

Faulkner Fisheries, St Ouen, Jersey
The Crab Shack, Jersey
Sumas, Gorey, Jersey
Banjo, St Helier, Jersey
Oyster Box, St Brelade, Jersey
Seafish Café, St Aubin, Jersey
Green Island Restaurant, Green Island, Jersey
Seymour Inn, Royal Bay of Grouville, Jersey
Balthazar, St Peter Port, Guernsey
Octopus, St Peter Port, Guernsey
Le Petit Bistro, St Peter Port, Guernsey
The Boathouse, St Peter Port, Guernsey
La Nautique Restaurant, St Peter Port, Guernsey
Stocks Hotel, Sark
White House Hotel, Herm

Ireland

Wild and Native, Rosslare & Wexford
Silver Fox, Kilmore, Wexford
Lobster Pot, Carnesore Point, Wexford
The Reg, Waterford, Waterford
Tannery, Dungarvan, Waterford
The Bulman, Kinsale, Cork
Blue Haven, Kinsale, Cork
English Market, Cork
Fish Kitchen, Bantry, Cork
Metropole Hotel, Cork
Síbín Bar, Baltimore, Cork
Out of the Blue, Dingle, Kerry
Fenton's on Dingle, Dingle, Kerry
Spa Seafoods, Tralee, Kerry
The Oyster Tavern, Tralee, Kerry
Alex Findlater's Oyster and Seafood Bar, Limerick City, Limerick
Gallagher's of Bunratty, Clare
Durty Nelly's, Bunratty, Clare
Linnane's, New Quay, Clare
Redbank Food Co (Flaggy Shore Oysters), New Quay, Clare
Monks, Ballyvaughan on the Pier, Clare
Keane's, Kilkee, Clare
Moran's on the Weir, Kilcolgan, Galway
McDonagh's Fish and Chips Bar, Galway City, Galway
Tartare Café, Galway City, Galway
Loam, Galway City, Galway
Hooked, Galway City, Galway
O'Grady's on the Pier, Barna, Galway
O'Dowd's Seafood Bar and Restaurant, Roundstone, Galway
Mitchell's, Clifden, Galway
Aniar, Galway
The Ardilaun, Galway

Ballynahinch Castle, Recess, Galway
Renvyle House Hotel, Renvyle, Galway
Delphi Lodge, Connemara, Galway
Radisson Hotel, Galway
Rosleague Manor, Letterfrack, Galway
Lodge Restaurant, Letterfrack, Galway
Keogh's, Ballyconneely, Galway
The Abbeyglen, Clifden, Galway
Cullen's at the Cottage, Cong, Mayo
The Chalet, Achill Island, Mayo
Coragh Patrick Seafoods, Newport, Mayo
The Grainne Uaile, Newport, Mayo
Clarke's Salmon Smokery, Ballina, Mayo
Towers Bar, Westport, Mayo
Woodfire, Westport, Mayo
Ashford Castle, Cong, Mayo
Cullen's at Ashford, Cong, Mayo
The Venue Bar and Restaurant, Strandhill, Sligo
Davis' Restaurant & Yeats Tavern, Drum, Sligo
Montmartre, Sligo
Sligo Oyster Experience, WB Coffee House, Sligo
Eithna's By the Sea Restaurant, Mullaghmore, Sligo
The Olde Castle Bar, Donegal
Smuggler's Creek Inn, Rossnowlagh, Donegal
Nancy's, Ardara, Donegal
The Mill Restaurant, Dunfanaghy, North West Donegal
Lobster Pot, Burtonport, Donegal
Kealy's Seafood Bar, Greencastle, Donegal
PJs The Anchor, Carlingford, Louth
Klaw, Dublin
Butcher Grill, Dublin
Matt the Thresher, Dublin
The Bank on College Green, Dublin
Porterhouse, Dublin

Bang, Dublin
The Merrion Hotel, Dublin
Union Café, Dublin
Sophie's at the Dean Hotel, Dublin
Portmarnock Hotel, Dublin
Barberstown Castle, Kildare

Northern Ireland

Harry's Shack, Derry
Pier 59, Derry
Katch 22, Kircubbin
The Quays, Portavogie
Mourne Seafood Cookery School, Kilkeel
Pier 36, Donaghadee
Mourne Seafood Bar, Belfast

London

Chiltern Firehouse, Marylebone
Richard Haward's Oysters, Borough Market (Tues–Sat)
Rules Restaurant, Covent Garden
Wright Bros, Borough Market and city-wide
Bentley's Oyster Bar, Swallow Street
Bob Bob Ricard, Soho
Hix Oyster and Chop House, Farringdon
Hix Soho, Brewer Street
Allegra and The Stratford, Stratford
Hawksmoor (various locations)
Neptune, Bloomsbury
Lore of the Land, Fitzrovia
Cornerstone, Hackney
The Laughing Heart, Hackney
Oystermen, Covent Garden

Maldon Oysters (Duke of York Square, Chelsea, Saturdays only)
Oyster Boy (market stalls: Broadway Market, Sat; Columbia
  Road, Sun)
Wiltons, St James
Wheeler's of St James's, the city
Scott's, Mayfair
Bibendum, South Kensington
Bonnie Gull, Soho
London Shell Co, King's Cross
J. Sheekey, Covent Garden
Randall and Aubin, Soho
Parsons, Covent Garden
Quo Vadis, Soho
Orasay, Notting Hill
The Cow, Notting Hill
Dorset Oyster Bar, Borough Market (market stall)
Seabird, The Hoxton, Southwark
Louie, Covent Garden
Caviar House & Prunier Seafood Bar, Selfridges, Oxford Street
The Ritz, Piccadilly
Estiatorio Milos, St James's
The Oyster Shed, City of London
Le Pont de la Tour, Bermondsey

Organisations Championing Local Producers

Taste the Atlantic Seafood Trail, Ireland
Seafood Trail, Scotland
England's Seafood Coast, England
Wild About Argyle, Scotland
Ireland's Seafood Festival Calendar

Oyster and Seafood Festivals

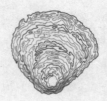

Mersea Island Food Drink & Leisure Festival, Essex (May)
Dublin Bay Prawn Festival, Dublin (May)
Caernarfon Food Festival, Wales (May)
The Colchester Medieval Festival & Oyster Fayre, Essex (June)
London Seafood Festival, London (June)
Portsmouth Seafood Festival, Hampshire (June)
Whitstable Oyster Festival, Kent (July)
Dorset Seafood Festival, Weymouth Harbour (July)
Carlingford Oyster Festival, Louth (August)
Wine Festival at New Hall Vineyards, nr Maldon, Essex (August/
    September)
Maldon Oyster and Seafood Festival, Maldon, Essex (September)
Food Rocks, Lyme Regis, Dorset (September)
Stranraer Oyster Festival, Loch Ryan, Scotland (September)
North East Oyster Festival, Durham (September)
Clarinbridge Oyster Festival, Galway (September)
Galway International Oyster and Seafood Festival, Galway
    (September)
Mersea Dredging Match, Essex (September)
Plymouth Seafood Festival, Devon (September)

Aldeburgh Food and Drink Festival (Woodbridge Shuck), Suffolk (late September)
England's Seafood FEAST, Devon (September/October)
Falmouth Oyster Festival, Cornwall (October)
Seafish Seafood Week, UK (October)

Shuckers for Hire

Most oyster farms will offer shucking for private events, so make them your first point of contact.

Oystermeister (UK)
Oyster Boy Events (UK)
Oysterman Sam (UK)
The Oystermen (UK)
Shuckin' Bell (London)
Boutall Bivalves (Luton/London)
The Whitstable Oyster Company (Kent)
Cornish Oysters (Cornwall)
Menai Oysters (Wales)
HMS Oyster (Guernsey)
Caledonian Oysters (Oban/Perth, Scotland)
The Caledonian Oyster Co Ltd (Scotland)
Wild Atlantic Oyster Cart (Ireland)
Kelly Oysters (Ireland)
Achill Oysters (Ireland)
Flaggy Shore Oysters (Ireland)
Carlingford Oyster Company (Ireland)

Bobby's Good Hotel Guide

Princes Arms Hotel, Trefriw, Conwy, Wales

Wonderful hospitality and gastronomy by Lindsay and Ann Gordon. I cannot think of a more perfect experience than I had in this beautiful part of the world. Geordie Lindsay's warm spirit and Northumberland Ann's food are the perfect home from home and will set you up brilliantly to go and climb a mountain.

Blue Boar, Maldon, Essex, England

Quaint Tudor historic Essex coaching house in my hometown. Fantastic brewery just metres across the cobbles from the hotel reception. Try the Puck's Folly!

Outchester and Ross Farm Cottages, Northumberland, England

Gateway to the most beautiful coastline and county in the north-east. Run by Lindisfarne Oysters, just a stone's throw from the sweeping beaches and sand dunes fringing the North Sea.

White House Hotel, Herm Island, Channel Islands

The perfect, magical location to explore beautiful Herm within touching distance of the oyster beds.

White Horse, Brancaster, Norfolk, England

Excellent food, drinks and shelter right on the marshes. Beautifully refined hospitality in an Area of Outstanding Natural Beauty.

The George Hotel, Inveraray, Scotland

Authentic Scottish hospitality in a beautiful old building on the banks of Loch Fyne.

No. 15 B&B, Furnace, Inveraray, Scotland

A cosy B&B with hearty home cooking on the water's edge of Loch Fyne.

Bola-Na-Traigh, Islay, Inner Hebrides

Self-catering cottage run by Islay Oysters at the head of Loch Gruinart, a tidal estuary, well placed for exploring the island. Deer, otters and eagles all around.

Castle Murray House, County Donegal, Ireland

Get cosy on the Wild Atlantic Way. This place is a bit off the beaten track, but you have your own log fire to light, massive armchairs to snuggle into and watch the mussel farm bob up and down in the Atlantic waves. The food is out of this world, too.

Galmont Hotel, Galway, Ireland

Right in the heart of bustling Galway City. The plushest hotel I stayed in and highly recommended. It's only a hop and a skip into Quay St, where you'll find all the stout and Celtic music you'll ever want.

Mulranny Hotel, Mayo, Ireland

Perched on a hillside, the views of Clew Bay and Achill from this hotel are truly spellbinding.

Ferrycarrig Hotel, Wexford, Ireland

Relaxing hideaway on the estuary just out of town, the restaurant by the water's edge is the ultimate way to enjoy your first taste of Ireland if starting in Wexford.

Useful Websites, Organisations and Suggested Reading

Restoration and Environmental Protection

Native Oyster Restoration Alliance: www.noraeurope.eu/
  restoration-projects
Native Oyster Network: www.nativeoysternetwork.org
Blue Marine Foundation: www.bluemarinefoundation.com
Cuan Beo, Ireland: www.cuanbeo.com
Mumbles, Wales: www.mumblesoystercompany.co.uk
Dornoch, Scotland: www.theglenmorangiecompany.com/about-
  us/deep/
River Blackwater, England: www.merseanativeoysters.co.uk
Essex, England: www.essexnativeoyster.com

Charities

Fishermen's Mission: www.fishermensmission.org.uk
Surfers Against Sewage: www.sas.org.uk
Marine Conservation Society: www.mcsuk.org

Historical research and activism

The Scottish Aquaculture Forum (SARF): http://www.sarf.org.uk
Shellfish Growers Climate Coalition: www.nature.org/
    shellfish4climate
Kelp Dredging: https://stopkelpdredginguk.wordpress.com
Coastal Shell Middens and Agricultural Origins in Atlantic
    Europe: https://www.york.ac.uk/archaeology/middens/
3D farming: www.greenwave.org

Further Reading

London Oyster Guide by Colin Pressdee
Consider the Oyster: A Shucker's Field Guide by Patrick
    McMurray
The English, the French and the Oyster by Robert Neild
Oyster by Drew Smith
Alive, Alive-O by Noel P. Wilkins
Oyster by Rebecca Stott
The Glorious Oyster: Its History in Rome and Britain by Hector
    Bolitho
A Geography of Oysters by Rowan Jacobsen
*Eat Like a Fish: My Adventures as a Fisherman Turned
    Restorative Ocean Farmer* by Bren Smith

Industrial Bodies

Bord Bia (Irish Food Board): www.bordbia.ie
Ireland's Seafood Development Agency: www.bim.ie
Shellfish Association of Great Britain: www.shellfish.org.uk
UK Seafood: www.seafish.org
Association of Scottish Shellfish Growers: www.assg.org.uk
Seafood Scotland: www.seafoodscotland.org

Oyster Recipes

Oysters au Naturel (on the half shell) with Red Wine Mignonette

Ingredients:
   6 oysters
   1 x shallot
   Red wine vinegar
   Brown sugar
   Black pepper
   1 x lemon

Method:
   Finely chop the shallot and place in a mixing bowl.
   Slowly add red wine vinegar until the shallots are thick in the
      solution.
   Add brown sugar to taste.
   Finish with cracked black pepper to taste.
   Shuck the 6 oysters and dress with a squeeze of lemon and half
      a teaspoon of mignonette.

Roman Oysters (Portland Pearls)

Ingredients:

Rapeseed oil
Balsamic vinegar
Anchovy essence
Fresh bread

Method:

Freshly shuck the rock oysters.
Drizzle on rapeseed oil and balsamic vinegar.
Add a splash of anchovy essence.
Enjoy with some fresh bread.

Deben Blue Cheese Melt

Ingredients:

Large oyster (100g plus)
Stilton
Bread
Butter

Method:

Place a large rock oyster under a hot grill until it pops open
(about 7 minutes).
Remove the top shell, keep the juices and quickly smother with
Stilton; pop back under the grill to melt.
Enjoy with bread and butter.

Ockran Oyster's Kelpie with Noilly Prat Mignonette

Ingredients:
   White balsamic vinegar
   Noilly Prat Extra Brut
   Edible dried/ground seaweed such as gutweed or porphyra
   Tabasco Mild Green Pepper
   Lime zest

Method:
   Fill ½ a cup with white balsamic vinegar and a dash of Noilly
      Prat Extra Brut.
   Lightly stir in the seaweed and Green Tabasco (to your taste).
   Shuck the oysters (retaining most of the liquor).
   Dress the oysters with half a teaspoon of the mignonette.
   Add lime zest.

Iberian Tomato Oyster

Ingredients:
   Beef heart tomato
   Extra virgin olive oil
   Maldon salt

Method:
   Shuck oysters and leave them on the side.
   Cut beef heart tomato in half and remove all the seeds with
      your fingers.
   Dispose of the skin and grate the tomato flesh into a bowl.
   Add olive oil and salt and mix to create a juicy pulp.
   Spoon a healthy dollop of the tomato pulp on to each oyster
      and finish with a drop of oil and a pinch of Maldon salt.

Menai Oysters' Crispy Oyster and Tartare Sauce

Ingredients:

For the oysters

    Menai oysters (or other available oysters)
    Flour for dusting
    1 × egg, beaten
    Panko or ordinary breadcrumbs
    Vegetable oil

For the tartare sauce

    200ml mayonnaise
    3tbsp capers (drained/chopped)
    3tbsp gherkins (drained/chopped)
    1 × shallot (finely diced)
    Squeeze of lemon juice
    3tbsp chopped fresh parsley
    Sea salt
    Ground black pepper

Method:

    Shuck the oysters (tip the liquor off and save for a cooking sauce).
    Coat oysters in flour.
    Dip in the beaten egg.
    Roll oysters in panko/ordinary breadcrumbs.
    Deep fry in vegetable oil at 160°C–170°C until they float and are golden brown.
    Combine all the ingredients for the tartare and mix well to creamy consistency.

Pickled Porlock Oysters
(Courtesy of the Luttrell Arms' head chef Barrie Tucker)

Ingredients:
- 650g water
- 280g sugar
- 5g juniper
- 1 x cinnamon stick
- 5g star anise
- 2g cardamom
- 10 x black peppercorns
- 2g thyme
- 1g rosemary
- 1g salt

Method:

Bring all ingredients to the boil and simmer for 20 minutes.

Sieve out the aromatics, leave for 10 minutes.

Add the oysters and leave for 22 hours.

Remove and store.

Oysters Rockefeller

Ingredients:
- 12 x rock oysters
- 1 x chopped shallot
- 1tbsp chopped parsley
- 2 x cups of spinach (cooked and drained)
- Salt
- Pernod
- Tabasco
- Handful of breadcrumbs
- 3tbsp salted butter
- Lemon

Method:

Shuck all 12 oysters and place on a baking tray to one side (not under the heat yet and keep the oysters upright).

Mix/blend the chopped shallot, parsley, spinach, then add salt, a splash of Pernod, Tabasco and breadcrumbs.

Cook the mixture in butter for 5 minutes (do not let it burn).

Spoon the mixture over each oyster and bake at 200°C for 10 minutes.

Serve with lemon.

Hugo's Hebridean Fried Oyster

Ingredients:

20 Caledonian oysters
½ Chardonnay vinegar
2tbsp Colonsay Wildflower Honey
2 x eggs
Milk
Salt
White pepper
Cornmeal
½ cup of butter
½ cup extra virgin olive oil
Isle of Mull Cheddar (100g)
Lemon

Method:

Mix the Chardonnay vinegar with the Colonsay Wildflower Honey.

Shuck the oysters into a bowl (save the shells for your garden, or recycle).

Pour the vinegar honey dressing over the oysters, mix well and leave for 30 minutes to marinate.

Beat the eggs and mix with some milk in a bowl.

Add healthy pinch of salt and pepper.

Dip oysters into the egg mixture, then roll in cornmeal until thickly covered and put to one side.

Melt the butter in a deep pan and add ample olive oil until hot (be careful not to burn yourself).

Drop in the oysters 5 at a time and fry until they are golden brown and cooked through.

Place all fried oysters on a serving plate and grate the Isle of Mull Cheddar quickly so it melts (or place under the grill).

Serve with lemon wedges.

Orford's Angels on Horseback

Ingredients:

20 x oysters

10 x slices of thin-cut bacon

20 x wooden toothpicks

Toast

2 x lemons

Method:

Shuck the oysters into a bowl (save the shells for your garden, or recycle).

Cut the bacon rashers in half and half-cook them in a frying pan.

Heat the grill while you wrap the bacon round the 20 oysters and hold them in place with a toothpick.

Place the angels on a tray and grill for 5 mins on one side and 3 mins on the other.

Turn them until they are crispy.

Toast your bread and cut into oyster-sized soldiers.

Place the angels on the toast and sprinkle lightly with lemon.

Emsworth Beef, Oyster and Ale Pie

(Courtesy of Chef Giles Babb of the Bluebell Inn, Emsworth)

Ingredients:

1kg/2lb 2oz diced beef skirt

Salt

Freshly ground black pepper

50ml/2floz local rapeseed oil

175g/6oz smoked bacon, cut into large lardons

125g/4½oz chopped onion

125g/4½oz carrots, peeled and diced

75g/2½oz celery, peeled and diced

Garlic cloves, peeled and chopped

25g/1oz plain flour

500ml/17½fl oz Wodehouse ale (or any good ale)

2 litres/3½ pints fresh beef stock

1 large bouquet garni (bay leaves, parsley and thyme, tied
together with kitchen string)

12 large fresh oysters, shucked

250g/9oz ready-rolled shortcrust pastry

1 free-range egg, plus 1 egg yolk, beaten together with a pinch
of salt

Method:

Season the beef with salt and freshly ground black pepper. Heat
a large pan until hot, then add the oil and fry the beef for 2–3
minutes, turning occasionally, until browned all over.

Add the smoked bacon and fry for a further 1–2 minutes, then
add the onion, carrots, celery and garlic. Fry for 2–3
minutes, then add the flour and stir well to prevent any
lumps from forming. Cook for a further minute.

Pour in the ale, bring to the boil and cook for 8–10 minutes,
or until reduced by half, then add the stock to the pan along
with the bouquet garni. Bring to the boil and season with

salt and freshly ground black pepper, then reduce to a simmer and cook for approximately two hours, or until the beef is tender. Remove the pan from the heat and set aside to cool. Discard the bouquet garni and add the oysters, folding them gently into the beef mixture.

Preheat the oven to 200°C/400°F/Gas 6.

Roll out the shortcrust pastry until it is 3mm thick.

Grease and line a large pie dish with the shortcrust pastry or individual ones if preferred. Spoon the beef mixture in, then cut out pieces of pastry large enough to fit over the top of the pie dishes as a lid, with a bit of overhang. Crimp the edges with your fingers, securing the pastry to the dish.

Prick the surface of the pastry with a fork, then brush with the beaten egg. Place the pies on a baking tray and bake in the oven for 20 minutes, or until the pastry is golden brown and crisp.

Serve the pies with mash, any excess sauce and seasonal local vegetables.

Glazed Grande Herm Oyster, Spinach and Champagne Sabayon

(Courtesy of chef Mike Pesrin, Le Petit Bistro and Octopus, St Peter Port, Guernsey)

Ingredients:
    6 x Herm oysters ('Grande' Herm)
    Spinach chiffonade
    Lemon juice
    Noilly Prat
    Freshly ground pepper

Ingredients:
For the champagne sabayon
    2 x egg yolks

40ml champagne (20ml+20ml)
100g clarified butter
Espelette pepper

Method:

Over a bain marie, whisk the egg yolks with half of the champagne until creamy consistency.

On the side, add the clarified butter and a pinch of Espelette pepper.

Top up with the rest of the champagne.

Ingredients:

For the Seaweed Butter

2g dry seaweed flakes (dulse, nori, sea lettuce)

5ml Noilly Prat (dry Vermouth)

100g salted soft Guernsey butter

20g finely diced shallots

4g lemon juice

Lemon zest

1g Maldon salt

Method:

Infuse the seaweed flakes with the Noilly Prat.

Combine all the seaweed butter ingredients together.

Method for final assembly:

For each oyster, use 3g seaweed butter and 2g spinach chiffonade.

Shuck the Grande Herm oyster, cut the nerve, then add the spinach chiffonade (finely chopped).

Top up with the seaweed butter, a dash of lemon juice and Noilly Pratt.

Season with freshly ground pepper.

Place in a hot oven for 4–5 minutes.

Cover each oyster with the champagne sabayon, place the
oysters under a hot grill until the topping turns a golden
colour.
Serve immediately.

Negroni Sbagliato

*(Courtesy of Jack Adair Bevan, award-winning
drinks maker, writer and author)*

Ingredients:
   1½ fl oz Martini Rubino (chilled)
   1½ fl oz Campari
   1½ fl oz Prosecco or other sparkling wine

Method (served up):
   Add vermouth and Campari to a mixing glass filled with ice.
   Stir to combine and chill.
   Strain into champagne flute.
   Top with Prosecco and stir again.

Method (served on the rocks):
   Fill an old-fashioned glass with ice.
   Add vermouth and Campari and stir.
   Top with Prosecco and stir again.
   Garnish with an orange slice.

Seaweed V and T

(Courtesy of Jack Adair Bevan, award-winning drinks maker, writer and author)

Ingredients:

50ml Wermod dry vermouth or Noilly Prat Dry (chilled)
150ml Indian tonic water
Finger-length piece of dried kombu (kelp)
Wedge of lemon
Ice cubes

Method:

Fill a highball glass with ice cubes.
Measure in the vermouth and top up with the tonic.
Slide the kombu in and give the drink a little stir.
Squeeze the lemon over the drink zest side down then drop it into the drink.

Acknowledgements

Book

Thank you . . .

Nichola for the love and support;

Rachel Mills for bringing this oyster book to life and believing in the concept;

Claire Chesser for the guidance and the wonderful opportunity to contribute to my industry;

André Balazs for wanting an oyster cart outside your hotel – I have loved every minute of it;

Nuno Mendes for inspiration, believing in me and, of course, the punk rock chats;

Shaun Reynolds-Darwood for the world-class photography and companionship – 'Howay the Lads';

Hannah Wood and Neil Gower for the wonderful artwork;

Jon Davies for tidying everything up and and getting things ship shape;

Liane Payne for the map;

Clara Diaz and Aimee Kitson for helping me tell the world;

All at Constable and Little, Brown;

Fiona St George and Sara Golec at 84 for PR advice;

Imogen Cunliffe and Alex Conway at Hunter PR for the creative support;

Christian Brown and all at Tabasco for spicing everything up;

Dean at Fishermen's Mission for the collaboration;

Huw Gott at Hawksmoor for the encouragement;

Roddie Sloan for the Bute adventure which played a huge role in making me start the Oyster Isles process;

Turku Zorlutona for sitting in on that Fruits de Mer chat (just imagine if I had never wanted you to hear my book idea).

Bike

Thank you . . .

Triumph for their immense support and being up for the adventure;

Steve for all your help with the bike delivery;

Tobyn, for getting me into bikes and whose loaned bike gear kept me warm and safe for 5,000 miles (especially in the Cairngorms);

Performance Communications – Andy Murphy, Monique Clark and Nick Totten for sorting everything;

Grenfell Cloth for the touring coat;

Brian 'Magpie' Winthrop for his exceptional Zone 1 car park facilities;

David Alexanian for advice on touring and inspiration along with Russ, Ewan and Charlie;

Paddy Renouf for being an enabler and guzzling my oysters in the courtyard;

Glyn and Alison Collins.

Oysters

The support from the oyster industry has been so positive and diverse – here are the people I would like to thank:

David Jarrad and the SAGB for the advice and cups of tea at Fishmongers' Hall;

Kelsey Thompson for casting an eye over my route and the food and shelter in Ulverston;

Dr Janet H. Brown, Nick Lake at the ASSG for spreading the word of the trip and for lending me the keys to unlock the doors to Scotland;

Karen Devereux, Roisin Keane, Michelle Butler at Bord Bia and Richard Donnelly at BIM for your generosity and support;

Colin Pressdee for his expertise and friendship;

Richard Haward for the understanding and wisdom;

Stacey Belbin and the *Lady Grace* boat;

Daney for the immense support at Borough and beyond;

Mike Warner and his East Anglian seafood knowledge;

Jacob and Morven and all at Blue;

The Borough Market shuckers (Tom Haward, Sam Jezzard, Lamor Hylton, Joe Daw, Travis Tinney, Derek and Gintaré);

Bill Pinney for the understanding, Ipswich games and Butley Creek visits;

Irene at Pinneys for being on the end of the phone;

All at the Maldon Oyster Company past and present;

Big Ian and Maurice;

Ben and Cyril Sutherland;

Jonathan Simper and family;

Christopher, Helen and Daphne Sutherland (thanks for my painting, Daphne);

Tristan Hugh-Jones for sharing his knowledge, taking me dredging and my first pint of Cork Beamish;

Neil Reader;

Rob Lamont;

John Mills;

The Wallace family for afternoon tea;

Richard Hunt-Smith for going the extra mile to take the best photo;

Iain MacKay for talking to me about Loch Fyne;

Andre Hughes for the tour;

Seonaid Clark for the supper, shelter and Kilmartin Glenn knowledge;

Judith Vajk for the Hobnobs, dinner and chats – I will always be grateful;

Gordon and Nick Turnbull;

Andy Abrahams and his renegade Celtic bees;

Tony and Janet Archibald;

Ailsa McLellan, Joe Hayes and pooches in Ullapool;

Shaun Krijnen and family;

Jodie and Tommy in Bannow;

Joe Harty and the Harty family;

Michael and Robbie Murphy at Sherkin;

Michael, Thomas and Hannah Galvin at Moyasta;

Gerry O'Halloran, Ciara and Lorcan at Flaggy Shore;

Diarmuid Kelly and the Kellys;

Shane Ginty at Dooriel;

John and Mark Doran of Cahir Linn Oysters;

John Ward at Dooncastle;

Hugh O'Malley at Achill;

Glenn and Aisling Hunter in Sligo;

Lissadell House;

Marie-Aude at Triskell Seafoods;

Ed Gallagher of Donegal;

Kian and Mary Louët-Feisser of Carlingford;

Mike at Porlock;

Phoebe and Martin of Torridge;

Lindsay of Instow;

Tim and Luke Marshall at Porthilly;

Chris Ranger of Fal;

Adrián Saint Aubyn of Fal;

Barry and Matt Sessions of River Teign for the hot pasty and drying my clothes out;

Nigel Bloxham in Portland;

Gary Wordsworth in Poole for putting a good word in for me with John;

Pete Miles for our great day in Poole;

Charlie Mourant and Chris Le Masurier of Jersey;

Charlotte Dickson and Justin De Carteret in Guernsey for the most wonderful day out;

Craig Senior of Herm;

Tom Rawlings;

Lee Stewart;

Mark and Penny Dravers for Guernsey chats;

Chef Mike Pesrin;

James and Richard Green and the Whitstable crew: Luke Gillam, Matt Mace, Frances Lucey and Glenn Tyrell;

Delia at Wheelers;

The Walpoles of Faversham;

Lees Court Estate;

John Bayes for letting me sit with a true legend;

Giselle and Tilly at Seasalter;

Patrick McMurray for the whisky phone call;

Dan and Jo Notkin for connecting Canada to me;

Michael Moran for the shirt;

Ryan O'Toole Collett for the beautiful photography in Tommyfield; Jenna Ba at Talisker;

Adam Simha at MKS Knife.

Friends and family

Thank you . . .

Groves family: Tim for the rebellious intellect, Anne Marie for the love, Philip for teaching us all empathy, Ellie for being you and Ben for the walks;

Mike 'Skapa' Groves for the education on all things Iron Age to the late tenth century;

Jenny, Sean and Alana Richards for being great;

Joan Barons (Nan) for the sausage rolls, being endlessly supportive and loving, a true matriarch;

Darius Ashard for learning to shuck;

Zaven;

Robin and Diane Toop for family time in Northumberland;

Gil and Monica Hughes (and Muffin) for welcoming me into your home;

Lily and Michael Graham Stewart for Colonsay tips;

The Firm, The Feed and NUFWC for the camaraderie;

Steve Joy for always being there and, of course, some cheeky printing;

Gav for the world-class design;

Lindsay and Ann for my fondest childhood memories and being the benchmark in hospitality and food;

Chunk and Lorna for Devon shelter and blondies;

Chris and Anita Joy, Stuart, Mapi and Tristan Barona-Joy for Wiltshire shelter before tackling the rainy southwest;

Dee Richards for Manchester stories;

Adam Riley and all at Riley's Fish Shack for the friendship;

Lee Dixon and Yolande Yorke-Dixon for eating my oysters;

Graeme le Saux for Jersey help;

Freddie Woodman for enjoying the oysters and the Toon tickets;

Matt Carr for Raw Spirit and Pasties;

Kathryn Ollett;

Jay McAllister for the sabbatical and adventures;

Patrick Powell for hiring me and helping me switch from oyster farm/market to restaurant;

Dennis Craven for the Dr Martens;

Raoul Shah for immense creative support and punk rock chats;

Harry Handelsman for the positivity;

Tracy Lowry for being you;

Henrietta Lovell for your compassion in helping me get this over the line;

Ben Reade and Kieran Joseph MacInnes for the Scottish translations;

Edwina Eddlestone, Marc Plumridge, Davide Zanardo and Grace Hunt for inviting me to Marseillan;

Olivia Gerardin, Kelly Bevan and all at Noilly Prat for showing me your charming world;

Jack Adair Bevan for inviting me to contribute to *A Spirited Guide to Vermouth*;

Neal's Yard Dairy for the inspirational and celebratory knowledge of British and Irish cheese;

Francis and Isabelle Tribaut for impeccable hosting in Äy;

Nigel Wilkinson at Boutinot for unlocking the door to the Champagne region;

Lucie, Justin H, Justin D and Chris at Two Tribes;

Romain Audrerie and Daniel Illsley for wine advice;

Chandra Kurt for my first foreign press in Weinseller;

Conor Pearson, Dan Tissingh, Kez Piel, Gabriel Scot-Seguin and Toby Boutall for being shucking legends;

All the wonderful colleagues at Chiltern Firehouse – what a fantastic bunch you are;

Sue Utting for Conwy info;

Professor Danielle Schreve, Professor Clive Gamble and Professor Ian Candy for prehistoric information;

Dr James Bonsall, the midden man;

Professor Nick Milner for more midden info;

Greg Graffin, Jay Bentley, Brett Gurewitz, Brian Baker and BR for the 'No Control' while we 'navigate a tangled web of logic and passion'.